FOLK POETRY OF MODERN GREECE

FOLK POETRY OF MODERN GREECE

RODERICK BEATON

Ouranis Foundation Fellow in Modern Greek Language
and Literature, University of Birmingham

CAMBRIDGE UNIVERSITY PRESS

CAMBRIDGE

LONDON · NEW YORK · NEW ROCHELLE

MELBOURNE · SYDNEY

Published by the Press Syndicate of the University of Cambridge
The Pitt Building, Trumpington Street, Cambridge CB2 1RP
32 East 57th Street, New York, NY 10022, USA
296 Beaconsfield Parade, Middle Park, Melbourne 3206, Australia

© Cambridge University Press 1980

First published 1980

Printed in Great Britain at the University Press, Cambridge

Library of Congress Cataloguing in Publication Data

Beaton, Roderick.
Folk poetry of modern Greece.

Bibliography: p.
Includes index.
1. Folk poetry, Greek (Modern) - History and criticism.
I. Title.
PA5255.B4   398.2'09495   79-7644
ISBN 0 521 22853 0

For my mother

Contents

Contents

Contents

Preface

There is no lack of terms to describe what I have chosen to call the folk poetry of modern Greece. Folk songs, ballads, epics, epic ballads, traditional songs, oral songs, oral tradition, oral poetry, all are widely used and, at least in a general sense, clearly enough understood. The expression 'oral literature' has gained ground in recent years through efforts, particularly of anthropologists, to find a blanket term which would include all the others, although there are signs now that the general distinction between 'oral' and other kinds of literature is not as clearcut as was once believed. (As will be seen later, not all the songs discussed in this book are unequivocally 'oral'.) The more old-fashioned 'folk poetry' does not of course cover *all* types of unwritten 'literary' expression – the oral poems attributed to Homer, for instance, were surely sung to entertain the pre-classical Greek aristocracy rather than the 'folk' – but it does truly describe the oral songs of modern Greece, in that all of them seem to have been produced away from centres of power and learning. The political and social attitudes they embody are unsympathetic to authority, whether Greek, Turkish or ecclesiastical, and in their language and cultural referents they lie at the opposite extreme from the archaising book-culture of Byzantium which has dominated religious, political and scientific writing up to the present day. And I have referred in my title to 'poetry' rather than to 'song' only because there has been no space here to attempt to do justice to the vast range of music which is still to be found all over Greece and which raises a great many fascinating problems of its own. It must not be forgotten, however, that all of this poetry is in fact song, and that until the collectors began to write it down, it had no existence outside the sung performance.

This book is the result of field research carried out in Greece between 1974 and 1977. A fair share of the work was also done in libraries, in particular that of the British School at Athens and the Gennadion

Library, Athens – the one especially memorable for its congenial atmosphere, the other for an outstanding collection of works on Greece. As far as possible the facts on which I have based my analysis of folk poetry in Greece come from published sources; but the arguments and conclusions in this book are largely based on experience, listening to Greek folk poetry and song in tavernas and cafés, at village weddings and *paniyíria*, and taking part so far as I was able.

Very many people whose names do not appear in the list of published references have aided and abetted me in different ways, and I would like to record my gratitude to Dr Hector Catling, Mr Roderick Conway Morris, Mrs Litsa Dalla, Mr Markos Dragoumis, Mr Paul Halstead, Manolis and Renée Philippakis, Miss Domna Samiou, Dr Philip Sherrard, and the villagers, singers and musicians of many places in Greece and Cyprus. I am grateful also to Professor Meraklis, Director of the Folk Museum and Archive, University of Ioannina, for permission to quote the extracts which appear in Chapter 4; to Dr Ruth Finnegan who very kindly read and commented on draft sections of this book; to Mr Yorgos Ioannou in Athens and Mr Theodoros Papadopoullos in Nicosia for help in specific areas of my research; to Dr Michael Herzfeld and Dr Michael Jeffreys, both of whom allowed me access to unpublished material of their own; and, by no means least, to the Scottish Education Department, the Greek Ministry of Education, and the Ouranis Foundation in Athens, who have financed successive stages of my work. With sadness I have to record the death in June 1979 of Stavros Papastavrou, who first encouraged me to research in the field of modern Greek studies, and who was for many years a patient supervisor and valued friend. This book is offered as a tribute to his memory.

My thanks are due, finally, to Dr Margaret Alexiou, to whose unstinting support and generous criticism the appearance of this book in its final form owes a great debt. Needless to say, all errors, omissions and misguided flights of fancy are my responsibility alone.

Birmingham 1979   R.M.B.

A nation? says Bloom. A nation is the same people living in the same place ... Or also living in different places.

James Joyce, *Ulysses*

Ὁ ἕνας τὸ λέει ἔτσ' ὁ ἄλλος τὸ λέει ἀλλιῶς.
Μάστορη τὸ τραγοῦδ' δὲν ἔχ'.

That's how one man tells it, another will tell it differently. In song no one has the last word.

A singer from Kostí, East Thrace

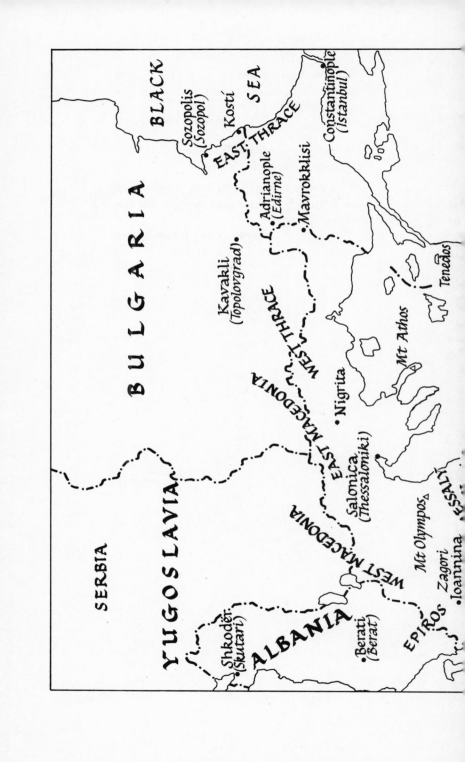

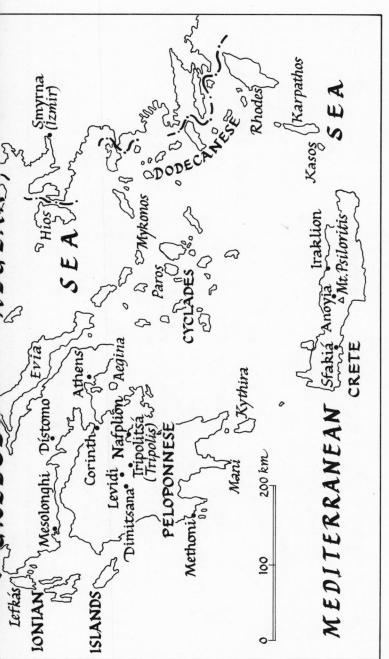

Map 1. Greece and the Eastern Mediterranean.

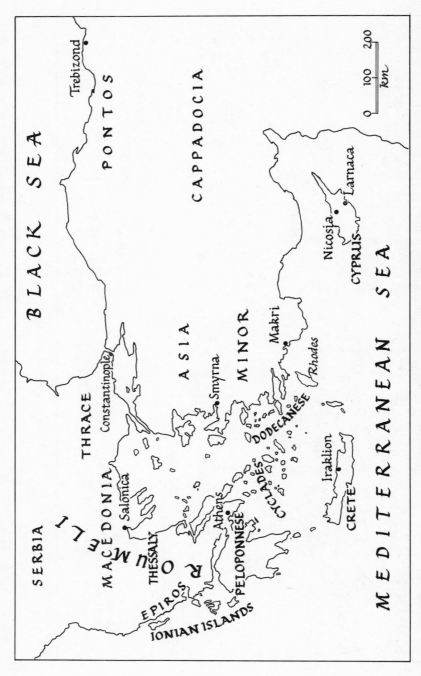

Map 2. Greece, the Southern Balkans, and Asia Minor.

1. Introduction

A. MODERN GREECE AND FOLK POETRY

Folk songs are not generally prone to abide within the boundaries drawn up by international treaties, and the provenance of many of the songs discussed in this book is often well beyond the political frontiers of Greece today. Outside the Hellenic Republic, the Greek language is spoken in Cyprus, Corsica and parts of southern Italy; before the First World War it was spoken in parts of Bulgaria, and before the 1922 defeat of a Greek invading force in Turkey it was widely spoken throughout western Anatolia and in Pontos (north-eastern Turkey). Since the songs people sing are determined by the language they speak far more than by the political grouping to which they belong, the traditions of Greek folk poetry belong equally to the Greek-speaking populations of all those places and to the refugees who at various times have been displaced from them. 'Modern Greece', at least where its folk poetry is concerned, is not geographical. Neither is it only contemporary. Greece (or to be more precise the Greek language) has a long history, conventionally divided into three periods – ancient (including the classical period), Byzantine, and modern. Modern Greece therefore begins with the fall of Constantinople, the capital of the Byzantine Empire, to the Ottoman Sultan on 29 May 1453. In a sense conveniently, the oldest dated manuscript of a 'modern' Greek folk song was copied seven years later (see below, pp. 82–6); and as we shall see there is good evidence for believing that the songs first systematically collected in the nineteenth century and still sung today come of a tradition which has lasted at least since that time. How much older this 'modern' tradition might possibly be is another question, to be discussed in Chapter 5.

As soon as one begins to consider folk poems (or songs) in Greek it is clear that a number of separate kinds are involved. Traditional Greek scholarship, which is still dominated by the pioneering work of N. G. Politis at the end of last century, has divided the vast body of sung

1

material into categories based on subject matter. Modern collections of songs follow a rigid format based on this classification: narrative songs in which the name Diyenis appears, or which seem to be related to other songs in which it is found, are known as *akritiká*, after the eponymous hero of the Byzantine epic *Diyenis Akritis*. Narrative songs in which this name is not found, but whose subject matter otherwise belongs to a similar vaguely historical or mythical past, are known as *paraloyés*, a word of uncertain derivation, rarely appearing in the songs themselves, but which has come into its own in the realm of scholarly taxonomy. Next come songs which appear to relate, or at least to be connected with, well-known events in Greek history (of which the earliest is usually taken to be the sack of Adrianople by the Ottoman Turks in 1361), and include the famous songs lamenting the fall of Constantinople. And the final category of narrative songs is that known as *kléftika*, the songs of the klefts, or bandits, who took part in the War of Independence against the Turks. Songs whose content is primarily lyrical rather than narrative are conventionally grouped under the headings of love songs, wedding songs, religious songs, lullabies, exile songs, gnomic songs, dirges and songs of the lower world.

The assumptions which gave rise to this system of classification are not hard to understand. Each folk song was thought to be the separate artistic creation of a member of the 'folk', which had been dispersed and transmitted by his friends and descendants. This archetypal song was therefore represented in the living tradition by a plethora of variants, and the original could be approximately restored by juxtaposing the best passages of all the available variants. For N. G. Politis, as for a great many prominent Greek and foreign scholars who came after him, each song was a separate entity; there was no question of a fluid tradition such as that more recently analysed by Milman Parry and A. B. Lord in Yugoslavia. Another assumption was of the historical character of the narrative songs. Politis was not alone in supposing that a single historical referent in the text of a song was a positive clue to the song's origin, geographically and in time.

In the following pages I hope to show that the internal structure of song texts, taken in conjunction with what can be deduced about their social function from internal evidence, may have more to tell us about the kinds of Greek folk poetry and the differences between them than the traditional method of extrapolating concrete referents whose occurrence is often little more than random.

In Greek folk poetry more than one tradition is discernible, tradition

2

being defined here and throughout what follows as a series of songs which show evidence of having been composed and re-composed over a period of time, and whose internal structure and external function are consistent. The tradition which I regard as the central one, and certianly the largest (although it need not be the oldest), may be termed the *demotic tradition*, and includes all those songs, both narrative and lyrical, whose internal structure consists of an interlocking system of formulas, images and themes, and whose characteristic external function, so far as this can be determined from internal evidence, can best be defined as the reflection and expression of cultural values and aspirations.

Although the bulk of Greek folk poetry conventionally grouped under the heading of *dimotiká tragoúdia* (folk songs) belongs to this tradition, there are, as we shall see, kinds of folk poetry in Greece whose structure or function diverges from this to such an extent that it is more helpful to regard them as separate, parallel traditions. Such are the epic-style, topical narrative poems of Crete and Cyprus, certain functional songs and, up to a point, the flourishing and versatile tradition of rhyming distichs. The next six chapters will be devoted to what I have called the demotic tradition, while in the later chapters I intend to discuss other kinds of folk poetry in Greece. One consequence of this, I hope, will be to challenge certain easily made assumptions concerning 'oral poetry' and 'oral literature' in general, and Greek folk poetry in particular.

B. PERSPECTIVES ON GREEK FOLK POETRY

In the past a variety of reasons have been put forward by both Greek and foreign scholars for studying or collecting Greek folk songs. Sometimes the reasons have been merely implicit, in other cases they have been explicitly stated. In general, though, it is impossible to separate the study of Greek folk poetry either from the widespread European interest in such matters which dates from the mid-eighteenth century, or from the movement, in Greece and abroad, towards the establishment and consolidation of the modern Greek nation.

In recent years the study of folk or oral poetry has begun to be recognised as an academic discipline, and I believe it is now possible to consider the folk poetry of another people apart from the romanticism or nationalism which provided the initial stimulus for such studies. Their value nowadays is not confined to particular peoples or nations,

3

but has to do with a more fundamental interest in the nature of folk (or oral) poetry. Particularly interesting is the relation between written and non-written poetry, which has an important bearing on the beginnings of what in Europe we are used to think of as literature, and demands a different perspective on folk poetry from those which traditionally have prevailed. A brief historical *résumé* of the development of interest in Greek folk poetry will, I hope, serve to illustrate the importance of this change in perspective.

Scholarly and antiquarian interest in folk poetry in Europe seems to have begun about the middle of the eighteenth century. In 1765 Bishop Percy published his *Reliques of ancient English poetry*, based on a manuscript which he claimed came into his hands in a rather curious way, and which he evidently edited considerably in deference to current literary taste (Wells, 1950, pp. 228–9). In Germany, as early as 1770 the young Goethe had begun to show enthusiasm for the German *Volkslied* (Swales, 1975, p. 12), and by the end of the century Macpherson's supposed translations of the ancient Gaelic bard Ossian (first published between 1760 and 1765) had become a bestseller all over Europe, being admired, perhaps significantly, by Napoleon among others. The debt of many European writers of the Romantic movement to what they knew of folk poetry was widely, if a little defensively, acknowledged, for example by Wordsworth, who stated categorically, 'I do not think that there is an able Writer in verse of the present day who would not be proud to acknowledge his obligations to the Reliques: I know that it is so with my friends; and, for myself, I am happy in this occasion to make a public avowal of my own' (Wordsworth, 1815, p. 78).

But the reasons which have justified the study of folk poetry have usually been more complicated than a matter of literary taste. Thus in western Europe romanticism tended to rebel not only against established literary conventions but also against the social order, and 'natural' and 'spontaneous' were terms applied to folk poetry and to the 'folk'. In Germany and eastern Europe the same interest tended to manifest itself as part of an emergent nationalism, and in many countries the history of the systematic collection and study of folk poetry is inseparable from the history of national independence and the establishment of a national consciousness. It is also noteworthy, at least in the case of Greek folk poetry, that it is the interest of the educated classes in folk poetry, and very rarely the songs themselves, that appear to have been inspired by the ideals of modern nationalism.

4

The earliest signs of scholarly interest in what we would nowadays call folk culture in Greece come from foreign sources, notably English and French, and appear to derive from the antiquarian interest in Greece itself which became especially fashionable towards the end of the eighteenth century. Not all of the dilettanti who travelled in Greece at this period were bent on archaeological plunder, and even those who were frequently give valuable information on the multi-racial society of Greece in the years before Independence, when the demotic tradition was flourishing.

Between the outbreak of the Napoleonic Wars and the Greek uprising of 1821, in particular, many visitors to Greece apart from amateur archaeologists wrote about their travels, and the claim made later by Claude Fauriel, in the preface to the first published collection of Greek folk poems, that he was the first to give due attention to contemporary Greece instead of to the ruins of its past, is also found in many of their prefaces. François Charles Pouqueville first visited Greece by accident when, taken prisoner by the Turks while serving with Napoleon's army in Egypt, he was held for a time at Tripolitsá in the Peloponnese before being taken to Constantinople and eventually released. Pouqueville immediately wrote about his experiences and his knowledge of the country, which was in fact slight; but largely on the strength of this publication, he was then appointed Napoleon's consul-general at the court of Ali Pasha in Ioannina, where he spent ten years from 1806 to 1816. In his later publications about Greece he shows himself conspicuously better informed than in his first (Pouqueville, 1813; Simopoulos, 1975a, pp. 324–5). Edward Dodwell, although a classical scholar, recorded much useful information on Greek life at the time of his visits in 1801, 1805, and 1806 (Dodwell, 1819); William Martin-Leake, who visited northern and western Greece between 1804 and 1810 on British government service, not only provided a wealth of topographical information but a grammar of modern Greek and information on Greek, Turkish and Albanian communities (Martin–Leake, 1814; Simopoulos, 1975, pp. 314–24). Henry Holland was for two years the personal physician to Ali Pasha of Ioannina (1815); and we possess at least two accounts of life in Corfu during the two periods when there was a French presence in the Ionian islands – between the years 1797 and 1799 (Bellaire, 1805), and later from 1807 to 1814 (Pernot, 1918). And from Dimo and Nicolò Stephanopoli, Corsican Greeks sent by Napoleon on a personal embassy to the Mani in 1797–8, who published an account of their experiences in French (1800), we learn much about the semi-autonomous Greek domain at this time. From these and other accounts of the period we gain some firsthand information about the performance of Greek songs and the circumstances in which they were sung.

The earliest serious attempts to collect and publish Greek folk songs were made by a German and a Frenchman respectively, neither of whom ever set foot in Greece. The sources on which Baron Werner von Haxthausen (1935) and Claude Fauriel (1824; 1825) drew for their collections were therefore the informal collections of educated Greeks, at this period either expatriates such as Theodoros Manoussis, Haxthausen's main source, or informants like Fauriel's close friend Andreas Moustoxidis, who came from the western-dominated Ionian islands. Thus, although the individual interest and the knowledge of Greek folk song existed for these collections to have been possible, there was no climate in Greece itself for the *publication* of folk songs until the second half of the nineteenth century.

Von Haxthausen, whose collection was abandoned on the publication of Fauriel's and did not appear in print until 1935, probably began first. The Baron does not seem to have been either a romantic or a liberal and, unlike Fauriel, his interest in collecting Greek songs appears to have come about casually. Encouraged by Jakob Grimm (to whom he was related) he succeeded as early as 1815 in interesting Goethe in some Greek poems he had collected, and vague plans were made for publishing a volume of songs. The prime motivation for this collection was not the events and repercussions of the Greek uprising of 1821 but the Romantic swing in European literary taste which, as already mentioned, had been gaining ground for half a century. Goethe's reaction to the poems von Haxthausen showed him admirably typifies the literary response of the period. 'I was visited by a friend of the modern Greeks', he wrote in 1815, 'who had with him some folk songs of that people, the most beautiful of all known to us from the point of view of lyric, dramatic and epic poetry. Yet these are folk songs!' (Kouyeas, 1932). Such a combination of admiration for the vitality and spontaneity of folk song with a civilised, incredulous disdain is characteristic of the Romantic response to folk poetry at this period.

Claude Fauriel, a man of liberal ideas and friend of the Italian Manzoni, set out in his preface three reasons for having undertaken the task of collecting and publishing modern Greek folk songs. Firstly and chiefly, to pay accurate and deserved respect to the manners, character and spirit of the contemporary Greeks; secondly, to counterbalance the exclusively antiquarian studies of Greece that had been published over the previous four hundred years (a claim which, as we noted, had also been made by several of his predecessors); and finally because of his belief that the living heirs of the ancient Greeks might be a source of hitherto unsought information about their illustrious ancestors (1824, pp. vii–viii). Whether or not the 1821 uprising provided the initial stimulus for Fauriel's work, it is certain that its prompt publication and instant success came largely as a consequence of political events in Greece.[1]

Following this publication, the cause of Greek folk poetry and that of Greek nationalism became inseparably linked. Charles Brinsley Sheridan, Fauriel's English translator, declared that the songs of the klefts are 'valuable as a collection, not so much of beautiful poems, as of historical documents, which prove the capacity of the Greeks to defend and govern their country, and, consequently, the injustice of shackling their freedom with the condition of receiving a foreign sovereign' (Sheridan, 1825, p. xviii). And the question of the most suitable form of government to be adopted by the future Greek state was also uppermost in the mind of Sheridan's reviewer the same year. On the songs themselves, the reviewer had this to say:

> To the name of *poetry*, a great many pieces of the collection have very little pretension, even that portion which the translator pre-eminently styles *ideal*; they are homely, inartificial descriptions of feelings, sometimes natural, sometimes not. The only sentiments which appear to kindle the poetic flame in the bosoms of the modern Greeks, are grief and the thirst of vengeance. Inspired by these, their bards *do* give birth occasionally to bold figures. But, upon the whole, their muse is a very matter-of-fact personage, who talks of balls and cartridges like a serjeant of dragoons! (*Oriental Herald*, 1825, p. 605)

In the wake of Fauriel other collectors outside Greece set to work with varying degrees of seriousness. The following year saw the appearance of Joss' *Specimens of Romaic lyric poetry* in a bilingual edition (1826). Many of these 'specimens' are patriotic pieces by writing poets associated with the War of Independence, but several convincing pieces of folk poetry are included, many of them apparently derived from Fauriel. Joss gives no hint of his sources, and the spectacularly appalling translations he added suggest that this collection was aimed at a popular market which had sprung up in the wake of events in Greece. And a year later, in Germany, the first of a series of collections was published

7

by Theodor Kind, in the periodical *Eunomia*. Like Haxthausen and
Fauriel, Kind depended entirely on educated expatriate sources, but all
five of his collections, published between 1827 and 1861, contain previously unpublished material and were edited with care and intelligence.

In Greece after Independence it was some time before any advance
was made on the pioneering work of Fauriel. Even Manoussis,
Haxthausen's informant who later became a professor at Athens University, seems never to have published the folk songs that he knew. It is
true that Moustoxidis published two folk songs in the Ionian Anthology
in 1834 (Ibrovac, 1966, p. 235), and an *Anthology of heroic and erotic
songs* was published by Andreas Koromilas in Athens (1835). But it is
clear from the latter's remarks to the reader that his interest was primarily in collecting poems, mostly on patriotic subjects, by popular
poets rather than traditional folk songs. A further collection was published by a Greek expatriate in Russia (Evlampios, 1843).

But it was in the Ionian islands, where the first modern university
in Greek lands had been founded under the British Protectorate, that
the systematic collection and study of folk songs by Greeks was first
undertaken. The motives for this study were different again. Unlike von
Haxthausen and Fauriel, the poet Dionysios Solomos and his followers
were not interested in folk poetry for itself but as a stepping stone
towards the creation of a national Greek literature. Thus in the Hepta-
nesian school the European trends of a new literary taste and nationalism in politics were combined. In a letter to his friend Giorgios Tertsetis,
dated 1833, Solomos unequivocally stated his own interest in Greek
folk songs. Speaking of his compatriots, who inclined merely to imitate
the songs of the klefts in their poetry, he wrote:

> I am glad that they take folk songs as their starting point; but I
> should like whoever uses the kleftic language to do so in its essence,
> and not formally, do you understand me? And as for writing poetry,
> attend to this, my Giorgio; certainly it is well to put down one's
> roots upon these traces, but not to stop there: one must rise perpen-
> dicularly . . . Kleftic poetry is fine and interesting as an ingenuous
> manifestation by the klefts of their lives, thoughts and feelings. It
> does not have the same interest on our lips; the nation requires from
> us the treasure of our individual intelligence clothed in national
> forms. (Politis, L., 1956, p. 32)

Such an interest is by no means that of the antiquarian or dilettante,
and the importance of Solomos' stand for the subsequent development
of modern Greek letters cannot be overestimated. It is largely as a result

of this that the universal propagation of folk poetry in Greek education from this time onwards has made available to Greek poets, musicians and even political orators a whole language of associations and references, comparable to that afforded in classical times by Homer and in certain periods of European literature by the Bible. But this perspective also meant that, while Solomos and his contemporaries collected and studied folk songs with close attention, it was only as something of an afterthought that they came to see the songs as worthy to be publicised in their own right.

It is known that Solomos provided the Dalmatian collector Niccolò Tommaseo with some of the Greek songs which appeared in the third volume of his wide-ranging collection of folk poetry (1842), among which appeared Solomos' own poem 'The Death of the Shepherd'; and an unauthenticated report states that the Ionian collector and pupil of Solomos, Antonios Manousos, possessed in 1851 a copy of Fauriel's collection with annotations by the poet (Kairofylas, 1952). It cannot be established how much folk poetry Solomos knew, or precisely how he came by it, since he too never set foot in the mainland of Greece; but Solomos was diffident enough about publishing his own poems, and the idea of publishing the folk songs he knew seems never to have occurred to him.

The first major collections of folk songs to be published in Greece both appeared in Corfu, and both were by younger members of Solomos' circle. Antonios Manousos, whose *National songs* appeared in 1850, was the first collector to engage in field work, and a number of his songs were recorded directly from singers. Although Manousos was erratic in acknowledging his sources he was careful to record divergences from the texts of Fauriel and Tommaseo. Two years later Spyridon Zambelios published a further volume of songs (1852), which was later heavily criticised on the grounds that Zambelios arbitrarily 'improved' his texts (Apostolakis, 1929). It is in fact unlikely that *any* of the versions of songs published up to this time corresponds exactly to an oral performance, but comparison of Zambelios' texts with those of other collectors of the period suggests that the charges may have been over-zealous. Many of the objections which were made to Zambelios' texts were actually based on a literary impression of what the 'true' folk style was, and these would be poor grounds today for emending texts which otherwise appear satisfactory.

The second half of the century saw the publication of many collections from different regions, without significant interference on the part of their editors, the most important being those by Hasiotis (1866)

9

and Aravantinos (1880) from Epiros, Ioannidis (1870) from Pontos, Jeannaraki (1876) from Crete and Sakellarios (1868; 1891) from Cyprus. The same period also saw the publication in Germany of the collection of Arnold Passow (1860), based largely on texts already published and the most scholarly edition so far,[2] and the development of academic interest in the historical origins of certain Greek folk songs.

As early as 1866 the German scholar Max Büdinger suggested that the song 'The Sons of Andronikos' referred to historical events and characters of the Byzantine period (Büdinger, 1866); and then came the discovery by George Sathas and Emile Legrand of the Byzantine epic *Diyenis Akritis* (first published 1875), which seemed to open out a new historical perspective on a number of Greek ballads in which the name Diyenis is found. It may be said that from that time onwards one branch of Greek folk song studies has had to do with the supposed historical origins of individual songs, placing them in some cases well back into the Middle Byzantine period; and this line of research, too, was not without political and cultural implications. It was not entirely fortuitous that the interest of Greek and foreign scholars in establishing this link with Byzantium developed during the decades when the *Megáli Idéa*, the Great Idea of recapturing Constantinople for Greece, became a serious factor in Greek political life, culminating in the Greek invasion of Turkey in 1920.

Towards the end of the nineteenth century, Nikolaos Politis, the founder of the science of *laografía*, or folklore, began the enormous scholarly task of coordinating the material that more than half a century of collection, in many different branches of folklore, had brought to light. In addition to collecting and collating versions of songs, his work included the establishment of a taxonomy of folk songs and collections of proverbs and folktales, which he classified and published with commentaries. Politis' work was both meticulous and on a grand scale, such that all later scholars of the subject owe him a considerable debt. Unfortunately, however, this very fact and the resultant awe in which his memory has been held by his successors, have delayed questioning of his basic assumptions.

Politis' vast labours on Greek folklore were motivated, throughout his career, by a deep commitment to Greek nationalism, a commitment which clearly affected his scholarship and to some extent that of his successors also. One result of Politis' nationalism, as far as songs are concerned, was determined by the assumption that the modern Greek state is the direct heir to the Byzantine Empire, with the implication that songs of other Balkan peoples, when they show any similarity to those of the Greeks, must have derived from them at a time when Greek culture was disseminated in those areas under Byzantine rule or influence. Politis did not ignore comparison with the songs of other peoples; in fact he took a great deal of trouble to collect and study them. But although his evidence was collected and presented with impeccable scholarship, his conclusions were inevitably dictated by his original motivation for research. This was the beginning of a curious 'isolationism' in Greek folklore studies, which has led several fine Greek scholars to divert valuable comparative studies to the end of demonstrating the Greek origin of particular songs.

Another consequence of Politis' nationalist convictions can be seen in his commentaries on the songs themselves. Songs, he tells us, have a special place in the folklore of

> our people; not only insofar as they mightily move the soul in contemplation of their unsurpassed beauty, unforced simplicity, originality, force and energy of expression, but because they reveal with greater accuracy than any other spiritual creation of the people the unique character of the nation . . . The songs reflect faithfully and perfectly the life and manners, the emotions and the thought of the Greek people and rekindle memories, refined by their poetic invention, of national vicissitudes. (Politis, N. G., 1914, p. 5)

Since he understood the songs in this way, it is hardly surprising to find that Politis often read into them the kind of historical and social information he believed they contained, and tended to assume that the nationalism of his time had also been shared by their composers.

Politis' *Selections from the songs of the Greek people* (1914) is notable both for its high quality of scholarship (it contains a list of sources for every known variant which he used in the compilation) and for its unusual method of establishing texts. This was to conflate existing variants of each song, so that gaps or inferior lines in one variant could be made good by adding or substituting lines from another. As Politis himself commented, 'My task is like that of the editor of a literary text who, on the basis of what is written in the manuscripts, refurbishes it, limiting myself to establishing a text (*recensio*) only, and not venturing upon correction (*emendatio*)' (1914, p. 7). Politis further believed that the result of this process would be the closest possible text to the 'original' which a modern editor could achieve.

Politis was attacked for this approach by Yannis Apostolakis (1929), who nevertheless persisted in applying methods of literary textual criticism without questioning whether they were really appropriate to the material; and the editors of recent collections (Petropoulos, 1958, 1959; Academy of Athens, 1963; Ioannou, 1966) have taken this criticism into account, although in other matters there has still been little serious reaction against Politis' general approach.

As can be seen from this brief summary, the history of collecting and studying Greek folk poetry is complicated by several factors. In particular, the impact of the early collections and the partisanship of folk song by Solomos and Politis for literary and cultural purposes respectively, have meant that a knowledge of folk culture is a prerequisite for approaching almost any aspect of modern Greek cultural life. There are two further factors which have contributed to my own involvement with the subject. For historical reasons folk poetry in Greece (or rather, in *Greek*) has probably been better preserved than comparable traditions in western Europe, and is still sung in the village setting where one may fairly assume it used also to be composed. Greek song is relatively accessible, therefore, through the many published collections of texts, a few of music and, most important of all, as a living, although declining, art in Greek villages. And the other factor is the unquestionably high quality of many songs, both as poetry and as music.

2. The Demotic Tradition: the Songs

We have already noted the characteristics of folk poetry emphasised by commentators whose inspiration was Romantic or nationalist, or a combination of the two. The Romantic view of folk song as 'spontaneous' has been considerably modified by modern studies of oral tradition, and yet the notions of charming simplicity and a hirsute sort of artistry have by no means been dispelled by the post-war British and American revival of folk singing. Very few Greek songs, it must be said at once, are either charming or simple. Most are formal and highly organised, although as with any well-developed art form, these characteristics are not always immediately apparent. The ideas they express are complex, often hauntingly elusive; and alongside their lyricism and fine imagery there is a violence and an uncompromisingly pragmatic outlook which are not easily sentimentalised.[1] Some of these qualities will be apparent in the song of Mikrokostantinos, or Little Constantine, which I quote in full.

A. 'MIKROKOSTANTINOS': STYLE AND ARTISTRY

Ὁ Κωσταδῖνος ὁ μικρὸς κι ὁ μικροΚωσταδῖνος
μικρὸ δὸν εἶχ' ἡ μάννα δου, μικρὸ δ' ἀρραβωνιάζει,
μικρὸ δὸν ἦρτε μήνυμα νὰ πάῃ στὸ σεφέρι.
Νύχτα σελλώνει τ' ἄλογο, νύχτα τὸ καλλιγώνει.
Βάν' ἀσημένια πέταλα μαλαματένιες λόθρες.   5
Καὶ ἡ καλὴ δὸν ἔλεγε ἀπὸ τὸ παραθύρι.
– Ἐσὺ διαβαίνεις, Κωσταντῆ, καὶ μένα ποῦ μὲ 'φήνεις;
– Φήνω σε πρῶτα στὸ Θεὸ κ' ὑστερινὰ στοὺς ἁγίους,
'φήνω σε κι ὁλοΰστερα στὴν ἐγλυκειά μου μάννα.
– Μάννα μου, μάννα μου καλή, μάννα μου ζαχαρένια,   10
ὅπως ἐμένα εἶχες παιδί, νὰ 'χῃς καὶ δὴ καλή μου,
νὰ 'χῃς καὶ δὴ γεναῖκα μου, τὴν ἀγαπητική μου.

13

Πήδηξε, καβαλλίκεψε σὰν τὸ γοργὸ πουλάκι.
Ὥστε νὰ πῆ σᾶς 'φήνω γειά, σαράντα μίλλια πῆρε
κι ὥστε νὰ ποῦνε στὸ καλό, ἄλλα σαραντατρία. 15
Ἀκόμα κρότος του βαστᾶ κ' ἡ πιλογιὰ κρατιοῦντο
κι αὐτὴ ἡ σκύλα ἡ γάνομη, ἡ γόβρέσσας θυγατέρα
ἀπὸ τὸ χέρ' τὴν ἄρπαξε, στὸ μπερμπεριὸ τὴν πάει.
Πὰ στὸ σκαμνὶ δὴ gάθισε κι ἀντρίκεια δὴ ξιουρίξει,
μιὰ gούκλα dὴν ἐφόρεσε καὶ βέργα dήνε δίνει. 20
Τὴ δίνει δέκα πρόβατα καὶ κεῖνα ψωργιασμένα,
τὴ δίν' καὶ τριὰ σκυλιὰ καὶ κεῖνα λυσσασμένα.
Τὴν παραγγέλνει στὰ γερά, γερὰ τὴν χωρατεύει.
- Θὰ πάης πάνω στὰ βουνὰ καὶ στὰ ψηλὰ κορφᾶτα,
πὄχουν τὰ κρύα τὰ νερά, τὶς δροσερούς τοὺς γήσκιους 25
κι ἄ δὲ dὰ κάνης ἑκατὸ κι ἄ δὲ dὰ κάνης χίλια
καὶ τὰ σκυλιὰ βδομηνταδυὸ στὸ gάμπο μὴ gατέβης.
Σὲ οὕλους πόρους πᾶνε τα, σὲ οὕλους πότισέ τα
καὶ στὸ Γιορδάνη ποταμὸ μὴ bᾶς καὶ τὰ ποτίσης,
γιατ' ἔχει φίδια κι ὄχεντρες, θὰ ξέβουν νὰ σὲ φᾶνε. 30
- Ἔλα, Χριστὲ καὶ Παναγιὰ μὲ τὸ Μονογενῆ σου.
Πὰ στὰ βουνὰ ποὺ βρίσκουμαι νὰ φτάνη ἡ εὐκή σου.
Πῆρε καὶ πῆγε στὰ βουνὰ τὰ δάκρυα φορτωμένη.
Ἀρνάδα ἀρνάδα γέννησε, ἀρνάδα πέντε δέκα,
γίνηκαν χίλια πρόβατα καὶ γίδια πεντακόσια 35
καὶ τὰ σκυλιὰ βδομηνταδυό, στὶς κάμπους ἑκατέβη
καὶ στὸ Γιορδάνη ποταμὸ πάει καὶ τὰ σταλίξει.
Κι ὁ Κωσταντῖνος ἤρχουντο ἀπὸ τοῦ σεφεριοῦ dου.
Κοιτάζ' αὐτὰ τὰ πρόβατα, μαλαμοβραχιολᾶτα,
κοιτάζει καὶ τὰ σκυλιὰ ἀσημοgερδανᾶτα. 40
- Καλημερά σου, λυγερή. - Καλῶς τὸν Κωσταντῖνο.
- Τινοὺς εἶναι τὰ πρόβατα, μαλαμοβραχιολᾶτα,
τινοὺς εἶναι καὶ τὰ σκυλιά, ἀσημοgερδανᾶτα;
- Τοῦ Κωσταντίνου τοῦ μικροῦ, τοῦ μικροκωσταντίνου,
ὅπου μικρὸς παντρεύτηκε, μικρὸς γυναῖκα πῆρε, 45
μικρὸ dὸν ἦρτε μήνυμα νὰ πάη στὸ σεφέρι,
τὴ μάννα dου παρέγγειλε, τὴν καρδιακιά του μάννα
καὶ στὸ σκαμνὶ μὲ ἔκατσε κι ἀντρίκεια μὲ ξιουρίσε,
μ' ἔδωσε δέκα πρόβατα νὰ πὰ νὰ τὰ φυλάγω.
(Ὕστερα αὐτὸς τὴν πῆρε, τὴν ἔβαλε στὸ ἄλογο, γνωρίστηκαν 50
κεῖ πέρα τὴν πῆγε στὸ σπίτι.)
Στὸ ἄλογο τὴν κάθισε, στὸ σπίτι τήνε πάγει.

14

Κάτου τὴν ἄφησε κι αὐτὸς πάγει ἀπάνου.
Βρίσκει τὴ μάννα του, κρατοῦσε στὴν ἀγκαλιά της ρόκα.
- Μάννα μ' ποῦναι ἡ γυναῖκα μου, ποῦναι καὶ ἡ καλή μου;   55
- Γυναῖκα σου ἀπόθανε, γυναῖκα σου ἐθάφτη.
- Πόναι, μαννά μ' τὸ μνῆμα δης νὰ πάγω νὰ τὴν κλάψω;
- Τὸ μνῆμα δης χορτάριασε καὶ γνωρισμὸ δὲν ἔχει.
Στὴ μέση τὴν ἔσκισε, στὸ μύλο τὴν πηγαίνει.

                                                      (Megas, 1961, pp. 488–90)

Kostantinos the Little, Little Kostantinos
was little in his mother's arms, and little when she betrothed
        him,
and little when a summons came to him to go to war.
By night he saddled his horse, by night he shod it.
He put on silver horseshoes and nails of gold.   5
And his beloved called to him from the window,
'You are going, Kostantis, and to whom do you leave me?'
'I leave you first to God and then to the saints,
I leave you last of all to my sweet mother.
Mother, good mother, mother sweet as sugar,   10
as you looked after me as a child, look after my beloved,
look after my wife, my loved one.'
He leapt into the saddle, and rode off like a swift bird.
No sooner had he said goodbye than forty miles went past,
no sooner had they said farewell, than another forty-three.   15
The sound of hooves could still be heard, his voice was still in
        the air
when that impious bitch, the child of a Jewess,
seized [his wife] by the hand and took her to the barber,
made her sit upon a stool and cut her hair like a man's,
dressed her in a shepherd's cloak and gave her a staff.   20
She gave her ten sheep and those were mangy,
she gave her three dogs and those were rabid.
She commanded her loudly, and loudly mocked her,
'You shall go up to the mountains and to the high peaks,
where the streams are cold and the shadows cool   25
and if you don't make them a hundred, and if you don't make
        them a thousand
and the dogs seventy-two, don't come down to the plain.
Take them to all the fords, at each one water them,

                                      15

but to the River Jordan do not go to water them,
because there are snakes and vipers there, they'll come out and   30
   eat you.'
'Come Christ, come Holy Mother with your Only Begotten Son.
Even in the mountains where I'll be, may your blessing reach me.'
She set out and went to the mountains weighed down with tears.
Lamb gave birth to lamb, lambs in fives and tens,
they became a thousand sheep and five hundred goats   35
and the dogs seventy-two; she came down to the plains
and by the River Jordan went to rest them.
And Kostantinos came by, returning from the war.
He looked at those sheep with their collars of gold,
and he looked at the dogs, with their ribbons of silver.   40
'Good morning, pretty girl.' 'You're welcome, Kostantinos.'
'Who owns the sheep, with their collars of gold,
and who owns the dogs, with their ribbons of silver?'
'Kostantinos the Little, Little Kostantinos,
who was little when he married, little when he took a wife,   45
and little when a summons came to him to go to war;
he left orders with his mother, his own heart's mother
but she made me sit upon a stool and cut my hair like a man's,
she gave me ten sheep to go and watch over.'
[The singer glosses part of the story in prose:] Then he took   50
her, set her on his horse, they recognised one another there
and he took her home.
He put her on his horse and took her home.
He left her below and himself went up [to the house].
He found his mother, with a distaff in her arms.
'Mother, where is my wife, and where is my beloved?'   55
'Your wife is dead, your wife is buried.'
'Where, mother, is her grave that I can go and weep?'
'Her grave is overgrown and can't be recognised.'
He stabbed her through the middle, and took her to the mill.

Regarding this song, for the moment, purely in stylistic terms, a
number of features attract attention. The tale is well told, and there is
no feeling either of 'padding' or of important material being left out.
On the other hand the first part of the song includes much more detail
in proportion to the events described than does the last part, and the
collapse of the metre in several places towards the end, as well as the

interpolation of a prose summary of a short part of the story, indicate that the singer was flagging by this time. This is a problem often encountered in recording songs, and has less to do with the singer's technique than with the simple fact that it has become customary at village festivals to sing only the opening few lines of a long song such as this. In my own experience of the Anastenaria, the festival with which this version of the song is associated, I have not heard more than half a dozen lines sung, although the accompanying music can be kept up for several hours at a time.

But although the end is telescoped, particularly in comparison with the first part of the song, the opening lines do not digress from the main theme. A further look at the opening reveals how this effect has been achieved. The lines of the song are built up not only in narrative units, but in balancing verbal patterns. Thus the second half of l. 1 repeats exactly the same information as is contained in the first half, but the different metrical requirements of the unequal halves of the line make possible the artistic satisfaction, for singer and audience, of an exact 'mirror-image' which is at the same time a repetition and a new invention. Then the word *mikró* (little) is again repeated as a key-word, uniting the three following items of information about the hero – his closeness to his mother, his engagement, and his impending departure. In a device very widespread in Greek songs, the third and most important of the three facts is given particular emphasis through occupying a whole line instead of a half-line.

A pattern similar to that of the opening line is created in l. 5, where instead of telling us merely that Kostantinos prepared his horse for the journey, the singer has concentrated on specific details. In l. 4, two balancing half-lines united by the repetition of the word *nýhta* (night) show us with some immediacy two 'stills' from the sequence of Kostantinos preparing his horse. Then in the following line (l. 5) the second detail, of his shoeing the horse, is further elaborated into two images which are hardly realistic (the silver horsehoes and golden nails) but form a balance through the repetition of related ideas (silver and gold, horseshoes and nails). The effect of such repetitions is first to focus on a single detail in the narrative, then to stop the narrative and expand upon the chosen detail, by means either of a verbal pattern, or of a pattern of images. A similar effect is found in l. 20 (the cloak and staff), ll. 21–2 (*mangy* sheep and *rabid* dogs) and l. 25 (*cold* water and *cool* streams).

Line 12 is a repetition, completely unnecessary for the development

17

of the narrative, of l. 11, but again it serves a double function. Not only is the patterning of different words for Kostantinos' wife effective at the level of verbal craftsmanship, but the emphasis that she is close to him both as a member of the family (his wife) and as his loved one (*agapitikí mou*) heightens the effect of the mother's cruelty to her when he has gone.

The tendency of the singer to dwell on the specific detail, even at the expense of narrative flow, can be seen throughout this song and is general in the demotic tradition. The examples quoted from the beginning of the song show how the singer chose to expand his material by verbal play or concentration on a single image, rather than by adding incidents peripheral to the story. Later in the song there are instances of a corresponding economy: in ll. 38-9, for example, the dramatic effect hinges on Konstantinos returning from the war and coming upon the healthy flocks and the shepherd who turns out to be his wife, and no details are introduced to make the coincidental meeting less abrupt or more natural. Where the singer has chosen to hold up the narrative is in the balanced questions and answers of Kostantinos and the shepherd, and the latter's close but not exact repetition of the opening lines of the song, by which Kostantinos recognises that she is his wife. And a further, highly dramatic, economy is found in the shepherd's reply to Kostantinos, where in repeating the first part of the narrative Kostantinos' wife ceases to be 'she' and silently admits that she is 'I'. She allows him to recognise her in mid-stream, as it were, and the great dramatic moment of the song is conveyed by the change of a pronoun.

Characterisation in this song, as in the majority of Greek narrative songs, is kept simple; and it is quite common for major characters, such as Kostantinos' wife in this song, not even to be named. Dramatic effect is obtained primarily by contrast (Kostantinos' faith in his mother, and his mother's cruel behaviour; Konstantinos' loving references to his mother and his brutal murder of her when he discovers the truth), and by hyperbole, often expressed in terms of vivid but non-realistic images in which the singers obviously delighted. Such are the silver horseshoes and golden nails, and the few mangy sheep and rabid dogs which miraculously multiply and come to have collars of gold and ribbons of silver.

Beyond the style and content of the song, as printed here out of context, the discussion inevitably leads on to other questions. This version of the song has a ritual as well as a narrative function, and how is one to understand the role of the song in relation to the Anastenaria ritual in which it plays an important part, as well as to the wide range of variants existing elsewhere and quite unconnected with any ritual?

B. LOCAL FUNCTION: THE ANASTENARIA

The festival known as the Anastenaria traditionally began in Kostí on 21 May, and was dedicated to the saints Constantine and Helen, whose day it is. In the late nineteenth century the festival took place in several Greek and Bulgarian villages in Thrace, in what is now the south-eastern corner of Bulgaria, and was dedicated to the patron saint of the village (Megas, 1961, p. 491). Kostí was the largest and most influential of the villages, and according to one informant the festivities there used to last for a whole week. The Anastenaria are still held in Greece, by refugees who left Kostí in 1914 and their descendants.

The festival begins on the morning of the saint's day, with the sacrifice of a young uncastrated bull and ram, which are to be eaten by the Anastenarides during the three days of the festival. During the sacrifice and the skinning of the animals the musicians play the *lýra* and the *daoúli*, a large side-drum; the sacrifice over, the animals' horns and hooves are cut off and buried in secret. About noon on the saint's day and the two following days, the men and women known as Anastenarides gather in the *konáki*, the house of their chief, where the icons of the saints are kept. During the day the musicians play for spells of about half an hour at a time, while one by one the Anastenarides begin to dance. This is when the 'Mikrokostantinos' tune is played, but when I was there very few lines of the song were actually sung. Towards dusk a fire is built of logs outside in the square, and when this has burnt down and the red-hot embers have been raked out to form a large circle, the dancers, headed by their chief and then by the musicians, come out from the house, holding the icons of the saints. Since there are not enough icons to go round, most of the dozen or so dancers carry the red silk scarves which during the rest of the year are draped over the icons, and are believed to contain the power of the saints. After first dancing in a circle round the burning embers, the dancers, now in bare feet, begin to cross the fire. The fire-dance lasts for about twenty minutes, until the fire begins to lose its heat, when the Anastenarides return to the *konáki*. Sometimes the music and dancing continue there long into the night.

This festival, with the spectacular element of fire-dancing and the ability of the Anastenarides, during the dance, to tread on and handle red-hot embers without suffering the slightest burns, has in recent years attracted the attention not only of folklorists and tourists, but of scientists from a variety of disciplines, students of the occult and sceptics.

This apparently pagan ritual, which the Greek Church condemns as idolatrous and orgiastic,[2] is also in many respects deeply Christian, in the intense and visible veneration of the Anastenarides for the icons of their saints, and their literal belief that Saints Constantine and Helen are present with them protecting them from the fire. The views of scholars on this complicated question, as well as on other aspects of the ritual, cannot adequately be discussed here. What is of immediate interest for our purposes is the part played by the song 'Mikrokostantinos'.

It will be immediately apparent that none of the details of the ceremonies at the Anastenaria correspond to details in the narrative. The only exception is the name of the hero in the song, which is also that of the principal saint honoured in the ritual. But the Kostantinos of the song is not specifically equated with the saint, nor is there any mention of the other saint celebrated – St Helen, the mother of Constantine the Great. The behaviour of Kostantinos' mother in the song, and his treatment of her at the end, surely preclude any identification between her and St Helen.

Two recent commentators have discussed the song as a source for information about the nature of the ritual, implying that the one is integrally related to the other. Maria Mihail-Dede, whose thesis is that the Anastenaria are an essentially Christian phenomenon, suggests that Kostantinos in the song is a humanised version of Kostantinos the saint, and sees him as a heroic moral exemplar (1973). And Professor K. Romaios, who regards the ritual as Dionysian in origin, has suggeested that the song was originally not about Kostantinos but about Diyenis, whose name he attempts to derive from Dionysos (1964, pp. 224–5).

As regards the equation of Kostantinos with the Christian saint, it seems to me that his final action in the song, that of murdering his mother, absolutely disqualifies him from this role. Only two other Christian references are found in the song: at the point where Kostantinos entrusts his wife first to God and then to the saints, and later when his wife, cast out of doors with the mangy sheep, prays to Christ and the Virgin Mary that the flocks may increase, leaving the implication that it is through divine agency that the miracle in fact takes place. Both of these themes are found, however, in other versions. The second, in particular, is subject to an interesting degree of variation. In Cypriot versions the references to God and the Virgin are *more* specifically Christian, and the multiplying of the flocks is explicitly attributed to God's intervention (Pantelidis, 1910, pp. 73–6). In another version God and fate together are responsible (Jeannaraki, 1876, pp. 225-6), although in others again the Christian reference is entirely absent. In other words, the Christian references are not unique to the Anastenaria version of the song – but neither is their inclusion obligatory in all other versions. This makes it very unlikely that the Christian references either have special importance in the version of the song used or composed by the Anastenarides, or are an essential ingredient of the song throughout all its versions, as one might have expected had its inspiration been specifically Christian. It would be interesting to discover whether versions of the song were also sung at villages which celebrated the Anastenaria on other saints' days and, if so, whether the name of the hero was changed accordingly.

The argument of Professor Romaios meets with similar objections. No other version of the song has any recorded connection with ritual, Dionysian or otherwise, and although his explanation would account for the Anastenarides changing the name of the hero to Kostantinos (since the pagan Dionysos, according to Romaios' theory, had been superseded by St Constantine in the ritual), it ceases to be convincing when we consider that the same change must have been made, quite fortuituously, all over Greece and as far away as Cyprus.[3]

It may be suggested that the song of Mikrokostantinos was adopted by the Anastenarides, rather than created specially for that ritual. A superficial reason for this would be the common occurrence of the name Kostantinos in the song; but it would also be appropriate to consider whether the song, in the various versions recorded from the tradition, perhaps contains some latent meaning or possibility of interpretation which would further explain its suitability for the ritual of the Anastenaria. Although in this local variant it is a ritual song, its form and content have not been dictated by ritual, but may nonetheless have an actual or potential mythical content which qualifies the song for its ritual purpose.

C. 'MIKROKOSTANTINOS' IN THE CONTEXT OF THE TRADITION

It is hardly surprising that, since the variant versions of this song were collected over a time-span of at least a hundred years and come from widely separated areas, no two recorded versions are exactly alike. But the whole idea of 'variants' is apt to be misleading. One tends to think of a 'variant' as a song which tells substantially the same story in substantially similar but not identical words; and many 'variants' of 'Mikrokostantinos' share this characteristic. But how is one to distinguish between a 'variant' in this sense, and a song which includes themes also found in 'Mikrokostantinos', and to which they are no less integral, but tells a slightly different story? Or which uses common phrases or imagery for an entirely different purpose? An examination of the 'variants' of this song will serve to show how the one category merges into the other.

(1) *Skriperó, Corfu, 1850.* Little Constantine, married in May, is called in May to go on a journey. His wife asks him in whose care he will leave her, to which he replies that he leaves her to God and the saints, to his mother and his two brothers. The brothers are not mentioned again, having no role to play in the story. As soon as Kostantinos has gone 'they' (unspecified) make his wife sit on a stool and cut off her fine hair, give her diseased sheep, goats and dogs and mouldy bread and send her off to the mountains, with the command not to descend to the plains until the flocks have multiplied. They do indeed multiply, thanks to fate, and she descends to the plain to water them under an olive tree. Here she meets Kostantinos returning from his journey. In a series of questions and answers he asks her whose are the fine flocks, but she fobs him off with the reply, 'They belong to the wilderness.' Kostantinos then rides off home where a further question and answer series with his mother elicits the information that his wife is dead and her grave is overgrown and unrecognisable. Kostantinos then asks his mother what he is to do to her if his wife is still alive, and she replies that he may cut off her head. Kostantinos rides back to the shepherd, and repeats his series of questions. This time she replies that she is under a parental curse not to reveal the truth, but since he has asked twice she may as well answer. She tells him that everything belongs to Kostantinos, and he takes her back to confront his mother, who concedes that he may now cut off her head. The editor comments, 'Here we do not see the terrible act of her murder carried out, and it is better so', implying that he knew other versions of the song in which it was described. In some of the following versions, which were recorded subsequently, the matricide is depicted with horrific detail (Manousos, 1850, II, pp. 37–42).

(2) *Corfu, 1921.* The first part of the story is very similar to example 1. Kostantinos returning from the war meets his wife (dressed as a shepherd) at the sea-shore, and the returning husband is compared to the

sun, an eagle and a prince. The recognition is quickly effected but then he rides off to his mother without another word. The dialogue with the mother is also similar to that of example 1, but after the confrontation between mother and wife Kostantinos stabs the former, cuts off her head and chops it into small pieces. He takes the remains of the head to the mill, and as he grinds the pieces he sings an incantation to the mill to grind up the head of the evil woman, apparently as an example to others (*Laografía* 8, 1921, pp. 523–4).

(3) *Nigrita, East Macedonia, 1915.* The opening sequence of this song is similar to that of the Anastenaria version, except that Kostantinos again leaves his wife in the care of his mother and *brothers*. There is no preparation of the horse or description of his departure, nor is there any prayer or explanation of the miracle by which the flocks increase. The wife, again dressed as a shepherd, takes the flocks to rest beneath a great tree 'which had a storm at its top and mist at its root, where neither birds nor nightingales come and go'. This is where she meets Kostantinos. The ensuing dialogue is again brief, and she tells him merely that the flocks belong to Kostantinos. His mother, asked what has become of his wife, tells him that she has gone back to her own mother. Kostantinos then goes to his mother-in-law, who tells him that she has not seen her daughter in the three years that have elapsed since her marriage. Kostantinos returns to the shepherd, who reveals her identity and tells him of his mother's action. Leaving her again with the flocks, Kostantinos goes back to his mother, whom he cuts into small pieces and takes to the mill. An invocation similar to that of example 2 accompanies his grinding up her remains (*Laografía* 5, 1915, pp. 582–3).

(4) *Aegina, 1913.* The song begins in the present tense. Now it is May and the ships are leaving, and Kostantinos has the urge to travel. Slipping into narrative form, the song goes on to tell how his wife asks what will become of her, as in the Anastenaria version, and he leaves her to the care of his mother and brothers. As his wife is sceptical of the arrangement, Kostantinos gives his mother specific instructions to treat his wife well in his absence. There is no description of the preparation or the departure, but we learn that it is by sea. The mother's treatment of the wife follows the general pattern, but there is no prayer. Unasked, 'God saw the wrong done to her and the great wickedness' and so caused the flocks to multiply. At length the shepherd–wife descends to the plain and takes her flocks to a well, where she meets Kostantinos who has just disembarked from his ship. The dialogue takes a very simple form, Kostantinos inquiring to whom the flocks belong

and the shepherd telling him that they are his. The song breaks off at this point and the end of the narrative was summarised by the singer in prose. According to this version Kostantinos then confronts his mother with his wife, complains bitterly to the former of her behaviour, and has her torn apart between two horses (*Laografía* 4, 1913, pp. 77–8).

(5) *Crete, 1876.* Kostantinos, newly married, is told he must go to war, and is visibly upset. Asked by his mother what is the matter, he tells her and entrusts his wife to her care. The narrative then moves abruptly from a bare mention of Kostantinos' departure to the incident of the cutting of the wife's hair, thus leaving some confusion as to who actually does this. The same unnamed person gives Kostantinos' wife a few sheep and dogs and the usual instructions that they should multiply. There is no prayer, but the miracle is brought about by God and fate. In addition to the flocks multiplying she herself gives birth to two soldiers. Finally she meets Kostantinos on the plain and a lengthy series of questions and answers, in the form of alternate lines, leads to mutual recognition. The song ends with a brief lament by the girl for the twelve years she has spent as a shepherd (Jeannaraki, 1876, pp. 225–6).

(6) *Mavrokklisi, West Thrace, 1970.* The song begins with an introduction: Curses on you, king, for calling up an army of brave young men, including Kostantinos who is newly married. Kostantinos tells his mother that he must go and instructs her briefly to take good care of his wife. The mother, however, either doesn't hear or doesn't listen, and takes his wife to the barber to have her hair cut (as a shepherd). The barber, who is reluctant, says a 'good word' for her – a sort of prayer or incantation to the effect that her flocks may increase. After twelve years Kostantinos returns and meets her in her shepherd's hut. In a brief dialogue he asks whose are the sheep, and she tells him they belong to Kostantinos. He goes straight home, and is told by his mother that his wife is out minding sheep. Kostantinos asks why she didn't hire a shepherd for the job, and kills her. He then returns to the hut and his wife, who, we are explicitly told, does not know who he is. He declares his identity but she is unwilling to believe him and asks to see a birthmark by which she might recognise him. At this point the song ends (*Thrakiká* 44, 1970, pp. 252–3).

(7) *Cyprus, 1910.* The first part of the narrative is told in the second person, directly addressing Kostantinos. He goes to his mother, who asks him why he is sad, and he tells her he must leave. Detailed instructions follow as to how his wife is to be looked after in his absence. The mother's behaviour follows the general pattern, except that the wife is

dressed not as a shepherd but as a monk. Sent out to look after and increase the flocks, the wife puts up a prayer to God and Christ, who, we are told, hear her. As a result the flocks increase and she takes them to the water-hole where she meets Kostantinos on his return. Kostantinos first asks for water, then inquires whose are the flocks, but she rebuffs him and sends him away. He goes first to his mother, who tells him his wife is away, then to the neighbours, who tell him that they haven't seen her since he left and finally back to his mother who tells him to sit down and eat, and then reveals that his wife is dead. Kostantinos goes to the church to look for his wife's grave and, since he cannot find it, asks an old priest where it is. The priest instructs him to go home and call a feast, to whom everyone must be invited including the monk who looks after the flocks all by himself, and to ask this monk to sing. All this is done, and the monk sings the whole song up to this point to the assembled company. At the end of this word-for-word repetition of the story so far, the mother interrupts and tries to send the monk back to take care of his sheep, but Kostantinos says that they are now his reponsibility and ties his mother between two mules which tear her apart (*Laografía* 2, 1910, pp. 73–6).

(8) *Cyprus, late nineteenth century.* This version shares many of the characteristics of example 7, notably the curious device by which the recognition takes place and the exact repetition of, in this case, eighty-one lines of the song.

The opening is in the third person in this version, and Kostantinos, upset that he must shortly depart, goes not to his mother but to his wife, whom he commends to his mother's care. In an additional line, unique to this version, he adds that if she doesn't like his mother she can go back to her own. Once again there is a substantial prayer and direct divine intervention. Then, in response to her wish, the wife, once again dressed as a monk, meets her husband returning from the war. The ensuing dialogue is simple. On his asking whose are the flocks she replies that they are his. Without another word he goes home to his mother, who tells him that his wife has gone back to her own mother (thus picking up the suggestion earlier that she might do so). The wife's mother has not seen her since the day she married, so Kostantinos returns to *his* mother who now tells him that his wife is dead. As in the previous version Kostantinos goes to the church and receives similar instructions from the priest, except that the request that the monk should sing is not included. The instructions are carried out and the company asks the monk to sing. The monk/wife then sings the whole story up to this point, where this version breaks off (Papadopoullos, 1975, pp. 178–82).

(9) *Pontos, 1946.* The hero in this version is called Marandon. The story begins with Marandon's night-time preparation of his horse which is interrupted by his wife calling to him to ask where he is going. There follows a long dialogue in alternate lines, in which he offers to leave her in the care, first, of his patron saint, St Constantine, then of 'my mother, the Holy Virgin', and finally of 'my brothers, the twelve Apostles'. All of these she rejects, so in the end he says he will leave her his golden-belled ram, five sheep and fifteen lambs and tells her they must multiply while he is away. He also leaves her a silver ring to sell for food and a golden cross to pray to. No sooner has Marandon left than 'they' (unspecified) cut his wife's hair, give her a little bread, five empty walnuts, five sheep and fifteen lambs, with instructions to take care of them and never return. (In all other versions, it will be remembered, the instruction was merely not to return until the flocks had multiplied.) The flocks increase miraculously, and after seven years Marandon returns and meets his wife 'on the ridges'. He asks who she is and whose are the flocks, at which she orders him back from her and threatens to have the dogs tear him in pieces. Then she says that her flocks belong to Marandon, but it's been seven years since he went. 'If he comes, he comes,' she says, 'if not, I'll take the veil.' The scene then cuts to his mother's house, where Marandon is told by his mother that his wife is dead. The final line is cryptic, but probably contains an ironic threat (Lampsidis, 1960, pp. 40–3).

Despite considerable variation in detail and emphasis, all of these versions, even the enigmatic example 9, tell a similar story to that told by the Anastenaria song. In the two examples which follow it could still be maintained that the story is the same, but the extreme brevity of both songs (eleven and eight lines respectively) and paucity of narrative information relate them far more to those lyrical songs whose theme is lamentation for the plight of the exile.

(10) *Sarakatsan nomads, Epiros, 1928.* Yannis was born in May, married in May, and in May a message came to him to go abroad. He then 'unleashed' his wife, gives her rough shepherd's shoes to wear, and the usual five sheep and five goats. The lambs and goats multiply a thousandfold and she give her shepherd's stockings (*tsorápia*) to her dogs to wear as ribbons (*giortánia*) and her keys to the sheep for bells.[4] Yannis is seen returning from 'wretched foreign parts', asks whose are

the flocks and is told they belong to Yannis who is lost (Tziatzios, 1928, p. 31).

(11) *Epiros, 1866.* The weather is bad and my loved one wants to travel. The rest of the song is in the form of a dialogue. She asks him in whose care he will leave her, to which he replies that he leaves her to God and his friends and finally to his mother who will feed her. She replies that she doesn't want his mother to feed her but only to go with him and prepare his meals for him. In form this song, like the previous one, is a classic lament for exile, but in terms of the situation it describes and even some of the wording, it must equally be regarded as a 'variant' of 'Mikrokostantinos' (Hasiotis, 1866, p. 77).

All the songs we have so far considered can be regarded as 'variants' insofar as they tell all or part of the same story, although it is clear in the case of the last two that the story has been subordinated to a non-narrative purpose. In the examples which follow, we have to consider songs built out of some or all of the essential ingredients of 'Mikro-kostantinos', but which tell significantly different stories. These songs cannot strictly speaking be regarded as 'variants', since they are well attested in their own right, yet it is possible to see how a series of small variations may produce a graded series of songs which by the end have no visible point of contact with the first. In all this it is important to remember that all these songs span the same period of time, and there is no reason to believe that one song is necessarily derived from another. Rather we must suppose that a range of different songs may be composed out of common elements.

(12) *Makri, Asia Minor, 1910.* Mikrokostantakis, married in May, is summoned in May to go to war. His wife comes out and asks him where he is going and who will look after her. He replies that he leaves her in the care of God and men, and finally of her father-in-law (τ' ἀρχοντο-πεθθεροῦ σου). She asks how long he will be gone and he answers that if he is not back in twelve years she may remarry. After twelve years, when he has still not returned, the 'evil parents' decide that the girl must remarry, and she, in her grief, takes a silver jar to the well to fill it. On her way she prays to the Virgin that Mikrokostantakis may appear with his troop. Mikrokostantakis and his troop then ride up, and he asks the girl for water for his horse and his men. He notices her state of grief and is on the point of taking offence, when she replies that she is unhappy because she is waiting for someone to come back from abroad. He asks for a sign by which the man can be recognised, and she holds up a ring which has his name on it. He takes her by the hair,

mounts her on his horse and carries her off to his palace (*Laografía* 2, 1910, pp. 177–8).

The story is no longer the same as that of the Anastenaria song, since the themes of the ill-treatment of the wife by the mother, the multiplying of the flocks and the hero's revenge are all absent. But not only are parts of this song verbally close to versions of the Anastenaria song, but many of the themes are common. The differences between the two are not as great as at first sight appears. The wickedness of the girl's in-laws is not so strongly emphasised, but is still present in the phrase 'evil parents'. And in this song Kostantinos leaves his wife not to the care of his mother but of his father, since the threat has changed from that of minding sheep to remarriage against her will, and this is the responsibility of the father as head of the household. And another difference, really only a change of emphasis, lies in the increased weight given here to the recognition scene. But the main ingredient of this scene here, the asking for a token as proof of identity, was also found in example 6.

Taking this song now as a starting point, it is possible to list a series of versions of a similar story, some of which can be related back to 'Mikrokostantinos', while others, according to the traditional classification into songs and variants, can only be regarded as separate songs.

(12a) *Hios, 1949.* Mikro Konstantaki, while still very young, is summoned to the war. His wife treats him with great affection and asks how long he will be gone. He says that if it is one year, he will return, if two, she is to wait for him; if he is away longer than that she mustn't expect him back. Fifteen years go by and his wife goes to the dyer and comes out dressed all in black – a sign of voluntary mourning, which in its imagery and verbal expression is reminiscent of the compulsory cutting of the girl's hair in 'Mikrokostantinos'. She goes to the well for water and there meets Konstantinos. A dialogue ensues, in which he asks for signs by which her lost husband may be recognised. She tells him and he at first pretends to her that her husband is dead and that it has been decreed she must marry him. She replies that she would rather die or turn Turk than marry anyone but Konstantinos, so that he rejoices in her fidelity and the song ends (Argenti and Rose, 1949, pp. 732–3).

(12b) *Region unknown, 1844.* A beautiful girl is weaving at a golden loom. A merchant reins in his horse as he passes and greets her, asking why she doesn't get married. She replies that she has a husband who has been away twelve years and that if he does not return she will become a nun. First of all he tells her that her husband is dead, and that before he died he recommended the merchant to ask his widow to repay the favours he had done the dying man. Then he reveals that he is in fact her husband and she asks him to tell her specific signs about the house and her person before she believes him. At the end of a long dialogue the recognition takes place (Passow, 1860, pp. 321-3). Passow also noted a variant (pp. 323-4) in which the story is told by the man in the first person. He is not specifically a merchant, and the encounter takes place at a well, where he asks the girl to draw him water. To this may be compared the meeting by the well in examples 4, 7 and 12, in the last two of which Kostantinos also asks for water; the lengthy dialogue leading to recognition (examples 5, 9, and 12); and the demand for a token in example 6.

(12c) *Sozopolis, 1909.* A man complains that someone has got him drunk, and that he slept outside the door of his loved one's house. He bends down to kiss the keyhole and prostrates himself before the door, begging the girl to open it. She asks who he is and he replies that it was he who sent her a number of gifts. She doesn't accept this as proof that he knows her and asks for signs about the house and her body. Finally convinced she allows him in to sleep with her (*Laografía* 1, 1909, p. 615).

(12d) *Cyprus, 1868.* Yannis, three days married, goes on a journey which is supposed to last thirty days. He is gone for thirty years, however, during which time his armour rusts, his house is shuttered and barred, and his wife is to be remarried. His father goes out and prays that Yannis might return. The hero returns and asks the old man if he will be in time for the wedding. The two do not recognise one another, and the old man tells him that if his horse is fast he may just be in time. Yannis rides on, arrives at the bride's house and identifies himself to his wife's mother by a series of signs (Sakellarios, 1868, pp. 14-15).

(12e) *Sozopolis, 1909, and Crete, 1876.* A galley slave sighs and the ship comes to a stop. Asked by the captain why he sighed and caused the ship to stop he replies that he was married only a very short time before becoming a slave. Twelve years have now passed and he has seen in a dream that his house (Sozopolis) or his clothes and weapons (Crete) are to be sold off and his wife remarried. The captain sets him free and leaves him on the shore, where he mounts his horse and heads for home. On the way he meets an old man (his father) and, in the Thracian version, an old woman (his mother) whom he asks if he will be in time for the wedding. The reply is standard – if your horse is swift enough you will just be in time. He arrives at the crucial moment, and his wife recognises him by the whinnying of his horse (*Laografía* 1, 1909, pp. 600–2; Jeannaraki, 1876, pp. 203–4).

Another version tells how a hero is seated at table when his horse whinnies and his sword breaks. This is a sign that his wife is being remarried in his absence, so he chooses his fastest horse and rides at miraculous speed to the wedding. His wife recognises him by his horse's whinny, and before the threatening father-in-law can stop her she joins him on the horse, which rides away, again at miraculous speed (Fauriel, 1825, p. 140).

(12f) *Published in Constantinople, 1891.* Three lords are sitting in the prow of a ship, when one of the slaves sighs and the ship comes to a stop. One of the lords asks who has sighed and caused the ship to stop, and the slave replies that it was he. Asked the reason, the slave says that he was married for three days and then a slave for twelve years, and now he has seen in a dream that his wife is being married off to his enemy. The master sets him free (*Zográfios Agón* 1, 1891, p. 73).

(12g) *The Song of Armouris, fifteenth century.* This is a long ballad which tells of the recognition and rescue of a father by his son. Armouris, the father, is imprisoned in a tower and his son takes on the whole Saracen army in order to rescue him but is eventually unseated from his horse. The horse goes straight to the tower, or castle, where Armouris is imprisoned, arriving before the son, who in fact is unharmed. Recognising the horse, Armouris thinks his son must be dead. and sighs deeply, causing the whole castle to shake. In words very similar to those of the ship's captain and the lord in examples 12e and 12f, the Emir, his gaoler, gently asks him what is the matter: is he not being treated well in captivity? Armouris replies that he has recognised his son's horse and believes his son to be dead. The Emir promises to find the son and not to harm him and the story ends happily (Destouny, 1877).

This chain of variants has now been followed to the point where the last few songs summarised bear no direct relation whatever to 'Mikrokostantinos' as sung by the Anastenarides. There is no sense in which 'Armouris' can be usefully described as a variant of 'Mikrokostantinos'. But at what point in this chain are we to draw a firm line, and say, up to this point all the songs are variants of 'Mikrokostantinos', beyond it they are something else? To speak of variants presupposes a belief that there exists an archetypal or original version of each song, from which individual versions diverge. But to assign many of the 'variants' I have mentioned to particular archetypes (whose existence and form must inevitably be only theoretical) would be largely arbitrary. The evidence so far considered suggests that, rather than being grouped as variants around a hypothetical archetype, the narrative songs we have looked at should be considered as independent creations drawing on a common body of themes, imagery and even verbal expressions.

The final set of examples consists of songs in which themes from 'Mikrokostantinos' are used to tell a different story, not just by combining with other themes, but through internal change or inversion. We have already seen one example of this in example 12, where the evil mother-in-law was replaced by an evil father-in-law, and the replacement was followed by a corresponding change in the subsequent theme of ill-treatment.

(13) *Karpathos, 1928.* A girl goes to a festival and then to church. On her way she is stopped by a shepherd who says he has been waiting for her and is going to marry her. The song is very brief and contains little narrative detail (Mihailidis-Nouaros, 1928, p. 272). The meeting between a girl and a shepherd on the road corresponds to that between Kostantinos and the shepherd who is in fact his wife, and the statement that he has been waiting for her is reminiscent of songs in which a girl whose husband has been absent a long time meets him by chance on the road or at a well. The theme of the meeting is a simple inversion of that found in 'Mikrokostantinos'. (It is also noteworthy that, insofar as this story corresponds to that of 'Mikrokostantinos', it relates only to the last part of the narrative, so that this 'deviant' version cannot be accounted for by the frequent habit in recent times of truncating narrative songs and performing only the first part.)

(14) *Pontos, 1946.* Exile, death and parting are weighed in the balance and exile is found to be the most grievous. Curses on you, exile; if one becomes an exile one is lost. The story begins, and the narrative is in the first person. The hero went abroad an orphan and stayed there in a foreign family who finally reject him. So he returns home and meets his mother, all in black, at the crossroads. He declares his identity, they embrace and go home together. Then he asks her about his wife, whom his mother says is dead. Asked about the grave, she says it is over-grown. Finally he tells his mother to light a candle and put it in the lamp, then whips up his horse and rides off (*Arheíon Póntou* 12, 1946, p. 141).

(15) *Pontos, 1946.* Mikro Kostantinon goes off for a short journey and is gone for thirty years. He arrives back, and Eleni, to whom he

31

had been betrothed or married before his departure, tells the story in the first person: she addresses him first as 'my eyes', a term suitable to a husband or a lover, and he does not answer. She then addresses him as 'brother' and he turns and tells her to be quiet. He has fallen in love with someone else, he says, and tells her to dress in black and come to the wedding. She replies in obscure terms, interpreted by the collector of the song as a curse. Eleni builds herself baths of gold, washes and changes her clothes, clothing herself with the dawn and the day and on top she wears the cloak of the sun. She wears the moon in her face and the stars for rings, and the brightest star of all is on her breast. When she appears at the church for Kostantinon's wedding, everyone is amazed, and Kostantinon faints. He then changes his mind and tells the priest to marry him to her instead of to the intended bride (*Arheíon Póntou* 12, 1946, p. 93).

This song includes themes that we have already encountered, such as the long absence of the hero and the threat of remarriage, although in this song inverted. The returning hero, instead of preventing his wife's remarriage against her will, himself wishes to remarry and is prevented by his former wife or mistress. But the crux of the story, to which these themes have been integrated in this song, is found in a great many other songs usually entitled by editors, 'The Bridesmaid who Became the Bride' (Petropoulos, 1958, pp. 107–9). In these songs a rejected mistress or fiancée dresses herself in a hyperbolic manner to go to her lover's wedding, and there creates such an impression that she is at the last moment substituted for the bride.

(16) *Karyes, district of Kavakli, 1903.* Kostantinos is ordered to turn Turk. As he refuses, he is forced to part from his wife and go to gaol. In gaol his hair grows (a direct inversion of what happens to his wife in 'Mikrokostantinos'). He is subsequently sold as a slave (cf. examples 12e and 12f) and set to work in the vineyards, while his wife is forcibly married to his master. The theme of the wife's remarriage is also found in examples 12d, 12e and 12f, while being set to work on the land as a mark of indignity is also found in those songs where Mikrokostantinos' wife is put to minding sheep. Kostantinos is redeemed through recognition by his wife, as Mikrokostantinos redeemed his wife from the role of shepherd or from a threatened second marriage, and she takes him to the barber to cut off the unseemly long hair he has grown as a slave. In the 'Mikrokostantinos' songs also, the cutting of hair accompanied an explicit change of status, from wife to shepherd. Here the change is from slave to free man (Louloudopoulos, 1903, No. 50).

These last examples, unless one is prepared to dismiss them, on arbitrary grounds, as 'deviant', suggest that themes integral to a given song (in this case 'Mikrokostantinos') can be used not only in a new context to create a 'new' song (such as examples 12–12g) but can also be inverted to create 'new' themes. This was undoubtedly an important process in the composition of Greek folk poetry, and examination of a wide enough range of 'variants' shows how new variants and entirely new songs could be created out of the same traditional material. The use of the word 'new' in this connection is purely relative of course: the dates at which the songs I have quoted were first collected, although spanning a considerable period of time, give no evidence of a simple progression from one type of variant to another; and it is reasonable to suppose that different songs (and 'variants') drawn from the same fund of thematic material have always coexisted, as indeed they do in modern collections.

As a final example of the important common ground between songs whose local function is quite different, it is interesting to compare the lines in 'Mikrokostantinos' where the returning husband asks whose are the sheep with golden collars, with a rhetorical question in a praise-song (*paínema*) for Epiphany recorded in Macedonia.

Τινοὺς εἶναι τὰ πρόβατα, μαλαμοβραχιολᾶτα,
τινοὺς εἶναι καὶ τὰ σκυλιά, ἀσημογερδανᾶτα;   (ll. 42–3)

Who owns the sheep, with their collars of gold,
and who owns the dogs, with their ribbons of silver?

– Τὸ τίνος εἶν' τὰ πρόβατα τ' ἀργυροκουδωνάτα;
– Τ' ἀφέντη μας τὰ πρόβατα τ' ἀργυροκουδωνάτα.

(Abbott, 1903, p. 89)

'Who owns the sheep with their bells of silver?'
'Our master owns the sheep with their bells of silver.'

Perhaps the most important fact to emerge from this examination of a single song, both in its local context and in relation to the song tradition, is that the factors governing both content and expression do not seem to be much affected by the song's apparent function. The process by which songs come to be repeated in different versions appears to be common to the Greek-speaking world and to apply equally to songs dealing with a wide variety of subject matter. This common pool of themes and expressions cuts across the scholarly boundaries which demarcate categories of songs, and also across local classifications, which

33

are often mutually contradictory. In different areas versions of the ballad 'The Bridge of Arta' are sung as a dirge or a dance tune; versions of 'Kitsos' Mother', a song of the klefts published by Fauriel and according to him already widely known and sung all over Greece (1824, p. 96), are sung as a kleftic song in Epiros, a 'table song' in Karpathos, where it is sung by men only, unaccompanied, after the psalms with which a wedding feast traditionally begins, and as a lullaby in Thrace (*Thrakiká* 11, 1939, p. 205).

In these cases it is impossible to tell whether this diversity of apparent function for versions closely enough related to be regarded as 'the same song' is a recent phenomenon. In the case of 'Mikrokostantinos' and its association with the Anastenaria, it almost certainly has a long history, and it is especially significant to note how little divergence there is between versions from the Anastenaria and others from quite remote areas, despite what must be a long-standing difference in function. To understand these similarities in content and structure and the differences in function, it is necessary to look beyond either the local or the scholarly classification of particular songs to a deeper, more generalised function which underlies very many songs of different types, rendering them suitable to be adopted, rather than adapted, for a specific purpose, whether for ritual or for entertainment.[5]

3. Structure of the Demotic Tradition: the Formula

A. COMPOSITION AND TRANSMISSION

We cannot know for certain how Greek folk poetry was composed. It is clear, however, that by the mid-nineteenth century, when songs began to be written down and published in large numbers, a corpus of songs already existed which must have been composed without the aid of writing and in which variations occurred which could not be explained by any process of transmission applicable to a written text. The question of the origin of the song tradition, which it may as well be admitted at once is probably insoluble, will be discussed more fully in Chapter 5; here it is enough to mention that songs roughly of the type recorded during the past century and a half appear to have been sung in Greek-speaking lands for at least four hundred years before they began to be collected and edited. The evidence of the variants discussed in the last chapter suggests that, although the singers may have been conservative in introducing radical innovations into songs, there was never any particular insistence on the exact repetition of an established text.

This is a point worth making, since oral transmission, in the sense of handing down 'texts' without the use of writing, can take different forms. In Yugoslav tradition, for example, it has been shown that singers substantially alter songs which they have heard. But they are not conscious of doing so, since the story remains the same. In other parts of the world, however, there is evidence that word-for-word accuracy in transmission has been actively pursued. The most famous case of this is the oral transmission of the Indian *Rgveda* (Finnegan, 1977, pp. 135–6), but traditions are also known from Africa, New Zealand and Polynesia in which systems of rewards and sanctions were used to encourage as exact a repetition as possible of oral 'texts' (Vansina, 1973, pp. 33–4); and a recent article on an epic tradition from India shows how in one instance the use of a formulaic style coexists with deliberate memorisation (Smith, 1977). That this is not the case with the Greek tradition is clearly indicated by the variants discussed in the last chapter.

The introduction of published texts of songs into Greek primary school education has undoubtedly affected modern practice regarding composition and the transmission of songs. But a hint of what may be an older attitude was given by the informant who provided the version of 'Mikrokostantinos' cited above:

Ὁ ἕνας τὸ λέει ἔτσ᾿ ὁ ἄλλος τὸ λέει ἀλλιῶς. Μάστορη τὸ τραγοῦδ᾿ δὲν ἔχ᾿! (Megas, 1961, p. 490).

That's how one man tells it, another will tell it differently. In song no one has the last word.

Clearly this singer did not consider transmission to be the same thing as exact memorisation, a discovery which leaves the way open for the kind of composition-in-performance which was found, at least until relatively recently, to have been practised in parts of Yugoslavia. But this is a comparatively rare instance, and external evidence for this kind of composition is not easily found in Greece today. In my own experience, aside from the improvisation of rhyming distichs, I found no indication that singers took an active part in reshaping the words of songs. Sometimes an informant would insist on writing down the text of a song before singing it, so as not to forget the words; and on one occasion a recording session was interrupted by a twelve-year-old boy just back from school, who tried to correct his elders' version of a song to that which he had been taught in class.

Oral composition-in-performance cannot be proved in the case of Greek songs, although it can certainly be inferred from the variations in recorded texts. In the absence of external indications to the contrary, one may suppose that, before they came to be written down by collectors and published, Greek demotic songs were indeed composed and transmitted orally, in a manner analogous, but not identical, to that found in Yugoslav epic poetry.

B. THE ORAL FORMULA

The existence of frequently recurring phrases in Greek songs was first remarked by Fauriel (1824, p. cxxix), and throughout the nineteenth century was generally recognised as a characteristic of all folk poetry.

But the full significance of these recurrences was not really understood until Milman Parry first applied the findings of Yugoslav and Russian scholars on contemporary oral heroic poetry to the study of Homer, and developed the theory of the oral formula. A formula, according to Parry's now famous definition is 'a group of words which is regularly employed under the same metrical conditions to express a given essential idea' (Parry, 1930, p. 80). The theory goes on to assert that the oral poet, who unlike his literary counterpart does not have time to reflect upon what he is going to say and find a new and satisfying means of accommodating it to the requirements of his verse, has no choice but to create his whole poem out of a reservoir of formulas, in which commonly recurring ideas have already been tailored to fit the verse. This reservoir of formulas, and not whole 'texts' of songs, is what the apprentice *guslar*, the Yugoslav epic singer, learns, and having acquired a working knowledge of a set of formulas, his task is then to work with them flexibly, readapting and varying them to fit the requirements of the poems he sings (Lord, 1960, pp. 13–29).

The studies of Yugoslav oral poetry by Parry and Professor A. B. Lord, in particular, give due attention to the subtleties involved in this method of composition and have gone a long way towards dispelling the erroneous impression of many critics of the theory, that composition using formulas must be a dull, mechanical business, devoid of genuine artistry. In their work on Yugoslav oral epics, Parry and Lord have convincingly shown how the 'formulaic style' works, and that, at least as employed by the Serbian *guslari*, its final product is readily distinguishable from a poem composed by more familiar methods. Since the late fifties, however, the 'oral-formulaic theory' has had many repercussions in fields not directly related either to Yugoslav epic poetry or to Homer. (The impact of the theory on Homeric studies, to which it was originally intended as a contribution, has rightly been enormous, and need not be gone into here.) The most significant feature of recent developments of the oral-formulaic theory is that it has been applied almost exclusively to works of *literature*. A great deal of ink has been spilt in efforts to identify formulas in poems such as *Beowulf*, the *Chanson de Roland* and Greek vernacular poems of the late middle ages, which do not at first sight appear to be oral poems, in order to show that, like the Homeric epics, they are the products of oral tradition (Haymes, 1973; Lord, 1975). As a result, the term 'formula' is now frequently understood in such a narrow sense that one may question whether it any longer means anything at all.

Under the banner of objectivity, some adherents of the oral-formulaic theory now believe that the percentage of formulas in a poem of some length can be used to determine whether the poem was originally oral or written. Lord has claimed that the Yugoslav epics he has recorded and studied are '100 per cent formula or formulaic', while the Homeric poems are 'around 90 per cent' (Lord, 1960, pp. 47, 144; 1968, p. 19). As a contrast to these examples of oral poems, Lord further states, 'So far, I believe, we can conclude that a pattern of 50 to 60 per cent formula or formulaic, with 10 to perhaps 25 per cent straight formula, indicates clearly literary composition. I am still convinced that it is possible to determine orality by quantitative formulaic analysis, by the study of formula density' (1968, p. 24).

In order to be analysed in such terms, the formula, from being an adaptable poetic tool, has had to be defined, implicitly or explicitly, as nothing more than a repetition. Only exact verbal repetitions are susceptible of the kind of rigorous quantitative analysis advocated by Lord; but exact verbal repetitions are not formulas. Parry himself was quite clear on the point: 'It is important to remember that the formula in Homer is not necessarily a repetition, just as the repetitions of tragedy are not necessarily formulas. It is the nature of an expression which makes it a formula' (Parry, 1930, p. 122). Parry adds that, in this particular article, he was 'taking up the problem of the Homeric formulas from the side of the repetitions' because repetition makes a formula easier to identify. But two things are clear: a formula according to Parry may be used only once; and must be qualitatively identified before there is any purpose in quantifying its occurrences.

In seeking to apply the theory of formulaic composition to Greek folk poetry, I am not concerned to prove that the tradition is oral. What will be of greater interest will be to examine how formulas are used in the structure of folk songs. Since the application of the theory to the material needs no special justification, it is to be hoped that this discussion of formulas in a non-literate tradition may provide further qualitative insight into their nature and possible use.

C. FORMULA SYSTEMS AND THE LANGUAGE OF SONGS

The problem of how a formula may be identified except through its repetitions was not fully solved by Parry. While it was unavoidable that frequently recurring phrases in Homer should be singled out in order to make the whole theory objectively impressive, some of the most interesting parts of Parry's seminal essays are those where he discusses phrases which are metrically identical and syntactically parallel, but which do not repeat the same words. Such a series of parallel phrases Parry called a 'system of formulas' (1930, p. 86), and their significance became clear in the part of his analysis where he discussed the way in which an oral poet could use formulas. Starting out with easily demonstrable formulas (repetitions) Parry concluded that 'in showing the usefulness of the repeated expressions we did nothing more than find the systems of formulas to which they belonged' (1930, p. 132).

Despite opposition from Lord on the grounds of subjectivity, a few scholars recently have taken Parry's lead and some theoretical work has been done on the formula system. The most important development which they have brought about is that the formula system is no longer thought of as deriving from an archetype by a process of analogy (Parry, 1930, p. 145). J. A. Russo maintains that an 'oral formulaic style may depend . . . on structural repetitions as well as on literal ones' (1966, p. 233), and his 'structural repetition' is different from Parry's 'system of formulas' only in that it does not imply the multiplication of a single literal formula by analogy. Where two non-identical phrases have the same metrical and syntactical structure, Russo maintains, this does not mean that one has been created on the analogy of the other, but that the recurring structure is itself formulaic.

More important still is the position taken up by M. N. Nagler (1967), which consists 'in looking vertically to a deep structure underlying the production of two similar or identical phrases rather than horizontally from one phrase to the second'. Nagler had the advantage of Parry in that the terminology and concepts of Gestalt psychology and structuralism were available to him, thus offering a model capable of illustrating, in modern scientific terms, how identical, related or merely structurally similar phrases could be created without dependence on a small number of archetypes. Nagler's 'generative' view of the formula demonstrates what Parry and Lord had always emphasised – that formulaic composition is a creative process. But he was able to go beyond Parry and show that it is creative not merely in the continual reshaping of stories out of existing formulas with the occasional 'new' formula thrown in, but in the capacity of the system itself for renewal through the generation of new formulas. As Nagler sums up, 'oral-formulaic composition is a language . . . the training of the oral bard is more like the acquisition of a linguistic skill than the memorization of a fixed content'.

This conclusion was also borne out by an examination, in terms of linguistic theory, of the songs of the Todas, a south Indian community. In an article on style and meaning in oral tradition, M. B. Emeneau analyses the difference between the structure of the Toda spoken language and that of their songs (1966). In the case of the Todas, both expression and content in song are far more restricted than in any European parallel, but in such an extreme case it is possible to analyse, relatively simply, how the two kinds of expression, song and speech, differ. Emeneau discovered that the linguistic restrictions imposed by the traditional structure of their songs meant that the sung language of the Todas is a closed system in which the range of expression, although large, was theoretically limited in extent. Drawing his conclusions not from oral-formulaic theory or from counting repetitions in Toda songs, Emeneau found that 'the song language is *in theory* completely formulaic' (my italics). The discovery is not an empirical one but derives from a fairly formal proof that Toda song language is different in structure from any spoken language. Emeneau goes on, 'The formulaic character means, in theory, that no song-unit can occur that does not occur elsewhere in the corpus, nor can a combination of song-units in a sentence occur that does not occur elsewhere.'

From this account it is evident that the song language in question is different at least in the *degree* of restriction involved, from that of Greek songs, Yugoslav epics, or Homer. But Emeneau's study is most valuable in that it suggests very forcefully that when we speak about oral composition as a 'language' this is probably more than mere analogy. And it is worth considering the more general implications: that a similar qualitative, but objectively demonstrable, distinction separates the language of traditional song from that of speech.

D. FORMULAS AND FORMULA SYSTEMS IN GREEK SONGS

It has been emphasised by Lord, in particular, that each oral singer has his own repertory of formulas. Although the bulk of these will presumably be traditional, and common to a number of singers in a locality, it is to be expected that an individual will both add formulas of his own and perhaps alter some existing ones (Lord, 1960, p. 49). This has led to the common practice, in identifying formulas, of restricting oneself to a single poem or at most to a group of poems which there are grounds for regarding as the work of a single singer. In dealing with an epic tradition where songs run to many thousands of lines, or with a written text of comparable length, this is both feasible and desirable. In the Greek tradition, however, the most that we can ever attribute to a single singer is a single version of a song. Many of the songs which are purely lyrical are extremely short, and even narrative songs in the Greek tradition rarely run to as many as a hundred lines, with the very longest just over two hundred.

First of all, what evidence have we that these rather brief songs are formulaic? An analysis of a version of the ballad 'The Dead Brother' (Passow, 1860, pp. 394-6) according to Lord's quantitative system reveals that of the sixty-seven lines of the song, thirty-seven half-lines are exactly repeated, while a further sixteen half-lines occur more than once with slight variations. In quantitative terms this would yield approximately 38 per cent formula or fomulaic, with 27 per cent straight formula, a result which falls just short of Lord's requirements for an oral poem. Are we then to fly in the face of probability and such evidence as we have, and declare that this version of 'The Dead Brother' was originally *written*? Surely not.

If formulas can be identified in a tradition of this kind, I do not believe that they are to be found in the repetitions and near-repetitions which occur in individual songs. Instead we must look at the tradition as a whole, or at least at a cross-section of it, in order to recognise formulas as the variable manifestations of underlying patterns in the minds of singers, which shape *all* songs sung in the same tradition. This sounds rather less objective than the procedure recommended by Lord and students of the oral epic, but if Nagler's view of formulaic composition as a generative process is accepted, then it may be that a formula is the more readily identifiable if it is found to exist in a series of variations. While exact repetition can be explained in a number of ways (one recalls Parry's remarks on the repetitions in ancient tragedy) the frequent recurrence of the same *patterns* in phrases which are structurally similar but not identical in content can only be put down to the operation of a common system of formulas in the minds of all the singers involved.

Something of the range of variation to be expected within such a system can be seen from the following:

(1) Εἶδα τὰ φίδια σταυρωτὰ καὶ τὶς ὀχιὲς κουβάρια
   I saw snakes crossed and vipers wound into balls

(2) ποὺ 'ταν τὰ φίδια σταυρωτὰ καὶ οἱ ὀχιὲς πλεγμένες
   where snakes were crossed and vipers twined

41

The formula

(3) ἤβρα τὰ φίδια πλεχταριὰ καὶ τὶς ὀχιὲς γαϊτάνι
I found snakes [like] twine and vipers [like] braid

(4) Θὰ βρεῖς τὰ φίδι' ἀγκαλιαστά, ὀχιὲς περιπλεγμένες
you'll find snakes embracing, vipers intertwined

(5) κι ἀκούω ἀέρες ποὺ τραβοῦν καὶ τὰ στοιχειὰ ποὺ σκούζουν
and I hear winds blowing hard and ghosts howling

(6) Ἀκούω τ' ἀέρι πὄσκουζε, καὶ τὶς ὀξυὲς ποὺ τρίζουν
I heard the wind howl, and the beech trees creaking

(7) 'κούγω τὰ πεῦκα καὶ βροντοῦν καὶ τὲς ὀξυὲς νὰ τρίζουν
I hear pinetrees thundering and beech trees creaking

(8) καὶ βρίστ' ἀθρώπω κεφαλὲς καὶ γυναικῶ πλεξοῦδες
and finds men's heads and women's tresses

(9) ἀκούω τὰ φκιάρια ποὺ βροντοῦν καὶ τὰ τσαπιὰ ποὺ σκάβουν
I hear shovels thundering and pickaxes digging[1]

Examples 1–4 can easily be seen to belong to a formula system such as those described by Parry in Homer and by Lord in the Yugoslav epics. In each case the first half-line (one formula) describes snakes, while the second (another formula) describes vipers. In the first half of each line, the verb form filling the first metrical foot varies so that the formula can be used in a number of grammatical contexts. Similarly with the adjectives which replace *stavrotá* (crossed, examples 3 and 4). Not only do they occupy the same number of syllables, but their meanings are similar and their final *sounds* (the accented *a* at the mid-line caesura) are the same. So much can also be said for the second half of the line in examples 1–4. All the words used to describe the vipers share the same general meaning. The verb form introducing the first half-line in example 2 requires *i ohiés* (nominative) in the second half of the line, which under stricter rules of elision would have disrupted the metre. But it is a feature of oral composition that once a singer has begun a line in a certain way it is too late to go back and change it: since this adaptation of the formula in the first half-line posed no problems, it would be natural for him to continue the line in the way he was used to, even though the grammatical change in this second formula means that it no longer quite 'fits'.

In the remaining examples the syntactical and architectonic pattern by which the two half-lines are joined is constant. But there are other factors which show that despite their different words they belong to the same formula system. In examples 5 and 6 the first half of each line begins with the same words, and the meaning of the verb which completes the half-line is roughly similar in each case, because of its context. That is to say, *travó* and *skoúzo* do not in everyday speech mean the same thing at all, but *travó* applied to the wind means 'blow hard', thus bringing it close to the meaning of *skoúzo* (howl). *Vrontoún* (thunder, examples 7 and 9) shares this general meaning, and example 7 is further related to examples 5 and 6 by the opening word 'hear'. Only in example 8 do we find no familiar words in the first half of the line, although their syntactical arrangement is the same as in the other examples; but the word *plexoúdes* (tresses) in the second half of the line strikes an echo with *plegménes* (twined, example 2), *periplegménes* (intertwined, example 4) and *plehtariá* (twine, example 3). A similar echo arises in the second half of the line in examples 6 and 7, where *ohiés* (vipers) has been replaced by the similar-sounding *oxiés* (beech trees). This device of substituting a word of different meaning but similar sound in a formula is one of the most obvious indications that we are dealing with *oral* composition, and it is interesting to notice that although the meaning of the words in examples 6 and 7 is quite different from those of examples 1–4, they are used to create a similarly sinister effect. It is probably no accident either that all of these examples come from songs which refer in one way or another to the theme of death and the lower world.

What these examples suggest is that formulas in Greek songs are not fixed and memorised units but may be derived by the singer, perhaps during a performance, from a system, or a series of systems, of stylised language and syntax. Considering formulaic composition in this way, it may be difficult to fix the boundary of a formula system without seeming to be arbitrary. Starting from any given formula in a Greek song, I believe it is possible to identify other formulas which belong to the same system, expanding outwards from the original formula in such a way as quickly to overlap with what seem to be other systems, rather as we found variants of a song expanding outwards from our chosen starting point until they began to overlap with other songs. Clearly the Greek singers did employ memorised phrases or 'straight formulas', but these relatively stable formulas must also at one time have been derived from the underlying system, which can be more generally defined as a stylisation of language according to fixed patterns. In adapting the possibilities offered by this system to the requirements of performing a

The formula

song, I believe we can detect three main factors which, consciously or unconsciously, determine the singer's choice of expression. These are architectonic patterns, syntactical patterns, and sense.

(i) Metrical and architectonic patterns

A formula in the Greek tradition is never more nor less than a half-line. By far the most common metre in Greek folk poetry is the 'political verse' (politikós stíhos) of fifteen syllables, which contains two half-lines in the following metrical pattern:[2]

The stress patterns in the first and second feet of the first half-line and in the first foot of the second may be inverted, but the mid-line caesura is always clearly marked. There is practically no enjambement and both caesura and the end of the line regularly coincide with the end of syntactical and sense units. An invariable metrical rule is that the first half of the line should have an iambic ending ($\cup'$ or $'\cup(,)$) while the second half always ends in a trochee ($'\cup$). Since each half-line comprises a self-contained unit, in terms of syntax and sense, it is natural to find that songs are constructed out of architectonic patterns, often of considerable complexity. As a general rule, a line of political verse consists of two units, or formulaic expressions, whose arrangement in the line is in some sense symmetrical.

The architectonic patterns open to the singer of folk poetry were clearly very many, and frequently encompass many lines of a song. Considering for the moment only the more limited case of the single line, we notice that these fall into two broad types: those in which the two half-lines establish an architectonic balance – by repetition of the general sense, or of one or more words in both halves of the line, or by an exact parallelism of expression, where the sense of the second half-line may be either complementary or antithetical – and those in which the second half-line adds new information rather than establishing a pattern.

The different types can be seen in the opening lines of the ballad 'The Bridge of Arta':

(10) Σαρανταπέντε μάστοροι κι ἐξήντα μαθητάδες
τρεῖς χρόνους ἐδουλεύανε τῆς Ἄρτας τὸ γιοφύρι.
Ὁλημερὶς ἐχτίζανε κι ἀπὸ βραδὶ γκρεμιέται.

Μοιριολογοῦν οἱ μάστορες καὶ κλαῖν' οἱ μαθητάδες:
- Ἀλίμονο στοὺς κόπους μας, κρῖμα στὲς δούλεψές μας,   5
ὁλημερὶς νὰ χτίζωμε, τὸ βράδυνὰ γκρεμιέται.
Καὶ τὸ στοιχειὸ ποκρίθηκεν ἀπ' τὴ δεξιὰ καμάρα:
- Ἂν δὲ στοιχειώσετ' ἄνθρωπο, τοῖχος δὲ θεμελιώνει·
καὶ μὴ στοιχειώσετ' ὀρφανό, μὴ ξένο, μὴ διαβάτη,
παρὰ τοῦ πρωτομάστορα τὴν ὤρια τὴ γυναίκα,   10
πόρχετ' ἀργὰ τ' ἀποταχιά, πόρχετ' ἀργὰ στὸ γιόμα.

Forty-five master-craftsmen and sixty apprentices
for three years worked on the bridge of Arta.
All day they would build, and in the evening the work
    fell down.
The master-craftsmen lamented, the apprentices kept
    weeping:
'Alas for our efforts, alas for our labours,   5
all day to build and in the evening have the work fall
    down.
And the spirit [of the river] spoke up from the
    right-hand arch:
'Unless you sacrifice a human, no wall stands firm;
and don't sacrifice an orphan, nor a stranger, nor a
    passer-by,
nor anyone but the master-builder's beautiful wife,   10
who comes here slowly in the morning, who comes here
    slowly at mealtime.'[1]

Lines 1, 4 and 5 are built out of parallel expressions where the words are different in each half of the line but the sense is repeated. Lines 3 and 6 are built in a similarly parallel way but the two halves of the line are antithetical. Line 11 is an example of parallel phrases introduced by the same initial word. The remaining lines belong to the second type, in which new information is provided by the second half of the line.

It is interesting to note that so strong was the instinct of the singer for establishing patterns rather than adding narrative information in the second half of the line, that just under half of the total number of lines in the song are of the patterned type. Lines 8–11 are an example of a larger, more complex pattern, based on what K. Romaios has termed the 'rule of three' (1963). Line 8, of the non-patterned type, states a simple condition: if someone is not sacrificed no wall will stand firm. The next line *as a whole* establishes a pattern by the repetition of the verb of the previous line, so that the two lines now form a structural pattern similar to that which we saw between the two halves of l. 11. In the next line, l. 9, a pattern of three is established (orphan, stranger, passer-by), which is then resolved, by the addition of l. 10, into a larger pattern of three, in which the two halves of the preceding line are 'capped' by the whole line in which it is spelled out that the person to be sacrificed must be the master-builder's wife. And the final line, l. 11, with its additional description of the master-builder's wife alters the balance again, so that the two lines of build-up (ll. 8–9) are balanced by the same number of lines (ll. 10–11) actually devoted to the victim herself.

The fact that the singer was evidently constructing such patterns as he went along, both at the level of the two halves of a line and on a larger scale, clearly affected the formula systems available to him in each case. The first line, for example, belongs to a formula system in which the first half-line very frequently evokes the second. Thus we find,

(11) Σαρανταπέντε Κυριακὲς κι ἐξηνταδυὸ Δευτέρες
      Forty-five Sundays and sixty-two Mondays

(12) μὲ ξηνταπέντε κάτεργα, μὲ ξηνταδυὸ φεργάδες
      with sixty-five galleys, with sixty-two frigates

(13) μὲ τετρακόσια δυὸ φλουριά, μ' ἐξηνταδυὸ ρουμπιέδες
      with four hundred and two florins, with sixty-two gold
      coins

(14) πὄχει τριακόσια δυὸ φλωριὰ καὶ πεντακόσια γρόσια
      who has three hundred and two florins and five hundred
      groats[1]

It is much more common to find these two formula systems together in a line, balancing one another, than to find them used with other formula systems, but examples are found which show that the whole line does not represent a single formula system but a pattern set up by two such systems:

(15) Σαρανταπέντε λεμονιὲς στὸν ἄμμο φυτεμένες
      Forty-five lemon trees planted in the sand

(16) Τρακόσι' ἀρκούδια σκότωσα κι ἐξηνταδυὸ λεοντάρια
      Three hundred bears I killed and sixty-two lions

46

(17) νὰ σοῦ χαρίσω τά φλουριά, ἑξηνταδυὸ ρουμπιέδες

I'll give you the florins, <u>sixty-two gold coins</u>[1]

These examples serve to show that the first line of 'The Bridge of Arta' is made up of two component parts. A count of repetitions would have suggested that the whole line was a formula but what in fact has happened is that two formula systems, which may exist separately, have become a relatively standard pair because of the architectonic pattern set up between them.

The second line of the same song is of a different type. The formula systems which make up each half of the line do not form a pattern and are connected only by their sense. It would be a reasonable prediction that the pattern of the whole line in this case will be much less often repeated than that of the previous line. And this is in fact the case. There is no difficulty, though, in finding the formula systems to which the two halves of the line belong. For the first half-line we find,

(18) Τρεῖς χρόνους ἐπερπάτησα γιὰ 'ν' ὄμορφο κορίτσι

For three years I went on foot [to find] a beautiful girl

(19) Τρεῖς χρόνοι πᾶνε σήμερο, τέσσερις πορπατοῦνε

Three years have gone by today, and rising four[1]

This analysis is not intended to be quantitative and these examples do not represent the whole extent of a formula system. But in these first half-lines we find the same pattern as is found in the line we are considering. The change of 'years' from the accusative to the nominative affects the formula not at all, and in both examples the rest of the formula is made up of a verb or a verb and a predicate which is metrically and syntactically parallel to that of the half-line in 'The Bridge of Arta'. It is also especially interesting to note that in example 19 the half-line is followed by an exactly balancing complement to create a whole line in the same architectonic pattern as the *first* line of 'The Bridge of Arta'. Here we have a good example of the choice facing the singer in shaping the patterns of his song. He could have continued his line with a formula introduced by the word 'four' and completed by a verb which repeated the general sense of 'worked'. That the singer did not choose to do so (in this version at least) was probably determined by the consideration that, following a patterned elaboration of the number of people working on the bridge, a similarly weighted description of the length of time involved would be anticlimactic. The singer in this version evidently preferred to keep the parallel effect for the succeeding line, in which the antithesis between building the bridge by day and its falling down by night has a far greater dramatic effect. The second half of the line falls into one of the commonest formulaic patterns in Greek song, a syntactical arrangement of two nouns describing either where something is, whose something is, or who someone is. In variants of the same song *Artas* (of Arta) is replaced by any two-syllable place-name which was considered to fit the context. In other songs, denoting place we find,

(20) στοῦ δράκ oda τὴν πόρτα   at the dragon's door

(21) στῆς Ἀραπιᾶς τὸν κάμπο   on the plain of Arabia

(22) στῆς λεϊμονιᾶς τὸ φύλλο   among the lemon leaves[1]

There are very many examples of each type, but taking just enough to illustrate the principle, we may note derivatives of the same formula system denoting ownership,

(23) στοῦ πιτσαχτσῆ τ' ἀκόνι   on the knife-grinder's whetstone

(24) Τὰ πρόβατά 'ναι τῆς βροντῆς, τῆς ἀστραπῆς τὰ γίδια
     The sheep belong to the thunder, the goats to the lightning[1]

and to indicate who a person is,

(25) τοῦ Μαυροειδῆ τὴν κάλην   Mavroidis' beloved

(26) μιᾶς χήρας δυχατέρα   a widow's daughter

(27) τοῦ Κώστα ἡ γυναίκα   Kostas' wife[1]

There is scarcely any restriction on the content of the first half-line where this formula system is used, apart from the obvious constraint that the line must make sense. But there are certain ideas, particularly in setting the scene at the beginning of a song, which naturally combine with this formula system. Examples 28–37 are all opening lines of songs:

(28) Μαῦρο πουλὶ ἐκάθουνταν   στοῦ Μπερατιοῦ τὸ κάστρο
     A black bird was sitting   on the castle of Berati

(29) Μαῦρο πουλάκι κάθεται   στῆς Κάσος τ' ἀγριοβούνι
     A black bird sits   on the wild mountain of Kasos

(30) Ἕνας ἀιτὸς καθότανε   στοῦ Ἅδη τὸ περβόλι
     An eagle was sitting   in the garden of Hades

(31) Ἕνα πουλάκι κάθουνταν   στοῦ Ζίδρου τὸ κεφάλι
     A little bird was sitting   on Zidros' head

(32) Τρία πουλάκια κάθουνταν   στὴ ράχη στὸ λημέρι
     Three little birds were sitting   on the ridge in the bandit's
                                       lair

(33) Τοῦ Κίτσ' ἡ μάννα κάθονταν στὴν ἄκρη στὸ ποτάμι
     Kitsos' mother was sitting   at the river at its edge

(34) Τρία πουλάκια κάθουνται   στὸν Ἔλυμπο στὴ ράχη
     Three little birds sit   on Olympos on the ridge

(35) Τρεῖς περδικοῦλες κάθουνται στὴν ἄκρη στὸ Λεβίδι
     Three little partridges sit   on the summit on Levidi

(36) Τρία πουλάκια κάθουνται,   τὰ τρία ἀράδα-ἀράδα
     Three little birds were sitting   the three all in a row

(37) Τρία πουλάκια κάθονταν   κάτω στὴν Ἀλαμάνα¹
     Three little birds were sitting   down at Alamana[1]

Looking first of all only at the formula systems occupying the second
half of each line, we can see at a glance that examples 28–31 conform
to the pattern of 'on the bridge of Arta'. In the case of examples 32–5
it may be argued whether the system is the same or different: the metrical pattern remains the same but the syntactical pattern changes so
that the two nouns have equal weight. The meaning is not really different, however, since 'at the river at its edge' means the same as 'at the
river's edge'. This is evidently a closely related formula system.
Examples 36–7 show how different formula systems can also be used in
combination with the same *first* half-line system. Turning our attention
now to the first half of each line, it can be seen that all the examples
with the exception of example 33 belong to the same broad system:
that is to say, they are alike in metre and syntax, the word nearest the
caesura does not change (although its grammatical form does), and the
meaning is constant in all except examples 28 and 29, where the adjective 'black' adds something to the meaning not found in the other
examples. Once again, example 33 has a different system, also very
common, which can be combined with the second half-line systems we
are considering.

How architectonic patterns are built up by juxtaposition of formulas is not difficult to see from these examples. Within this sample the commonest pattern is formed by the juxtaposition of the 'bird(s) sitting' with one of the two formula systems of place which are practically interchangeable. There must be very few places 'generated' by this formula system where one could not imagine a bird or birds sitting. Consequently there is a large number of formulas of this type with which the first half-line system may be combined. The first half-line system, 'Kitsos' mother was sitting', could also be followed by most of the second half-lines in the examples, with one exception – 'on Zidros' head', which would obviously be absurd. Thus there is a slightly greater limitation on the number of formulas deriving from the 'place' system with which the *person* sitting' can be combined, and we find this balanced by the correspondingly frequent substitution of a different system in the second half of the line, where the first includes the name of a person:

(38) Τ' Ἀνδρούτσ' ἡ μάνα θλίβεται,   τ' Ἀνδρούτσ' ἡ μάνα κλαίει
Androutsos' mother grieves   Androutsos' mother weeps

(39) Τ' Ἀνδρούτσ' ἡ μάνα χαίρεται,   τ' Ἀνδρούτσ' ἡ μάνα κλαίει
Androutsos' mother is glad,   Androutsos' mother weeps[1]

The wording in the first half of the line is different in these two cases, but the syntactical pattern is maintained, and in each case a second half-line system is used which forms a symmetrical pattern with the first.

In a similar manner the use of the formula 'the three all in a row' in the second half of the line (example 36) is restricted to those derivatives of the 'bird sitting' system in which the number three appears. On the other hand, if the analysis so far is correct, it should be possible to predict that this limitation will be compensated by the use of 'the three all in a row' to follow *any* first half-line in which the number three appears, irrespective of formula system. And this is precisely what happens:

(40) Τρία ντουφέκια τόδωκαν,   τὰ τρία ἀράδ' ·ἀράδα
Three rifle-shots they fired at him,   the three all in a row

(41) Τρία 'δερφάκια κρέμασαν,   τὰ τρί' ἀράδ' ἀράδα
Three brothers were hanged,   the three all in a row

(42) Τρία μπαϊράκια κίνησαν   τὰ τρί' ἀράδ' ἀράδα
Three banners set out,   the three all in a row

(43) 'Σ τ' Ἀλῆ πασᾶ τὰ ἔφεραν,   τὰ ἔξ' ἀράδ' ἀράδα
     They took them to Ali Pasha   the six all in a row[1]

The ability to predict combinations of formula systems through an analysis of architectonic patterns in songs suggests how it may be possible to approximate analytically to the intuitive processes of the traditional singer.

One final prediction. The examples of first and second half-lines we have been looking at suggest a large number of possible substitutions which would probably be legitimate so long as the rules of pattern and congruity were not violated. To bring this discussion back to its starting point, the ballad 'The Bridge of Arta', I wish to suggest only one:

(44) Τρία πουλάκια κάθουνταν   στῆς Ἄρτας τό γιοφύρι
     Three little birds were sitting   on the bridge of Arta[1]

This is in fact the opening line of a kleftic ballad.

(ii) Syntactical patterns

We have already looked at cases where the repetition of a syntactical pattern, in a fixed place in the metre, seemed to suggest the existence of a formula system. It might be argued of course that such syntactical repetitions are merely the result of using a relatively inflexible metrical scheme. But (although I can provide no quantitative data) it is my experience that the writing poet is normally as assiduous in avoiding such repetitions as in varying his diction. The writing poet is keenly aware of the dangers of monotony, and has the means at his disposal to prevent his verse from falling into too much of a set pattern. The folk poet, in Greece at least, was probably conscious of this danger, but the means available to him for circumventing it were different.

Certainly there are enough examples of the literary use of the political verse in which syntactical repetitions of this kind do *not* occur, or are found only rarely, for us to regard them as a characteristic of folk poetry. That such repetitions are indeed the product of formula systems can most easily be seen by looking at examples where a balance of two syntactical patterns forms a whole line – for example, in the line,

(45) Μοιρολογοῦσε κι ἔλεγε, μοιρολογάει καὶ λέγει
     He was lamenting and saying, he laments and says.[1]

Here the pattern of half-lines is one of verbal repetition, with the verb tenses changed in the second half-line in accordance with the metrical pattern. There are many lines in Greek folk poetry whose syntax and pattern are parallel to this – for example,

(46) Καὶ τοῦ Γιαννάκη μίλησε καὶ τοῦ Γιαννάκη λέει

And he spoke to Yannakis and to Yannakis he says

(47) Στὸν ὕπνο ποὺ κοιμόμουνα, στὸν ὕπνο ποὺ κοιμᾶμαι

In my sleep as I was sleeping, in my sleep as I sleep[1]

Given these examples it is easy to conceive of two formula systems, each the length of a half-line, the first of which is determined by a verb in the past tense, the second by a verb in the present. The tendency we have already observed, for about half of the total number of lines in a song to establish a pattern of complementation or antithesis, would naturally result in the frequent occurrence of lines such as this, where the verb of the first half-line is repeated with a change of tense in the second. In this case the selection of formal systems and the balancing of one by another is dictated purely by the requirements of the pattern in the singer's mind, and not by the sense of the song; since in none of these cases does the second half-line add anything to the information conveyed by the first.

There are instances, too, of substitution of words in what looks like a relatively fixed formula, while the syntax remains unaltered. In the line,

(48) καὶ πῆρε δίπλα τὰ βουνά, δίπλα τὰ κορφοβούνια

and he took to the mountains, to the mountain peaks[1]

often repeated in kleftic songs, it can be seen that the first half of the line has 'generated' the second as a suitable and relatively invariable complement. Verbal changes, which quite alter the sense of both halves of the line, produce the following:

(49) καὶ βγῆκα νύχτα στὰ βουνά, ψηλὰ στὰ κορφοβούνια

and I went out at night to the mountains, high among the peaks[1]

What has, presumably, determined the expression here is the syntactical structure which underlies both the formula system of each half-line and their combination to make a whole line.

As a final example of a repeated syntactical pattern, we may consider the description of a girl dressing for a special occasion, which is repeated with only minor variations in many narrative songs:

(50) Βάνει τὸν ἥλιο πρόσωπο καὶ τὸ φεγγάρι στῆθος
  She wears the sun in her face and the moon in her breast[1]

This can be varied to describe a beautiful girl irrespective of occasion:

(51) Ἔσει φεγγάριν πρόσωπο, τὸν ἥλιο μηλοβούτσια
  She has the moon in her face, the sun in the apples of her cheeks[1]

But the same syntactical pattern also underlies the line, unrelated in terms of sense,

(52) βγῆκε κι ὁ ἥλιος κόκκινος καὶ τὸ φεγγάρι μαῦρο
  The sun came out red and the moon black[1]

(iii) Sense

Parry originally defined the formula as 'a group of words which is regularly employed under the same metrical conditions to express a given essential *idea*' (my italics). Most of the examples of formula systems we have so far considered in Greek folk songs do not conform exactly to this definition, since in many cases we dealt with syntactical and architectonic arrangements rather than with groups of words expressing the same idea. But formulas in this narrower sense are frequent enough in Greek folk poetry – obvious examples would be the 'bird sitting' (examples 28–32, 34–7) and examples 1–4 describing the snakes in the lower world. Since there are many recurring ideas in Greek songs it is natural that we should find formulaic expressions, repeated from song to song, which are specially designed to handle them. In the series of songs where a galley-slave sighs, miraculously stopping the ship, versions from different parts of Greece have virtually identical lines describing the event:

(53) ὁ σκλάβος ἀνεστέναξε καὶ στάθηκ᾽ ἡ φιργάδα
  the slave sighed and the frigate stopped

(54) Γ·εῖς σκλάβος ἀναστέναξε καὶ στάθηκ᾽ ἡ φριγάδα
  a slave sighed and the frigate stopped

(55) Κι ὁ σκλάβος ἀναστέναξε κι ἐστάθη τὸ καράβι
  And the slave sighed and the ship stopped[1]

Perhaps one should suspect memorisation of a fixed text at this point; but the evidence that the line does *not* belong to a memorised text but is formulaic comes, not from the many cases of repetition, but from an instance of significant variation. In a manuscript of the oldest surviving Greek folk song, 'Armouris', a comparable incident occurs in which someone sighs and provokes a sympathetic reaction from inanimate nature:

(56) βαρέα βαρέα ἀναστέναξεν καὶ ἐσείστη ὁ πύργος ὅλος

Heavily heavily he sighed and the whole castle shook[1]

With the exception of the key-word 'sighed' the words are not the same in this example. But the *essential idea* is certainly the same, as is the syntactical pattern.

This is an example of conservative use of the formula system in Greek folk poetry, where the use and repetition of the formula are dictated by the meaning. Here we have a formula which corresponds exactly to Parry's definition of the epic formula – and yet we could not be certain that it was truly a formula, and not a memorised catch-phrase or part of a fixed text, until we had found a significant variation of its most common form.

The following are examples of formulas defined by their sense:

(57) δὲν ἐκιλάηδειε τὸ πουλὶ ὡς κελαηδοῦνε τ' ἄλλα,
μόνο κιλάδειε κι ἔλεγε (τσῆ νύφης μοιρολόγια)

the bird did not sing as other birds sing,
but sang and spoke (the bride's lament)

(58) Δὲν ἐκιλάηδε τὸ πουλὶ ὡς κιλαηδοῦν τ' ἀηδόνια,
μόνο κιλάηδε κι ἤλεγε (γιὰ τὰ ξενιτεμένα)

The bird did not sing as nightingales sing,
but sang and spoke (about those in exile)

(59) Δὲν ἐλαλοῦσε σὰν πουλί, σὰν ὅλα τὰ πουλάκια,
μόν' ἐλαλοῦσε κι ἔλεγεν ἀνθρωπινὴ λαλίτσα

It did not give voice like a bird, like all the little birds,
but gave voice and spoke with human speech[1]

The 'essential idea' in each case is that the bird did not sing as birds normally do, but spoke instead, and the words used to describe this are similar in all three examples. But the second line in each case shows how even a use of formulas determined by the 'essential idea' can be fitted into different architectonic patterns. In examples 57 and 58 the second line begins with part of the 'essential idea', but the singer has the choice in the second half of the line of either adding new information (*what* the bird said) or of spelling out how it spoke – with human voice. And example 59 gives a hint of what we can expect to find in the following examples – that when the sense is fixed the syntactical pattern of the words is likely to vary. 'It did not sing *like* a bird' in example 59 belongs in terms of words and general sense to the same system as 'the bird did not sing' but is syntactically different and requires a correspondingly different second half-line.

It is not surprising to find that the same idea may be expressed elsewhere by formulaic expressions which belong to quite different syntactical and architectonic patterns:

(60) a. κι ἕνα πουλί, χρυσὸ πουλί   b. ἀπανωθιὸ καὶ λέγει
      a. and a bird, a golden bird   b. [in the air] above says

(61) a. ἀκοῦν πουλιὰ καὶ κελαδοῦν,   b. ἀκοῦν πουλιὰ καὶ λένε
      a. they hear birds sing   b. they hear birds say

(62) Πάντα κελάηδ'ναν κι ἔλεγαν . . .
      [The birds] would always sing and say . . . [1]

That these lines are also formulaic is not hard to demonstrate, but there is no question here of 'the same group of words' being used to express a given idea. Example 60a belongs to the pattern also found in

(63) Ἕναν πουλλίν, καλὸν πουλλίν, ἐβγαίν' ἀπὸ τὴν Πόλιν
      A bird, a good bird, came out from the City

(64) Μωρὲ βουνί, κακὸ βουνί, πουτάνα Καταβόθρα
      Mountain, evil mountain, you whore Katavothra[1]

Examples 60b and 61b seem based on a common pattern, while example 61a belongs to the system shared by examples 5, 6, 7, and 9. And example 62 belongs to the same system as we saw in examples 45–7. This half-line could either be followed by *what* the bird said (as is in fact the case) or by a repetition according to the pattern of examples 45–7, for example, with the final verb repeated in the present tense.

E. THE ROLE OF THE FORMULA

From what has been said it will be evident that the formula, or formula system, in Greek folk poetry has more than a mnemonic purpose. Certainly it has *some* mnemonic function. One has only to become familiar with a number of folk songs to recognise recurring patterns, and it is surprisingly easy, when in doubt of the exact words of a song, to reconstruct a credible version by substituting words of one's own so long as the pattern of the lines has been remembered, or (as must surely be the case with an experienced singer) internalised to the point where conscious remembering is not necessary.

But what is most striking after even a brief analysis of Greek formula systems is their complexity. A single formula can be related to several formula systems at once – in terms of the architectonic pattern set up by its relation to other formulas, and in particular to the formula which complements it to fill a line; in terms of its syntactical arrangement; and in terms of the actual words used or their general sense. If a mnemonic purpose was all, surely we would have found a far more economical system in operation, even allowing for the diversity of regions and the number of singers involved in the tradition? In the Yugoslav tradition Lord identified a principle of 'thrift', which is also found in Homer, according to which a singer will tend to use one formula and only that formula to express his given essential idea (Lord, 1960, p. 53).

The formula systems we have looked at frequently do share an 'essential idea', but not necessarily a group of words. In attempting to understand the extent of variation found in Greek formulas we should not be tempted to impose too inflexibly the conclusions reached by Lord in analysing another tradition. The aims of the Greek singers cannot have been the same as those of the *guslari*, who sang on an epic scale, and consequently they may have solved the same problems of oral singing in a different way. It seems that the complex interlocking structure of formula systems in Greek folk poetry has been developed not simply to fulfil a functional role (as a mnemonic system) but rather as a formal system capable of affording satisfaction to singers and their audiences. The patterns underlying formula systems provide the singer not so much with a poetic 'language' as with a poetic 'syntax' which obeys its own rules and, like the 'syntax' of musical phrases, affords pleasure to singer and audience quite apart from the meaning conveyed by the words. In this way a technical device which seemed at first sight to serve only a rather mechanical function in the composition and transmission of oral poetry is central to the structure of Grek folk songs and also enables the singer to communicate at a different level from that of ordinary conversation – that is, to express himself in what we would call poetry.

4. Structure of the Demotic Tradition: Imagery and Themes

A. IMAGERY

One of the most immediately striking features of almost any Greek folk song is the prominent role of imagery. In the majority of cases this imagery is neither merely decorative nor does it offer a pictorial representation of the natural world. Frequently the architectonic patterns of a song or the progress of a theme are worked out in terms of images, and these images often invoke the natural world as a reflection of human emotions or attributes, and also perhaps as an arbiter of order. Although many images of this sort tend to recur with predictable regularity and seem to fulfil fairly standard functions, the range and subtlety of detailed imagery which we find in the songs show that the ability to create and vary images must have been a highly prized aspect of the art of composing and singing. It is this ingenuity in handling imagery, and the ability to develop a lyrical theme almost entirely through images, that most readily distinguishes the demotic tradition of folk poetry in Greece.

This can be seen by comparing two poems, one from a popular religious text of the twelfth century, the other a folk lament.

'Εμέν' οὐ πρέπει νὰ λαλῶ, οὐδὲ νὰ συντυχαίνω,
οὐ πρέπει ἐμὲν νὰ βλέπωμαι, οὐδὲ πάλιν νὰ βλέπω,
οὐδὲ νὰ τρέφωμαι τροφὴν τὴν πρέπουσαν ἀνθρώποις.
'Εμένα πρέπει νὰ θρηνῶ, ἡμέραν ἐξ ἡμέρας.

I ought not to speak, nor to converse,
I ought not to be seen, nor yet to see,
nor to eat food that is fitting to men.
I ought only to lament, day after day.

Δὲν πρέπει ἐγὼ νὰ χαίρωμαι, οὐδὲ κρασὶ νὰ πίνω·
μόν' πρέπ' ἐγὼ νἄμ' σ' ἐρημιὰ σ' ἕνα μαρμαροβούνι,

58

νὰ κείτωμαι τὰ πίστομα, νὰ χύνω μαῦρα δάκρυα,
νὰ γίνω λίμνη καὶ γυαλί, νὰ γίνω κρύα βρύση.

I ought not to be happy, nor to drink wine,
I ought only to be on a desolate marble mountain,
to crouch down head forwards, to weep black tears,
to become a lake, a piece of glass, to become a cool spring.

(Alexiou, 1974, p. 180)[1]

The Byzantine poem is a consecutive rhetorical composition, while the folk song expresses the same theme by an accumulation of images. The theme as such is stated in the first half-line; from there the imagery takes over. From 'drinking wine', an image whose associations are with happiness, we are plunged into a succession of images for grief: this progression provides the means for the singer to build up his song in balancing half-lines and patterns. It is also, as a result of this use of imagery, psychologically much more subtle than the Byzantine text, as each group of images reflects a different stage of grief – shock and deprivation in the second line, a violent outburst in the third, and calm resignation in the last.

This is by no means an isolated example, and many lyrical songs are constructed in this way from a pattern or series of images, which express the meaning of the song through associations rather than by direct statement. Sometimes the effect seems to be deliberately cryptic, as in example 1.

(1) Ὁ ἥλιος βασιλεύει στὰ παραθύρια σου
καὶ σὺ, διαβολοκόρη, βάφεις τὰ φρύδια σου.

The sun sets in your windows
and you, devil-girl, paint your eyebrows.[2]

The tone is clearly one of bitterness, but the first line also expresses admiration. The meaning seems to be both that the sun 'rises and sets' only for the girl, and at the same time that the girl herself *is* the sun for the singer. The second line is probably a deliberate anticlimax, but we are left with a rather sinister impression created by the association between the perhaps garish light of the setting sun on the window pane and the girl's make-up, strengthened by the vituperative epithet – devilgirl. A whole emotional tangle of admiration, bitterness, attraction and perhaps fear is concisely expressed by this juxtaposition of images.

A highly sophisticated play of associations occurs in a line which appears from time to time in narrative songs:

(2) Μαῦρος εἶσαι, μαῦρα φορεῖς, μαῦρο κααλλικεύγεις
    You are black (unhappy), you wear black, you ride a
    (black) horse[2]

To say that someone is black is a normal Greek idiom meaning that he is unhappy; to be dressed in black is a sign of mourning, thus adding to the total effect; and then follows a pun, since *mávro* (black) as a noun means a horse. And as we learn from the end of the song, Kostantinos in this line is advising his comrade Andronikos to forget the woman he loved and go to war instead: by a series of images the singer has suggested, with some subtlety, both Andronikos' state of mind and what the speaker, Kostantinos, thinks he ought to do about it.

The same idea (one might say, the same formula system) is also used in a number of dirges where the figure of Haros (Death) is described:

(3) Μαῦρος εἶναι, μαῦρα φορεῖ, μαῦρ' εἶν' καὶ τ' ἄλογό του
    He is black (unhappy), he wears black, his horse is black too[2]

The images are the same but the associations, although less subtle since there is no pun on 'black' and 'horse', have been shifted to allow for the difference of context. To describe Death as 'black' is a common enough image, but the extra connotation that the image has, of wretchedness and unhappiness, adds an element of poignancy to this humanised figure of Death. Similarly, to describe him as wearing black is again common enough, but the extra connotation of 'mourning' is both apt and ironic. That he also rides a black horse intensifies the general impression, but does not add further to the subtlety of the image.

It is interesting in this case to see how the associations of the same image can vary in different contexts. Equally important is the tendency, which seems to be general, for *different* images to be used in the same context when it recurs in a number of songs or versions. This can be seen in versions of the ballad 'The Dead Brother'.

The story, briefly, is of a mother of nine sons and a single daughter. The youngest son, usually called Kostantinos, persuades the mother to allow his sister to marry a suitor from abroad, by vowing that at need he will fetch her home. Kostantinos and his brothers all die of the plague, leaving their mother all alone in her extremity, and calling for her daughter to come back from abroad. The dead Kostantinos, still bound by his oath, rises from his grave and brings back his sister.

60

Imagery

Mother and daughter are reunited and, in most versions, die in one another's arms. One of the most graphic and dramatic parts of these songs is the description of the ride home, with the girl sitting behind her dead brother in the saddle. As they ride a bird sings with human voice, warning the sister in cryptic fashion that all is not well. In this fixed context there frequently follows an exchange between the brother and sister, in which she recognises some unnatural aspect of his appearance or demeanour and becomes afraid, while he attempts to reassure her. This theme obviously requires imagery for its expression, and of seventeen versions published by N. G. Politis (1885) just under half include this type of question and answer.

(4) – Θαρρῶ, θαρρῶ, κὺρ Κωσταντή, πῶς χωματιᾶς μυρίξεις.
– 'Σ τὴ στράτα ποῦ ἐρχούμανε μ' ἔπιασε μιὰ βροχοῦλα
καὶ βράχηκαν τὰ ροῦχά μου καὶ χωματιᾶς μυρίζω.
– Θαρρῶ, θαρρῶ, κὺρ Κωσταντή, πῶς λιβανιᾶς μυρίξεις;
– 'Σ τὴ στράτα ποῦ ἐρχόμανε 'μπῆκα 'ς ἐρημοκκλήσι
καὶ στέγνωσα τὰ ροῦχά μου καὶ λιβανιᾶς μυρίζω.

'I'm sure, I'm sure, Kostantis, that you smell of earth.'
'On the road as I was coming I was caught in a shower
and my clothes were soaked and I smell of earth.'
'I'm sure, I'm sure, Kostantis, that you smell of incense?'
'On the road as I was coming I went into a chapel
and dried my clothes and I smell of incense.'

(5) – Κώστα μου, τί εἶσαι κίτρινος καὶ τί εἶσαι λερωμένος;
– Ἀρέτω μου, ἤμουν ἄρρωστος, τώρα πεντ' ἔξη χρόνους.

'My Kostas, why are you yellow and why are you soiled?'
'My Areto, I've been ill, five or six years since.'

(6) – ποῦ'ν' τὰ ξανθά σου τὰ μαλλιά, κ' ἡ μαύρη σου γενάδα;
– 'Σ τὴν ἀρρωστιά μ' ἐπέσανε τώρα σαράντα 'μέραις.

'where is your fair hair, and your black beard?'
'They fell off in my illness, forty days since.'

(7) – Καὶ ντ' ἔπαθες, ναὶ ἀδελφέ μ', καὶ κούφαναν τ' ἐμμάτα σ';
– Τ' ὤμματά μ' ἐκούφαναν ἀπὲ τὴν ἀγρυπνίαν.
– Καὶ ντ' ἔπαθες, ναὶ ἀδελφέ μ', καὶ ξάγκωσαν τὰ 'δόντια σ';
– Τὰ 'δόντια μου ἐξάγκωσαν ἀς τὴν ἀνοφαγίαν.
– Καὶ ντ' ἔπαθες ξαν', ἀδελφέ μ', καὶ νέλλαξεν τὸ χρῶμά σ';
– Ἀτὸ 'δὲν 'κ ἔν' ἐλέρωσα ἀς σὴν ἀναπλυ 'σάδαν.

'And what's happened to you, my brother, that your eyes are hollow?'
'My eyes are hollow from not sleeping.'
'And what's happened to you, my brother, that your teeth are stained?'
'My teeth are stained from not eating.'
'And what else has happened to you, my brother, that you've changed colour?'
'That's not so; I'm dirty from not washing.'

(8)   - Φοβοῦμαί σ᾽, ἀδερφάκι μου, καὶ λιβανιαῖς μυρίξεις!
      - Ἐχτὲς βραδὺς ἐπήγαμε πέρα ᾽ς τὸν ἅη Γιάννη,
      κ᾽ ἐθύμιασέ μας ὁ παπᾶς μὲ περισσὸ λιβάνι . . .
      - Πές ποῦ, ποῦ εἶν᾽ τὰ μαλλάκια σου, τὸ πηγορὸ μουστάκι;
      - Μεγάλη ἀρρώστια μ᾽ εὕρηκε, μ᾽ ἔρρηξε τοῦ θανάτου,
      μοῦ πέσαν τὰ ξανθὰ μαλλιά, τὸ πηγορὸ μουστάκι.

'I fear you, little brother, you smell of incense!'
'Yesterday evening we went over to St George's,
and the priest sprinkled us with too much incense . . .'
'Tell me, where is your hair, your bushy moustache?'
'I've had a long illness, that brought me to death's door,
my hair fell out, and my bushy moustache.'

(9)   - Πέ μ᾽, ἀδερφέ μου Κωνσταντή, τί χωματιαῖς μυρίξεις;
      - Προχτὲς τἀμπέλι ἔσκαφτα καὶ χωματιαῖς μυρίζω.
      - Γιὰ ᾽πέ μου, ἀδερφούλη μου, τί λιβανιαῖς μυρίξεις;
      - Ἐψὲς ἤμουν ᾽ς τὴν ἐκκλησιὰ καὶ λιβανιαῖς μυρίζω.
      - Ἀμ᾽ ὥρας ὥρας, Κωσταντή, μυρίξεις καὶ κηρίλαις.
      - Ἐψὲς λαμπάδες ἔχυνα, μυρίζω καὶ κηρίλαις.

'Tell me, brother Konstantis, why do you smell of earth?'
'The other day I was digging the vineyard and I smell of earth.'
'Come tell me, little brother, why do you smell of incense?'
'Yesterday I was in church and I smell of incense.'
'But now and then, Kostantis, you smell of candle-wax too.'
'Yesterday I was making candles, and I smell of candle-wax too.'

(10) - Κώστα μου, τὰ ᾽ματάκια σου πολὺ κοκκινισμένα.
      - Τὴ στράταν ὅπου ἐρχόμουνα, ἐκεῖ γιομίσαν χοῦμας·
      Φύσαε ἀέρας καὶ βοριᾶς γιομίσαν τὰ σκουτιά μου.

'My Kostas, your little eyes are very red.'
'On the road as I was coming, they were filling compost;
the north wind blew and filled up my clothes.'[2]

Three further examples from the University of Ioannina Archive
might be added:[3]

(11) - Κώστα μου τί είσαι κίτρινος, μυρίζεις χωματίλια;
- Έχω τρεῖς μῆνες ἄρρωστος, τρεῖς μῆνες πλαγιασμένος.

'My Kostas, why are you yellow, and smell of earth?'
'I've been ill for three months, for three months I've been
lying down.'

(12) - Κώστα μ' ποῦ τὄχεις τὸν τσαμπά, τὸ φρύδι, τὸ μουστάκι;
- Αὐδόκω μου ἀρρώστησα καὶ πέσαν τὰ μαλλιά μου.

'My Kostas, what have you done with your hair(?) your
eyebrows, your moustache?'
'My Avdoko, I was ill and my hair fell out.'

(13) - Κώστα μ', μυρίζεις χώματα, μυρίζεις τοῦ χωμάτου.
- Άϊντε Ἀρέτω μ' άϊντε στὴ μάννα μας νὰ πᾶμε.

'My Kostas, you smell of earth, you smell of the soil.'
'Come, my Areto, come on, let's go to our mother.'[2]

It seems that in a case like this the singer was relatively free to use
his ingenuity and that, in a tradition which is in many ways conservative, the detailed imagery employed to express a given idea is one area
where quite radical changes do take place from one recorded version of
a song to another. But the freedom involved is a good deal less than the
freedom to improvise. Quite apart from the need for the singer, in con-
tributing images of his own, to do so within the stylised patterns of
language and syntax which govern all songs in the tradition, he seems
also to have been bound to keep his originality within the limits set by
a given theme or context.

Within these restrictions the presence or absence of this creative
contribution makes a considerable difference to the impact of a song.
In example 13 the imagery in question has been determined by the most
obvious association and the simplest balancing pattern. The earth association is the one which would spring to mind most easily, and whereas
in most versions the association is double (with the fact of Kostantinos'
being dead, and with an ironic excuse) here the singer has left out

Kostantinos' ironic answer altogether. Similarly, the antithetical pattern set up by the question and answer is avoided, and the internal pattern of the image is one of the simplest kind – a verbal balancing repetition.

By contrast example 7 shows, in its use of imagery, a full development of the dramatic possibilities of the theme. Here both the associations and the structural patterns are more complex. The singer plays first of all on the double association of the hollow eyes of a skull and the 'hollow' eyes caused by lack of sleep. The associations perfectly balance one another in the sister's question and Kostantinon's reply. A further level of irony is added by the basic truth of his reply. Since the dead don't sleep, his condition is in a sense the result of sleeplessness. In the same way the image of his stained teeth has a double association – with the decay of the grave and with lack of food. The balance is formed in the same way, and Kostaninon's reply contains the same ironic truthfulness. And in the final exchange the ironic use of imagery is sustained by Kostantinon's emphatic denial that he has changed colour. 'It's only that I haven't washed', he snaps back, still with sinister truthfulness.

In the case of these three images, each occupying two lines balanced by ironically related associations, a larger cumulative pattern can also be observed. Kostantinon's hollow eyes can be truly explained away with the least alarm; the state of his teeth is also truly explained, but taken together the two explanations now begin to point to the real truth, that his sister Erin is riding with a dead man. Kostantinon, in his attempt to hide this truth from her, has to deny her third hinting suggestion, that his colour has changed, but cannot deny its implication: he has still to make a true admission. The cumulative effect of these answers is exactly the opposite of what is *said* in each. It is the pattern of question and answer as a whole that reveals the real truth behind the individual statements. One may also note the internal structure of the lines, with Erin's interrogative first half-line repeated in each case, and the pattern of Kostantinon's repetition of the last, key word of the question as the first word of his answer, which is suddenly broken in the last case where he tries to avoid picking up Erin's implication. And in this version, the whole sequence is balanced by Erin's apparent acceptance and the journey which follows, the final part of the song exploiting a see-saw effect between her alternately growing realisation of the truth and regained faith in her brother.

B. THEMES

A. B. Lord defined themes in the Yugoslav context as 'groups of ideas regularly used in telling a tale in the formulaic style of traditional song' (1960, p. 68). The implication of this statement, which also holds good for Greek narrative songs, is that the song tradition is thematically as well as verbally stylised, and that many songs and variants will be made up of a relatively small number of component themes. We have already seen how songs which tell different stories are nonetheless related by the use of common thematic material, and that songs in the tradition are interrelated as much through the recurrent use of a restricted range of themes as through the all-pervasive formula systems.

As we saw in Chapter 2, there are two ways in which a theme can be transferred from one song, or context, to another. Either the same theme may be combined with a differnet set of themes so as to tell a different story, or a different song may be built up by transformation, or reversal, *within* particular themes. The first may be seen in these examples, taken from a group of songs which include the same theme, that of a girl pursued by a Turk or Saracen and given refuge by St George in his church. This theme remains invariable in combination with any one of three other themes, describing a dénouement, which may follow it: the Turk may offer to turn Christian, so that St George gives up the girl and the two are married; St George may give up the girl to the Turk unconditionally; or St George may keep the girl hidden and punish the Turk.

(14) - νὰ βαφτιστῶ στὴ χάρη σου ἐγὼ καὶ τὸ παιδί μου,
ἐμὲ νὰ βγάλουν Κωσταντῆ καὶ τὸ παιδί μου Γιάννη.
Γιὰ νὰ κερδίση τὲς ψυχὲς ἀφέντης ἅι Γιώργης,
ἀνοίξανε τὰ μάρμαρα καὶ βγάλαν τὸ κοράσι.

'[St George,] I'll be baptised for your sake, and my child
as well,
I'll let them call me Kostantis, and my child Yannis.'
So that St George could win souls
the marble [of the chapel] opened and disgorged the girl.

(15) - Ἅι μου Γιώρκη, ἀράπη μου, καὶ νὰ σὲ προσκυνήσω,
φανέρωσέ μου τὴ Ρωμιὰ καὶ νὰ σὲ λουτουρκήσω.
Νοιχτήκασι τὰ μάρμαρα κι ἡ κόρη μέσα φάνη.
Ἀπ᾽ τὰ μαλλιὰ τὴν ἔπιασε καὶ στ᾽ ἄλογον τὴ βάλλει.

- Ἄφησ' με, Τοῦρκ', ἀπ' τὰ μαλλιὰ καὶ πιάσε μ' ἀπ' τὸ χέρι,
κι ἂν εἶναι θέλημα Θεοῦ, θὲ νὰ γενοῦμε ταίρι.

'St George, my Arab, if you want me to worship you,
reveal the Greek girl and I'll say a liturgy for you.'
The marble [of the chapel] opened and the girl was revealed
inside.
He caught her by the hair and set her on his horse.
'Let go, Turk, of my hair and catch me by the hand,
and if it be the will of God, we'll marry.'

(16) Κι ὁ Τοῦρκος ἀπ' τὸν Ἄη-Γιώργη πέρασε καὶ τὸ σταυρό του
κάνει.
-Βόηθα μ', Ἄη-Γιώργη μ', βόηθα μὲ τὴν κόρη γιὰ νὰ πιάσω.
Σοῦ τάζω φόρτωμα κερὶ καὶ φόρτωμα θυμιάμα,
κι ἔνα βουβαλοτόμαρο νὰ σοῦ γεμίσω λάδι.
Κι ὁ Ἄη-Γιώργης βγῆκε ἄπιστος, τὴν ἔδωσε στὸν τοῦρκο.

And the Turk passed by St George's and made the sign of the
cross.
'Help me, St George, help me catch the girl.
I promise you a load of candles and a load of incense,
and a buffalo hide I'll fill for you with oil.'
And St George broke faith, he gave her to the Turk.

(17) Ποιὸς εἶδεν Ἅγιο ψεύτικο καὶ Ἅγιο προδότη
γιὰ νὰ προδίν' τοὺς χριστιανοὺς στὰ τούρκικα τὰ χέρια;

Who ever saw a Saint play false and a Saint a traitor
to betray Christians into Turkish hands?

(18) Ἀκοῦστε χῶρες καὶ χωριὰ 'κκλησιὲς καὶ μοναστήρια,
ποὺ βγῆκε ἀφέντης προδοτὴς καὶ Παναγιὰ γκουντόστα,
καὶ πρόδωσαν μιὰ χλωρασιὰ μέσ' τῶν Τούρκων τὰ χέρια.

Hear this, towns and villages, churches and monasteries:
a saint has turned traitor and the Virgin Mary a betrayer (?),
they've betrayed a young girl into the hands of Turks.

(19) Ἄϊ Γιώργη μὴ πιστεύετε κι Ἄϊ Γιώργη μὴ προσκυνᾶτε,
Ἄϊ Γιώργης βγῆκε ἄπιστος καὶ μ' ἔδωσε τοῦ Τούρκον.

Don't believe in St George and don't worship St George,
St George broke faith and gave me to the Turk.

(20) Ἀκοῦστε σεῖς Χριστιανοί, καὶ σεῖς μώρ' βαφτισμένοι,
ὅποιος δὲν πιστεύει σὲ τοῦτον, τὸν Ἅγιο Γεώργην.

[The Turk takes hold of the girl:]
Hear this Christians and you who have been baptised,
whoever doesn't believe in him, St George.

(21) κι ὁ Ἅη-Γιώργης τὸν τοῦρκο γκάβωσε καὶ γλύτωσε τὴν κόρη.
and St George blinded the Turk and saved the girl.

(22) - Ἄνοιξε Ἁγιώργη, ἄνοιξε τὴν κόρη γιὰ νὰ πάρω.
Μιὰ κατάρα τοὔδωσε καὶ κεῖ τὸν ἐμαρμάρωσε.

'Open up, St George, open up and let me take the girl.'
A curse he put on him and turned him to marble on the spot.[2]

Example 14, which comes from Lefkás and was published at the end
of last century, reveals a rather naive piety and chauvinism which is
markedly absent from the others. In example 15 the final theme is
ambiguous. St George gives up the girl in response to the Turk's promise to say the liturgy and the girl's final words suggest that the Turk
will indeed have to change his religion if he is to have his way with her.
But in examples 16–20 St George appears in a very bad light indeed. In
all of these the theme is constant – the saint gives up the girl in his protection to her pursuer – but the singer's comment on this behaviour
varies. In example 16 it is matter-of-fact, in example 17 it is expressed
in the manner of a traditional *adýnaton*, or paradox, while in example
18 the singer clearly wished to proclaim the saint's shortcomings to the
world. The singer in example 19 tells his story from the girl's point of
view, and thus was allowed greater rancour, and example 20, by a
curious reversal, presents this instance of treachery on the saint's part
as a proof of his power, and a reason why he deserves to be revered.
And in the last two examples the final theme is quite different.

This grouping of themes, in which a Christian girl is pursued by a
Turk, often attracts another theme whose separate existence in other
contexts is well attested. This is the theme of the 'valiant maiden', the
girl who joins a battle or fights alongside the klefts in man's attire. In
the common context of this theme, the girl's sex is accidentally discovered by one of her comrades, whom she may marry or kill or bind
by oath of silence. In example 14 the theme of the 'valiant maiden' and
that of the girl pursued by a Turk and given refuge by St George have
been placed together to form a different context. The resulting song

cannot be considered simply as a variant, and still less as a 'confusion' between preexisting songs. In combining the two themes in question, which for the sake of argument we will suppose a singer took from two distinct, preexisting songs, the bard if he is talented enough may give the themes a new significance, by playing on some aspect of the relation in which they now stand. This was done most effectively by the Cretan singer who began with the theme of the 'valiant maiden', using a formulaic opening and the form of the *adýnaton*, or paradox, commonly associated with the theme:

(23) Ποιὸς εἶδε κόρην ὄμορφη 'ς τ' ἄλογο καβαλλάρης;
Who ever saw a beautiful girl riding on horseback?

and at the end of the song, after St George has betrayed the girl, comments on the saint's behaviour by drawing attention to the symmetry between the two themes: both involve a contradiction of expected roles, something, in fact, paradoxical, and the singer plays on this to point his moral:

(24) Ποιὸς εἶδε τέθοιον ἄγιο σὰν καὶ τὸν ἅϊ Γιώργη;
Who ever saw such a saint as St George?

Here a singer has combined themes which in other songs are independent of one another, in order to create a new context and a new meaning by exploiting the symmetrical pattern set up between them.

This symmetry is an important feature of Greek narrative songs, even of those whose narrative sequence seems confused or incomplete, and suggests that at the broader level of grouping his themes in a song, the singer was accustomed to express himself in the same kind of architectonic patterns as govern his diction.[4]

The second way in which themes may be transferred from one song to another is by transformation or inversion. Such a transformation or reversal may be in response to a different context, as in the case of example 12 in Chapter 2, where the evil mother-in-law becomes a father-in-law to suit a changed set of circumstances. But there is a significant number of examples in which such a transformation seems quite gratuitous, at least as regards the architectonic pattern of the song. The most striking examples of this, which must be put down to a single singer's exercising his ingenuity, occur where a well-known theme takes an unexpected twist. This happens in a relatively small number of versions, but often with a powerful dramatic effect. In one out of the seventeen versions of 'The Dead Brother' published by Politis, Areti, instead of dying with her mother, becomes a bird (Politis, 1885, No. 4); in a few versions of the 'dying hero' theme, the hero on his deathbed is resurrected (Zambelios, 1852, pp. 700–1; Romaios, 1958); and in one version of a song where a husband returning after a long absence is recognised by his wife, which usually ends happily with the couple going to bed together, a simple transformation in the last line is used with electrifying effect. The wife wakes up:

(25) Γυρίζει βλέπει δίπλην τση τὸ χάρο κ᾽ ἐκοιμᾶτο
She turned and saw beside her Death as he slept[5]

C. 'TRADITION AND THE INDIVIDUAL TALENT'

In discussing the composition and structure of Greek songs we have been obliged to return again and again to the question of *variation*. At the levels of formulaic diction, imagery and themes, we have noted situations where the individual singer was most likely to substitute something of his own for what he had heard, and those where in the majority of cases he has been content to repeat a phrase, image or theme in exactly the form in which it had been used by other singers. It is unfortunate that we know so little about the processes of composition at a time before written versions of songs began to circulate. But from the internal evidence of the songs we can say with absolute certainty that they were composed in quite a different way from that in which a poem or narrative is written in the western literary tradition. 'Composition', as we can see from these songs, involves two apparently separate processes. Firstly there is the formation of the relatively standard groups of formulas, image-patterns and narratives which are so consistent all over the Greek-speaking world that we cannot suppose that they were independently arrived at by singers even working within a restricted traditional framework. And the second process, which must follow it in time, concerns the inventiveness of the individual singer in choosing among these traditional elements and varying them within certain limits.

It is unhelpful to equate these two processes respectively with the older notions of original or archetypal composition and the corruption and confusion which for some scholars is still implied by oral transmission. Rather, in the second process, which is closer in time to the recording of the particular version or variant in which it results, we can detect the operation of a selective principle: the singer 'composes' his version of the song by selecting from a wide range of elements which he knows to be part of the tradition. It is to be expected that most of these elements will be formulas, images and themes which he has actually heard from other singers; but if, as I have suggested, the formal structure of the tradition is generative, he has in theory also to select from a wide range of possibilities which he has *never* heard. In this sense he will be composing, in the more usual sense of the word, and it is to be expected that a proportion of his song, probably not a very large one, will consist of material that has never previously been actualised. But we can go on to imagine a further step. A particularly fine version of a song is actualised in this way and contains a number of formulas, uses of imagery and perhaps a theme or two either rearranged or internally transformed. In discussing the artistry necessary to create successful architectonic patterns (at all three levels) we have already suggested how, within the terms of the tradition, an individual version of a song may be superior in quality to another. It is to be assumed that this, in conjunction with external factors such as the personality and prestige of the singer, will influence his hearers also. For a subsequent singer, when he comes to make his selection of actual and potential elements for his song, these 'original' elements are already actual. They will therefore come to mind more easily, particularly if the first singer's version has been admired and praised, and so far as he is able (he may be more or less skilled in combining the elements of tradition to make a song) he will tend to repeat the 'new' version of the song, which now is no longer new or original but has become part of the received tradition.

Clearly this process can be endless, and by extending it backwards instead of forwards we can just as well use it to explain the first type of composition mentioned. We need not suppose that all the traditional material which is relatively invariable has been composed by a different process as an 'archetype', but that this too is the result of selection and endorsement.

Although writers on folk poetry, perhaps because of a traditional education in literature, are usually hesitant to admit the role played in composition by the fluidity of the 'texts' with which they have to deal, this approach to composition and transmission has more readily been adopted by their colleagues on the side of folk *music*. The Hungarian composer and collector of folk songs, Zoltán Kodály, said in 1941,

> In folk music, a new transcription, a variation, is produced by the singer on each occasion. An essential trait of folk song is this power

of unconditional ownership; but this used to exist also in high art – Shakespeare, Bach, Handel. At first it seems that the mode of production is entirely different: here we have a process of individual creation, there a slow variation of existing material leading to a new work through tiny changes. But let us look closer at musical history. Do compositions of such individual character, showing no likeness to anything already in existence, spring from the heads of composers like Minerva from the head of Jupiter? (Quoted in Lloyd, 1975, p. 64)

Kodály suggests that the art-composer is no less dependent than the folk musician upon his tradition and that the development of musical style is not necessarily any more rapid for the former. 'A new type of folk song develops from existing forms by slow variation, but hardly at a slower pace than that discernible in art music.'

The International Folk Music Council definition allows for a similar process: 'Folk music is the product of a musical tradition that has been evolved through the process of oral transmission. The factors that shape the tradition are: (i) continuity which links the present with the past; (ii) variation which springs from the creative impulse of the individual or the group; and (iii) selection by the community, which determines the form or forms in which the music survives' (I.F.M.C., 1955, p. 23).

Both of these are fair and accurate accounts of the process of transmission, but the role and meaning of originality in oral tradition still require discussion. Again in an article on folk music rather than on poetry, Bertrand Bronson makes the suggestive point:

The folk-memory does not recall by a note-for-note accuracy, as a solo performer memorises a Beethoven sonata. Rather it preserves a melodic idea in a state of suspension, as it were, and precipitates that idea into a fresh condensation with each rendition, even with each new stanza sung. There is no correct form of the tune from which to depart, or to sustain, but only an infinite series of positive realisations of the melodic idea. (1954)

The originality of the individual singing within a tradition is confined to the exercise of selection and judgement in the combining of elements given by the tradition, the majority of which have themselves become relatively stable parts of tradition as a result of a similar process of selection and endorsement. Expressed in this way, especially nowadays when the emphasis in many branches of art is on the discovery and exploitation of new forms and materials, the creative role of the traditional singer may sound quite insignificant. But we must be careful how we use the term 'original'. Even in English and European literature the meaning given to 'originality' has not always been what it most often is today.

We should also not forget the comment of Kodály, who suggested that musical styles, conventions and thematic material change no more rapidly in art music than in traditional folk music. It may be suggested that the role of tradition and the proportion of original innovation that is really acceptable in sophisticated art music or literature is not so very different from what we find in folk poetry. In this connection it is interesting to note the opinion of T. S. Eliot in the essay whose title I have borrowed (from tradition) as the heading for this section. Eliot was of course writing about the English literary tradition, which he saw as part of a larger tradition, that of European literature from Homer to his own day. And yet his remarks hold surprisingly true for folk poetry as well.

> No poet, no artist of any art, has his complete meaning alone. His significance, his appreciation is the appreciation of his relation to the dead poets and artists. You cannot value him alone; you must set him, for comparison, among the dead . . . The necessity that he shall conform, that he shall cohere, is not onesided; what happens when a new work is created is something that happens simultaneously to all the works of art which preceded it. The existing monuments form an ideal order among themselves, which is modified by the introduction of the new (the really new) work of art among them. The existing order is complete before the new work arrives; for order to persist after the supervention of novelty, the *whole* existing order must be, if ever so slightly, altered; and so the relations, proportions, values of each work of art toward the whole are readjusted; and this is conformity between the old and the new. (Eliot, 1932, p. 15)

Eliot's contention here may be perhaps the harder to grasp, although no less justified, as he was speaking of literature and not of traditional folk poetry. In an oral tradition, of course, there are no monuments of the past which directly invite comparison. Rather, as we have seen, these monuments are the selections made and endorsed by long-dead poets and repeated by later generations in their songs. The equivalent of literary monuments in folk poetry are the creative possibilities allowed by the stylised language, patterns and thought of the singer's culture that have already been actualised by older singers. And the modification of these past monuments which is effected by each new work is much more immediate in its impact on folk tradition than on a literary tradition: since the new work is itself the modification of the old. While both kinds of tradition are continuously modified by a similar process, it is only when written monuments survive that this development can be charted. In folk tradition the elements selected, endorsed and *retained* over, say, two hundred years, are bound to be extensively modified and updated in response to changes in circumstances and taste; but the singer, unlike the writing poet, cannot know this. He is not required to respond to song texts which are two hundred years old, but merely to those elements which seem to him timeless but which may in fact have been continuously changing.

There is indeed an interesting and important difference between oral and written traditions, but it does not concern the relation of individual creativity to tradition. As Eliot said elsewhere, 'The poem which is absolutely original is absolutely bad; it is, in the bad sense, 'subjective' with no relation to the world to which it appeals' (Eliot, 1928, p. 10); and this is precisely true for folk poetry as well. The significant difference lies in what Eliot called the 'historical sense':

> Someone said: 'The dead writers are remote from us because we *know* so much more than they did.' Precisely, and they are that which we know. (Eliot, 1932, p. 16)

They are just what the folk poet does *not* know, and therein lies the largest single difference between oral and literary traditions. The folk poet has no historical perspective beyond the previous generation from which he has learnt his songs. Although both types of tradition develop diachronically, the writing poet is conscious of the fact and has to measure himself against works which are no longer 'living'. For the folk poet only what is 'living' is handed down to him: in his eyes his tradition is synchronic and the songs he sings are ageless. He is unaware of his own creative contribution, and untroubled by the idea, because he has no monuments of the past against which to measure it.

5. The Emergence of the Demotic Tradition

It has generally been the practice, among scholars seeking to unravel the historical problems associated with Greek folk songs, to treat individual songs as special cases and either to extrapolate a hypothetical archetype for the song, or to discover ancient or medieval parallels from which songs are supposed to be derived. If the analysis of the nature and structure of the tradition in the last two chapters is accepted, the value of this line of arguing is limited. The songs of Yannis, reprieved from death on condition that his bride will lend him half the years of her life (Politis, N. G., 1909, pp. 250–1), and of Mavrianos, making a wager on his sister's chastity (Petropoulos, 1958, pp. 110–12) are most likely related respectively to the Alcestis story and a tale in the *Decameron*. But each of these stories has been retold by (presumably) generations of singers whose thought and expression were governed by considerations quite different from those which affected Euripides and Boccaccio. The point is that if a folk tradition is admitted to have been a creative process involving its own conventions and expectations, then we can no longer regard *transmission* as the progressive corruption of an original text. This is as true if the original is supposed to have been borrowed from literary tradition or to have been invented. Thus the appeal to Euripides or Boccaccio in these instances, and a great many similar appeals in more doubtful cases, brings us no nearer to the archetypal first version of the folk song. From a discussion of archetypes, the argument becomes one merely of sources. And the sources of folk songs no more help to explain the nature and quality of the song tradition than the sources of Shakespeare explain Shakespeare's qualities as a dramatist.

Lévi-Strauss' famous image for the savage, or mythical, mind, as a *bricoleur* is probably applicable to the folk poet or singer. He is prepared to use anything that comes to hand, provided it conforms to a type of thought-pattern, but without regard for what it is or where it

comes from (Lévi-Strauss, 1972, pp. 16–22). The tradition is this process, or technique, of *bricolage*, and it is the rise and development of
the tradition in this sense, and not the origins of particular songs,
themes or 'motifs', that I wish to chart in the present chapter.

A. ORIGINS OF THE POLITICAL VERSE AND BYZANTINE FOLK SONG

It would be optimistic to suppose that the origin of the predominant
metre of Greek folk poetry, the fifteen-syllable 'political verse', would
necessarily shed any light on the origin or antiquity of the modern folk
song tradition. In fact the range of theories which have been proposed
to account for the appearance and popularity of this metre from the
twelfth century or earlier makes it practically impossible even to form
hypotheses on the subject. However, the recently published view of
Michael Jeffreys (1974) must be mentioned as he has produced a considerable amount of suggestive evidence for the use of political verse
as a popular or folk metre much earlier than is often supposed.

Jeffreys believes that there is a continuous line of descent from the
Latin *versus quadratus*, used for mainly satirical purposes during the
triumph of a Roman general, through the later Byzantine 'acclamations' to the Emperor in the Hippodrome, to the political verse which
by the twelfth century was firmly established as a medium for popular
or low-brow didactic literature. Whether or not the connection with
Latin accentual verse is finally accepted, Jeffreys has offered evidence
for the attitude of the earliest *literati* known to have used political verse
to the medium in which they were working. Direct comments from
Planudes and Eustathios of Thessalonike, and attitudes extrapolated
from the voluminous writings of Tzetzes and others reveal a consistent,
almost standardised attitude to the fifteen-syllable accentual metre.
Such verses, according to these authors, are playful, common, rustic
and trite (Jeffreys, 1974, p. 161).

This attitude on the part of the *literati*, usually combined with a
grudging acceptance that the 'vulgar' metre had come to stay, and
coupled with the lack of any single author or text to which such an
important innovation could be attributed, suggest that the metre had
previously been established at a non-literate level. As Jeffreys sums up
this part of his argument,

> Just as nobody would now dispute the fact that Demotic Greek,
> bearing a surprising degree of resemblance to the modern language,

was spoken in Constantinople in the twelfth century and before, so there is, I think, little more reason to doubt the existence at that date of the vernacular political verse as a major medium of expression for the illiterate and half-literate members of Greek society – verse written, spoken, and sung by them and for them'. (1974, p. 161)

The rest of Jeffreys' argument is concerned with showing how the old Latin *versus quadratus* may have been preserved at least until the tenth century through the medium of popular acclamations chanted in the Hippodrome in praise of members of the Imperial family. The supporting evidence here is very scanty and the main difficulty with the argument, for our purposes at least, is that, since the *versus quadratus* was not the same as the political verse, Jeffreys has still to allow for an intermediate stage in the evolution of the latter. Thus the hypothetical derivation of the political verse from the Roman metre does not alter the fact that most of the acclamations and such fragments of apparently popular poetry as we have dating from before the tenth century are in mixed eight- and seven-syllable lines. For this reason, although I am inclined to accept Jeffreys' argument for the popular origin of the metre, its immediate derivation, and the evolution of the folk song style and structure which depend on it, must be the result of a systematic combination of existing eight- and seven-syllable units, probably no earlier than the ninth or tenth centuries.

A further point about the acclamations: although these tend to be in a markedly popular language for the period (fifth–tenth centuries), such accounts as we have of their *performance* in the Hippodrome point to something much more official and less spontaneous than could possibly be associated with folk song (Cameron, 1976, pp. 231–2). The singing was accompanied by large groups of wind instruments and at least two portable water organs (Cameron, 1973, pp. 33–4, plate 19) and was antiphonal in the organised manner of church music (Wellesz, 1949, pp. 103–4). Such music for them as survives (solely for acclamations with a religious purpose) is entirely within the tradition of Byzantine church music (Wellesz, 1949, p. 120; Tillyard, 1912, pp. 240–1) which, with its probable origin in middle-eastern religious chant, can have had little or nothing to do with folk music of the same period. Far from being a manifestation of folk poetry or reflecting its trends, the acclamations from the Roman period onwards are thought to derive from religious traditions of the middle east which go back to the Old Testament and Babylonian ritual (Wellesz, 1949, pp. 49, 365; Kraeling and Mowry, 1957, p. 290).

Other evidence that the folk tradition, in something resembling its present form, may have existed before the twelfth century is rare and in my opinion worthless. Apart from the controversy surrounding the epic *Diyenis Akritis* and the 'akritic' folk songs, which will be discussed in the next section, the information that we possess tells us no more than that folk songs of some kind existed – as, indeed, it would be surprising if they had not. In a now famous comment, one Arethas, Bishop of Caesarea, referred in the early tenth century to 'the cursed Paphlagonians who compose odes containing the deeds of famous men and sing them for an obol at every house' (Kouyeas, 1913, p. 239). But there is no evidence for this practice in the modern demotic tradition, which seems never to have been the province of professionals and is as summary in its dealings with historical characters as with historical events and places. Nor can we be certain that these Paphlagonians even sang in Greek.

One of the oldest surviving examples of political verse is a fragment of a dance-song sung in the Hippodrome of the Butchers at Constantinople, celebrating the return of spring and dated to the early tenth century:

Ἴδε τὸ ἔαρ τὸ γλυκὺ πάλιν ἐπανατέλλει,
χαρὰν ὑγίειαν καὶ ζωὴν καὶ τὴν εὐημερίαν,
ἀνδραγαθίαν ἐκ Θεοῦ τοῖς βασιλεῦσι Ρωμαίων
καὶ νίκην θεοδωρητὸν κατὰ τῶν πολεμίων.

(Jeffreys, 1974, p. 168; Politis, N. G., 1911, p. 649)

Behold sweet spring returns again,
[bringing] joy, health and life and well-being
valour and might from God to the kings of the Romans
and God-given victory over their foes.

The first two lines are quoted in two different places in the same manuscript and show the sort of variations one would expect in a song written down from memory. But the language, which is probably not quite the spoken language of the time, and the formal references to God and the Emperor suggest that this is a ceremonial rather than a folk song. Nor does it seem to be based, even remotely, on structural features similar to those of the modern demotic tradition.

The earliest surviving example which convincingly reflects the existence of a tradition such as that of modern folk songs is also reported by Jeffreys (1974, p. 160), and was recorded in Cyprus in 1180:

77

Πότε νὰ ὑπάγω ἐπὶ τὰ ἐμά, πότε νὰ ἐπαναλύσω! . . .
ὁ ξένος πάντα θλίβεται, ὁ ξένος πάντα κλαίει,
ὁ ξένος πάντοτε θρηνεῖ παραμυθίαν οὐκ ἔχων.

(Tsiknopoulos, 1952, p. 49)

When shall I go home, when shall I return! . . .
the exile ever grieves, the exile ever weeps,
the exile laments for evermore, having no consolation.

It comes as no surpirse to learn that the monk who recorded these lines
as they stood, and later worked them into a didactic poem of his own
in popular style, had heard them *sung* by a man who knew them by
heart. Both the sentiments expressed and the patterning of half-lines
belong without question to the later song tradition.

B. *DIYENIS AKRITIS*

At about the same time as they collected a number of folk songs in
Pontos whose hero was named Akritas, George Sathas and Emile Legrand
discovered the first manuscript of the medieval Greek epic *Diyenis
Akritis* in a monastery in Trebizond. The coincidence between the
names of the two heroes, and a very sketchy similarity of theme, suggested to the two scholars that the hero of the medieval epic and the
hero of the ballads were one and the same. Consequently, when they
came to publish the manuscript of the epic in 1875, they tacitly changed
the name of the hero on the title-page from Akritis ('Ακρίτης), as it is
in the medieval text, to Akritas ('Ακρίτας), as it is in the modern songs.

From such a small beginning a highly complex situation has developed. Over the next fifty years another four metrical versions of the
epic were discovered, as well as a prose version in Greek and others in
Russian. During the same period the number of recorded folk songs
multiplied, but practically nowhere outside Pontos had Akritas survived as the name of a hero. In a folk song discovered in a manuscript
of the seventeenth century, it is true, the name Diyenis Akritis occurs,
and one Cypriot song known to me ends with the declaration that its
hero, Dienis, is worthy to be the *son* of Akritis. But none of the evidence really supported the assumption, general among scholars at the
beginning of the century and still remarkably prevalent, that the folk
songs which mention Diyenis belong originally to the period of the
events described in the medieval epic – that is, to about the ninth century. These songs have come to be known as *akritiká*.

78

The epic tells the story of the abduction by an Arab Emir of the daughter of a Byzantine general, the efforts of her brothers to recapture her and the Emir's conversion to Christianity in order to marry the girl. The result of this union is the prodigious Basil, called Diyenis (born of two races) and later Akritis (frontiersman) because he chooses to live on the turbulent border between the Byzantine and Arab Empires. His exploits include killing wild beasts with his bare hands, abducting and marrying a girl who has been shut away in an impregnable tower to prevent just this eventuality, defeating several armies and miraculous monsters single-handed, and waging continual war with the bands of outlaws who roam the frontier area. Finally he settles down with his wife and builds a palace, in which shortly afterwards he dies, in one version as a result of taking a cold bath, in the others from unspecified but natural causes. It must be mentioned that Diyenis' role as a frontiersman does not seem to be to guard the frontier from Arab incursions so much as to glory in his own prowess in local feuds. Although a Christian, he is in no sense a defender of the faith, and the story has surprisingly little to say on the conflict between Christians and Moslems.

Even from this brief summary, it is evident that this Diyenis is at best a very distant relation of the Diyenis of the folk songs. Apart from the appearance in songs of a number of personal and geographical names belonging to the epic, the common elements are only three: Diyenis' abduction of his bride, the building of his palace and the fact of his death, although the most striking feature of the songs dealing with the death of Diyenis, the hero's single combat with Haros (Death), is entirely absent from the epic. All of these are themes common to many literary and folk traditions, and there are few immediate grounds for believing that the epic and the songs belong to a common tradition. The story of the epic undoubtedly belongs to the eighth and ninth centuries, but the often-repeated view that the songs must therefore be equally old has no easily observable basis in fact.

The detailed arguments and discussions concerning the precise relation between the hero of the epic and the hero of the folk songs have for the most part been scholarly, but their impetus comes from outside the field of objective research. With their slight change of the hero's name on the title-page of the Trebizond manuscript of the epic, Sathas and Legrand, probably inadvertently, gave birth to a modern myth which in the hundred years since has far outstripped that of either the epic or the folk songs. The hero of the modern myth is the composite

Diyenis Akri*tas*, who has become a symbol of attitudes and values prized by Greeks today and also of the uninterrupted existence of these values from a remote past. This is the Diyenis who appears in the poems of Palamas, Sikelianos, Ritsos and other prominent Greek poets, and who was to have been the hero of Kazantzakis' projected companion volume to his *Odyssey: a modern sequel.* This is not the place to discuss the significance of this modern myth, which fully deserves attention in its own right, but only to distinguish it categorically from the epic and the folk songs from which it originates and which at the same time it necessarily reinterprets.

This Diyenis, who is at once the borderer of the epic and the shepherd or brave young man (*pallikári*) who challenges Death to single combat in the folk songs, is depicted with complete seriousness in a recent article. The writer says it is his intention to talk about

> the Diyenis who was the champion of Hellenism and Christianity and became an everlasting symbol of youthful bravery, dignity and honour. This first Diyenis (who gave his name to today's Diyenis), Diyenis Akritas, together with all the other heroic frontiersmen, fought to preserve the Hellenic Christian state of Byzantium from the ceaseless incursions, raids and oppression of harsh tyrants and brigands of another race, to uphold and extend freedom and justice for the people, to bring security and happiness to the lives of men. His struggles became a legend, his life an epic, his passage through villages and memories indelible. (Prousis, 1972)

It is immediately apparent that this Diyenis, far from being the 'first' Diyenis, is quite different from the hero either of the epic or of the folk songs. But since attributes of the two are woven together into the fabric of this modern myth, it is not surprising that the close relation between the two traditions of epic and folk song, which has little objective basis, should so often have been assumed as a starting-point for the study of either.

The present position is most rationally summarised by John Mavrogordato in his bilingual edition of the Grottaferrata manuscript of the epic (1956) and by Professor L. Politis (1970). Mavrogordato's comments on the folk songs are curiously biased in favour of the epic (which not even in the Grottaferrata version can be regarded as a work of literary stature), but he clearly and rightly states that the common ground between the epic and folk songs is very small. Unfortunately his work has not provoked a reappraisal of the system of classification used by Greek scholars for the songs, nor has it scotched the notion that many of these 'akritic' songs existed in the eighth or ninth centuries in a form recognisably similar to that in which they are found today. This proposition was first seriously formulated by N. G. Politis (1909), although he qualified it with the view that the existing songs must be fragments of much longer pieces. His successor Stilpon Kyriakidis repeated this view in his standard work on folk songs (1965, pp. 100–3), but elsewhere he implied that songs may have existed in their present form in the eighth and ninth centuries (1934, p. 6). Henri Grégoire, whose frequently far-fetched attempts to tie down people, events and even monuments in the epic to historical origins seem to have been widely accepted, carried this view to extreme lengths (1942). On the one hand, he seems to maintain, persons and events in the songs as well as in the epic are closely related to those of Byzantine history; on the other, the epic was edited and expanded from versions of folk songs which still exist. It requires little understanding of the oral process to realise that proper names and historical events are the first things to be obscured and conflated, and that the sole case for the historical veracity of the epic rests on its composer having known his history from some more reliable source than present-day folk songs (cf. Politis, L., 1970, p. 552).

At this point a further complication arises. The discrepancies between versions of the epic found in the manuscripts are so great that they cannot be explained in terms of normal scribal transmission. Part of Grégoire's theory is therefore that the epic was *orally* transmitted, and more recently A. B. Lord has attempted to show in terms of formula-density that one or more of the versions conform to the rules of oral-formulaic composition (Lord, 1954; 1960, pp. 207–220; 1977). We are now faced with a question of probabilities. It is possible that the epic was at one time composed and/or transmitted orally. But none of the extant versions reveals consistently oral characteristics. Furthermore, the earliest of the manuscripts in date is that of Grottaferrata, which maintains a consistent, if scarcely distinguished, *literary* style. The manuscript dates from about 1300 (Politis, L., 1970, p. 554), while the events described belong definitely to the eighth and ninth centuries, since they take place on the Byzantine–Arab frontier in Mesopotamia. Whatever kind of transmission was involved in the case of the epic, it is not until at least seven hundred years later, in the manuscripts of the sixteenth century, that we find a significant number of elements in common with folk poetry. The most likely conclusion is that the folk song tradition only began to influence the texts of the epic at a very late stage of their transmission and in a correspondingly superficial manner.

In the later manuscripts of Diyenis, dated to about the sixteenth century, there are many signs of borrowing from folk songs, and a piece of rhyming doggerel included in the Athens manuscript seems to be a confusion of a love song and one in which the 'valiant maiden' theme occurs (Kalonaros, 1941, I, pp. 25-6, ll. 261-77). And in the Escorial manuscript there are many demotic formulas scattered among direct borrowing from literary texts, but no sign that they fulfil any integral function. This tendency shows a degree of give and take between the epic and folk song traditions, although at a late stage; and the shadowy awareness in folk songs that Diyenis and Akritas (or Akritis) are related names and suitable for a hero can be accounted for in the same way. It is also significant that *akritis* in the songs never has the significance of 'frontiersman' which is an integral part of the epic, nor do the songs ever include any play on the words Diyenis (literally, of double birth) and *monoyenis* (only-begotten son), which in the epic represent para-doxical aspects of the hero's dual nature.[1]

C. THE SONG OF ARMOURIS

Up until the fifteenth century any attempted reconstruction of the song tradition can only be conjectural. At that date the song of Armouris was recorded in two manuscripts, one said to date from the fifteenth century, the other dated 1461.[2] These are without doubt the oldest texts of a complete folk song, and although they show a number of features which are no longer commonly found in the song tradition, the evidence overwhelmingly suggests that 'Armouris' represents a slightly earlier stage of the same tradition. The narrative is simple, with many repetitions, and tells the story of a young man, Armouris Armouropoulos, who, although under age, accomplishes the feats of strength required by his mother before he can ride out against the Saracens single-handed, to rescue his father who is their prisoner. In his battle against the Saracens he is victorious, but is unhorsed in an am-bush. His horse reaches the captive father first, and the latter assumes that his son is dead. The Emir, whose chivalry is exemplary through-out, orders a search to be made for the missing son. The Saracen who had laid the ambush then tells his story, in almost exactly the same words as those used in the original episode, and the Emir reproves

Armouris *père* for the rampages of his son. The father writes to the son, asking him to cease slaughtering Saracens, but the latter haughtily refuses unless his father is freed. The Emir, impressed, agrees to let his prisoner go and offers the young Armouropoulos his daughter in marriage.

It has been suggested that the song 'refers not to Armouris, that is to the Emir (*Amirás*), but to his son, that is to say, to Diyenis' (Kalonaros, 1941, II, p. 213 n), but this wilful attempt to relate the song to the 'akritic cycle' is based on a misunderstanding of the text. In the song Armouris, far from being an Emir (as was Diyenis' father in the epic) is the captive of one; and his son is also called Armouris. The hero of the song is ὁ Ἀρμούρης ὁ Ἀρμουρόπουλος (ll. 75, 142), or Armouris, son of Armouris.

Most of the themes of the song are found in the demotic tradition; in more recent times variants of the initial theme have been recorded in Karpathos (Mihailidis-Nouaros, 1928, p. 56) and other songs deal in a similar manner with the theme of rescuing a father from foreign captors. The song contains many repetitions, sometimes consisting of several lines, and this is a device more commonly associated with oral epic than with the ballad style of the Greek song tradition. The closest modern parallels for 'Armouris', in fact, are the long Cypriot ballads, which combine a number of epic features with the style and structure of shorter Greek songs. Indications that the folk song structure exists, fully developed, in 'Armouris' are too numerous to quote in detail. A number of examples will suffice.

> Σήμερον ἄλλος οὐρανός, σήμερον ἄλλη ἡμέρα,
> σήμερον τὰ ἀρχοντόπουλα θέλουν καβαλλικεύσει·
> μόνον τοῦ κὺρ Ἀρμούρη ὁ υἱὸς οὐδὲν καβαλλικεύει.
>
> (Destouny, 1877, ll. 1–3)

Today the sky is changed, today is another day,
today the nobles' sons will ride out;
but the son of Armouris does not go riding.

This is how the song begins, and the interlocking structural pattern can be exactly paralleled in modern examples. The cumulative repetition of 'today' is a frequent device at the opening of a song, and this overlaps (in ll. 2–3) with another structural pattern where the content of two lines is contrasted, as in the demotic lines beginning a song,

> Οὖλες οἱ χῶρες χαίρουνται κι οὖλες καλὴν καρδιά 'χουν,
> ἡ Ρόδο ἡ βαριόμοιρη στέκει ἀποσφαλισμένη.   (Kriaris, 1920, p. 44)

All the towns rejoice and all are of good heart,
[but] ill-fated Rhodes stands beleaguered.

Equally certain examples of structures and ideas common to the folk songs are:

κλαίοντας ἀναιβαίνει τὴν σκάλαν, γελῶντας καταιβαίνει
(Destouny, 1877, l. 16)

weeping he climbs the stairs and laughing comes down again

ὥστε νὰ εἰπῇ ὅτι ἔχετε ὑγείαν, ἐδιέβη τριάντα μίλια,
ὥστε νὰ τὸν ἐπιλογηθοῦν, ἐδιέβη ἐξῆντα πέντε.
(Destouny, 1877, ll. 29–30)

no sooner had he said goodbye, than he travelled thirty miles,
no sooner had they replied, than he travelled sixty-five.

The first, which shows the standard structure of contrasting half-lines, may be compared with the demotic,

Παιζογελῶντας 'νέβαινε, κλαίντας κατεβαίνει
(Perdika, 1940, p. 197)

Playing and laughing he went aloft, and weeping came down
again,

and a close parallel to the second can be seen in ll. 14–15 of the song 'Mikrokostantinos' quoted on pp. 13–15 above.

In 'Armouris' there is a sufficient number of examples of structural features of the folk song tradition fulfilling the same structural role that one can fairly ascribe this song to an earlier stage of the same tradition, and contrast it decisively with the sixteenth-century Escorial manuscript of *Diyenis Akritis* which it superficially resembles.

This resemblance between two roughly contemporary manuscripts is nonetheless an interesting phenomenon which, if correctly understood, may help us to appreciate the confusing relation which must have existed at that period between oral and written traditions. First of all, both 'Armouris' and the Escorial version of *Diyenis* contain many unmetrical lines and unattached half-lines; and in neither, despite a popularising tendency, does the language correspond exactly to the vernacular of the day. In the *Diyenis* manuscript, these features have often been accounted for by the supposition that it was written down more or less directly from oral recitation. According to Gareth Morgan, the Escorial manuscript is in Cretan dialect and reflects features of present-day Cretan *rizítika* songs (1960, p. 54). On this analogy Morgan accounts for the unmetrical lines by the practice of modern singers of interjecting proper names or exclamations into their lines in singing, and he quotes a number of irregular lines in the manuscript which can be regularised by removing vocatives of this type. But interjections are comparatively rare in Cretan folk song and in any case the sort of emendation advocated by Morgan only works for a small number of the irregular lines in this version of *Diyenis*. While it is true that oral recitation (particularly in Cyprus) can produce a high proportion of unattached half-lines, the analogy with the manner of singing Cretan *rizítika*, in which at least half of each line is sung twice and always very slowly, cannot reasonably be applied to a poem of 1,867 lines.

Although the language of the Escorial manuscript includes more popular features than any earlier or contemporary version of the epic, it can also at times be just as literary as any of them. It has been shown that of all the versions, this is the closest to *literary* sources (Kalonaros, 1941, I, p. xxx; Politis, L., 1970, pp. 573-6), and I have already pointed out that many obvious demotic features are borrowings, at a superficial level, from the song tradition. Both the similarities and the differences between the Escorial *Diyenis* and 'Armouris' are, I believe, due to the effects of memory. In the case of the former the scribe was remembering something he had either read or heard, but which contained many unquestionably literary elements and direct quotations, and filled out the gaps in his memory with phrases vaguely remembered from current songs. His versification was inaccurate because he remembered the sense of a line but not the wording, the exact opposite of what the oral singer does in adapting his thought to formalised patterns which already fulfil the metrical requirements of lines and half-lines.

In the case of 'Armouris' it seems likely that a scribe who was not himself an oral singer was attempting to record a song in traditional style which he had heard, and many minor irregularities of the metre can be restored by substituting the modern demotic form of the words. Such has been the literary tradition in Greece from late antiquity onwards that anyone educated enough to be able to write at all would have come in contact with the conservative, purist notions inextricably bound up with the art of writing, and would probably, without perhaps even being aware of it, have made morphological changes in recording an oral song. Taken together with natural lapses of memory, this would drastically have disrupted the metre and sense of his text. In a number of cases in 'Armouris', in contrast to the Escorial version of *Diyenis Akritis*, the formulaic wording has been remembered accurately but confusion has arisen because the formulas, as reconstructed in the written language, are no longer metrical. Not all of the lines can legitimately be restored according to this principle, since in a number of cases the precise sense is dubious, and in the case of the unattached half-lines something has probably been lost; but a proportion of the metrical irregularities disappear if the words are rewritten or pronounced according to demotic morphology.

D. FOLK SONGS IN THE OTTOMAN PERIOD

Between the date of the song of Armouris and the early nineteenth century we have very little direct evidence for the folk song tradition. The only texts we possess from this period are a group of thirteen songs, most of them very brief, from a manuscript of the seventeenth century (Bouvier, 1960, pp. 86–9). These have been recorded with greater accuracy than 'Armouris' and are accompanied by musical notation. Evidently a scribe who was also a musician was recording songs which he knew well, and since the texts are so short (the longest contains only seventeen lines) he would have had little trouble in remembering them. Some of the songs are lyrics – laments for the plight of the exile – of which all but one (No. 1) can be paralleled by modern examples. The others appear to be the opening sections of ballads, for which, again, close modern parallels can be found. No. 3 is a song of a hero in prison, lamented by his wife, and may have ended either with the hero breaking out and recovering his wife just as she is about to be married to someone else, or in a lament for the impossibility of his doing so. The next song, whose hero is Diyenis Akritis, describes the preparations for a wedding feast and ends with a sequence usually found in songs of the 'Bridesmaid who Became the Bride'. (This is the only folk song known to me in which the full name of the hero Diyenis Akritis occurs.) No. 6 apparently begins the story in which a young man is taken to church by his mother, but is rebuffed by a voice from heaven because he is guilty of the sin of necrophilia, while No. 7 is a lament in a well-known style for the fall of the island of Paros.

In terms of themes and style all of these songs belong without doubt to the demotic tradition, although it is not surprising to find a number of old forms which have not survived into the nineteenth century. Some of these concern details of spelling which would not affect an oral rendering, and which must be the work of the scribe. But others, such as

καὶ δὲν εὑρίσκω 'δὲ τινάν	and I find no one
νὰ 'σέβω εἰς περιβόλι	to enter into a garden,

show that gradual changes in the spoken language have necessitated changes in the formulaic diction of the tradition. The modern song tradition does not show the same tendency to preserve archaisms as the ancient tradition of the Homeric poems, and this is only to be expected since the political verse is far more adaptable than the complex hexameter of the *Iliad* and the *Odyssey*. But, despite the evidence of a small number of phrases that the formulaic language of Greek songs was changing between the seventeenth and nineteenth centuries, the language and formulaic style of these thirteen songs are remarkably close to what we find in the nineteenth-century collections and even today.

Aside from this manuscript, there is a wealth of circumstantial evidence for the existence and wide popularity of the song tradition from the fifteenth century onwards. In Crete, which was not captured by the Turks until the second half of the seventeenth century, the great literary renaissance under Venetian rule shows many influences from folk songs, not least in the widespread use of the political verse, although generally with the addition of rhyme. The late sixteenth- or early seventeenth-century verse romance *Erotokritos*, although the work of a single author and based ultimately on a French source, contains many stylistic features of the folk songs, as do other works of the period. It is impossible to say whether this reflects the rise of the folk tradition itself or merely of a type of literature in which, for the first time, a truly vernacular style was acceptable to a reading public, although the latter is the more probable. Certainly after the fifteenth century there are clear signs that literary writers were aware of folk songs such as we know today and were to a greater or lesser extent influenced by them in their writings.

Other kinds of evidence, although tantalisingly few, suggest that the tradition during this period was creative. F. E. de Lusignan, in his description of Cyprus prior to the Ottoman conquest of 1570, distinguished between the musical entertainment of the ruling class, which must have been largely western, and that of the people. On the latter he has this to say:

Le peuple, & bourgeois, & autres de médiocre condition, après le manger estoient tousiours en recreatio dedans leurs iardins, amateurs des ieux & danses: & ont vn si enclin à la poésie, qu'ils composent gentiment, sans en avoir toutefois aucun art ou précepte. (De Lusignan, 1580, p. 220)

A hundred years later, in 1675, a group of Maniots led by the powerful Stefanopoulos family received permission from the Genoese to set up a small colony in Corsica on condition that they helped the Genoese to hold down the local population (Vayakakos, 1970, p. 152). Their descendants are still there, after three hundred years of virtual isolation from Greece. The songs that have been recorded from them (Fardys, 1888, pp. 169ff.) have the same structure as those found in Greece, and the same themes, although these are sometimes combined in unusual ways. This evidence suggests that the form and structure of the folk song tradition had become stabilised before the migration to Corsica. But the fact that the Corsican songs are often conspicuously different from the Greek, and the existence in Corsica of formulas not found in Greece, tends to confirm the view that the songs themselves did not have a fixed form and that the tradition has continued to develop in both places.

An account by the French traveller Tournefort, who visited Greece in 1700, tells us that songs were also composed to commemorate events which caught hold of the popular imagination. In Mykonos Tournefort was told the story of a *vrykólakas*, or *revenant*, who had recently plagued the islanders. This *revenant* created such havoc on the island that finally the authorities were obliged, contrary to Orthodox custom, to exhume the man's remains and burn them on the shore. After this there was no more trouble, and Tournefort concludes his story, 'and some Ballads were made to turn him into Ridicule' (1713, p. 107).

A century later, several European travellers provided useful information on the performance and composition of songs. Julius Griffiths, who was violently prejudiced against the music and songs he heard in Greece, quotes (and derides) the clearly more perceptive comment of an earlier traveller, a Mr Dalloway:

They reject notes [i.e. written music] – depending entirely upon memory; but are notwithstanding guided by strict rules of composition, according to their own musical theory. (Griffiths, 1805, p. 116)

And Pouqueville, in the condescending manner of the period, praised the inventiveness of Greek singers and musicians in the following terms:

> Notwithstanding their ignorance of the principles upon which the arts of poetry and music are founded, impromptus in both may occasionally be heard from the Greeks, which would not disgrace countries where the rules of these arts are better understood.
>
> (Pouqueville, 1813, p. 149)

His English contemporary Martin-Leake was more appreciative when he observed of the songs of 'the common people' that,

> as they are not printed, there is found an infinite variety of words, adapted to the same air; the lively imagination of the Greeks, their versifying talent, and the remarkable facilities of the language, readily supplying matter for the occasion. (Martin-Leake, 1814, p. 157)

One thing that is constant in almost all of these accounts is that songs were composed and performed in what we would nowadays call an oral manner. And another point that is frequently emphasised is their popularity. A not untypical case is that of Edward Dodwell, who, setting out from Athens for a tour of the Peloponnese in 1805, imposed on his guides and interpreters the firm condition that no singing should take place on the journey, commenting in his memoir of the trip that 'The traveller is sometimes tormented in this manner by his attendants, from sun-rise to sun-set!' (Dodwell, 1819, II, p. 18).

6. Function of the Demotic Tradition: the Songs and History

From the very beginnings of European interest in folk, or oral, poetry, it has been a common assumption that poetry or song which has been recorded from non-literate tradition is of ancient origin and preserves relics of a remote past. For Bishop Percy, the first English editor of such material, this claim to antiquity was clearly intended to justify its publication, as is evident from his title, *Reliques of ancient English poetry*. In the case of Greek folk poetry this notion that oral tradition preserves elements of a distant and perhaps glorious past was often the prime motivation for collecting and studying songs, and in particular, folk songs were used to provide evidence for racial and cultural continuity from classical times to the present day. As a result, scholars such as N. G. Politis, Kyriakidis, Grégoire and, sometimes, K. Romaios have sought in the songs for confirmation of known historical events with a view to establishing both the antiquity of the tradition, and its continuity from the time of the events in question.

I have already tried to show that isolated historical references in songs are not sufficient to demonstrate the antiquity of the tradition or of particular songs, and that the beginnings of the song tradition as we know it can only be dated by the occurrence of manuscript recordings of songs or quotations from songs which show the recognisable structural features of the tradition today. As we saw in the last chapter, the folk song tradition which we know in Greece today was definitely established by 1461, and there is reasonable evidence to suppose that it had also existed, perhaps in embryonic or transitional form, some three hundred years before that date. References or apparent references in song texts to historical events of an earlier period cannot be taken as evidence that the songs in which they occur were composed at that time.

The folk song tradition does however include a range of real historical references. Excluding the dubious significance of proper names associated with historical events before the fourteenth century, the earliest direct historical reference in a song is to the sack of Adrianople in 1361. Other songs refer to sieges and captures of cities from that time up to the present, while songs relating to the klefts describe conflicts which are sometimes historically documented. In this chapter I wish to discuss the significance of historical references, not as a possible source for historical information, but in order to gain some insight into the Greek singer's attitude to the past, which may in turn help us to understand part of the function of the song tradition as a whole.

A. ORAL TRADITION AND HISTORY

The view that oral tradition may contain useful historical information, either where no other sources exist, or as a supplement to written sources, is implicit in the traditional approach of many scholars to Greek folk songs, and in particular in the work of Henri Grégoire. This view has also been supported by students of oral traditions in other parts of the world. Jan Vansina has made the claim, based largely on his experience as an anthropologist studying non-literate societies in Africa, that historical information can indeed be gleaned from oral tradition, so long as the many possible types of distortion (from the historian's point of view) are fully understood. This claim has not been universally accepted, but Vansina's work is especially valuable in that he distinguishes different types of oral tradition and suggests ways in which their *relative* historical accuracy may be tested. Vansina is careful to insist, too, 'that, in a last analysis, every tradition exists as such only in virtue of the fact that it serves the interests of the society in which it is preserved' (1973, p. 78) – that is to say, that it has a synchronic function – and points out that all involved in the transmission of a tradition will be 'influenced by . . . their private interests and the interests of the society they belong to, the cultural values of that society, and their own individual personalities' (p. 76). Traditions, according to Vansina, have different functions in a society, and the historical veracity of a tradition can to some extent be determined by understanding its function.

That oral traditions of the type classified by Vansina as 'poetry' are not principally motivated by the desire to record historical facts seems to be generally agreed. Vansina himself points out what should perhaps already be obvious to the student of oral *poetry*, that in poetry the 'formal expression of the content plays as great a role as the actual content itself' (p. 147) and that, by its very nature, 'its psychological function and its aesthetic qualities distort the facts described' (p. 148).

For our purposes, the 'distortions' which occur will be of greater importance than the facts 'distorted', since it may be hoped that they will lead us to identify something of the 'psychological function' and 'aesthetic qualities' to which they are due.

A specific case of such 'distortion' is quoted by Jack Goody and Ian Watt in a non-literate society in Nigeria (1968, pp. 31-3). Legal disputes in this society were settled by reference to orally transmitted genealogies which detailed the rights of each family. This tradition seemed at first sight to have a historical function, in that its *apparent* purpose was to preserve information from the past as a means of arbitration in the present. Since these genealogies played such an important part in ordering the affairs of the society, the first British colonial officials went to the trouble of recording them in writing. Within little more than a generation, however, a new source of conflict arose, as the oral tradition and the written version no longer corresponded exactly. What had happened was that the oral 'historical records' of the tribesmen were continually updated as the fortunes of families changed. In other words, history was being 'rewritten'; and the function of this tradition turned out not to be the recording of information about the past, but the selection or invention of such information to provide a seemingly historical sanction for the contemporary (and changing) *status quo*.

According to Goody and Watt this is an instance of a phenomenon very commonly found in non-literate societies, and the writers suggest that this may be a general feature of traditions in such societies. As they summarise this and other cases,

> Myth and history merge into one: the elements in the cultural heritage which cease to have a contemporary relevance tend to be soon forgotten or transformed; and as the individuals of each generation acquire their vocabulary, their genealogies, and their myths, they are unaware that various words, proper names and stories have dropped out, or that others have changed their meanings or been replaced. (Goody and Watt, 1968, p. 34)

Even where an oral tradition has the *apparent* function of recording information about the past (as, with Greek songs, is assumed by the scholarly classification *istoriká tragoúdia*, historical songs) it may be that the 'distortions' from which Vansina hoped to free them are the

92

real determinants of the nature and function of the tradition, to which the seemingly historical content is only incidental.

B. THE SIGNIFICANCE OF ARCHAISMS

One of the most curious features of the *Iliad* and the *Odyssey*, which led Milman Parry to formulate his theory of oral composition, is the 'mixed' language of the texts. In these poems linguistic features of several distinct ancient Greek dialects coexist, as do words and grammatical forms which had disappeared from speech long before the poems were first written down. Parry explained this by reference to his theory of the oral formula, according to which the poems had been composed orally over a period of several hundred years, during which the bards who sang them had evolved and refined a complex system of formulas, suitable to be repeated or adapted to fulfil the requirements of metre and sense in rapid composition. As the prosody of the Homeric hexameter is highly complex, and as the language at that time required many times the number of inflections found in later vernacular Greek, the difficulties of composing a poem orally must have been enormous. The problem was eased, according to Parry, by the retention of formulas even after their characteristic words or inflected forms had fallen out of use. The language of the songs became a specialised language, whose features were determined not so much by the spoken usage of any one time or place, but by the existence of traditional formulas suitable for expressing particular ideas according to the requirements of the metre. Thus archaic and newer forms exist side by side in Homer, as do dialectal features characteristic of different geographical areas. One effect of this was that isolated pieces of historical information were 'embedded' in the Homeric texts, and have in many cases been confirmed by archaeology.

Parry thought that this principle, although with variations of degree according to the nature of different traditions, must be universal in traditional poetry (Parry, 1932, p. 12). It is not, however, found in the contemporary Yugoslav oral epics, whose style and structure are in many respects analogous to those of the Homeric poems, and it now seems that the historical archaisms preserved in the texts of Homer are an extreme and unusual case.

The erroneous impression that the language of modern Greek folk songs is similar to that of the Homeric poems in this respect probably

derives from Fauriel. In his introduction to the first published collection of Greek songs Fauriel echoed the view fashionable among educated supporters of the demotic, or vernacular, Greek language, that dialectal differences in modern Greek are not strongly marked: 'On peut
donc considérer la langue dans laquelle sont écrites les pièces de ce
recueil, comme une langue régulière et fixe, une et homogène . . .'
(Fauriel, 1824, pp. cxii–cxxiii). There is no reason, however, to believe
that the language in which the songs are *written* in Fauriel's collection
is identical to that in which they were originally sung. We must remember that Fauriel himself had no first-hand experience of Greece, so that
his information about the lack of dialectal differences must have been
taken on trust. And we know that informants such as Moustoxidis, who
was a friend and admirer of the poet Solomos, were actively promoting
a common demotic form of the language in the teeth of opposition
from neoclassical purists. Fauriel's informants, like Solomos, would
therefore have played down the importance of dialects in Greek, and
we must also remember that it was from the same educated sources
that he drew the texts of his songs. None of Fauriel's texts, accurate
though they are in comparison with those of other collectors, can possibly be an *exact* transcription of a performance, and most of their
dialectal features would naturally have been smoothed out or 'corrected'
by his educated informants.

The same impression was further fostered by N. G. Politis who included in his *Selections from the songs of the Greek people* (1914) an
appendix entitled 'Songs in the Greek dialects', implying that these
were an exception to the general rule. And more recently James
Notopoulos made the quite unjustified claim that: 'It is a well-known
fact in modern Greek folksongs that adherence to a dialect is not strict,
especially where metre and rhythm are involved' (1959, p. 15).

We know from the satirical play by Dimitrios Vyzantios, *Vavylonía*
(Babylonia), first published in 1836, that the differences between regional dialects at the time could cause considerable misunderstandings,
which are exploited in the play to comic effect (Vyzantios, 1972). And
that these dialectal differences are equally present in folk songs is immediately apparent when one hears an actual performance, or consults
one of the more conscientious transcriptions that have been made since
the time of Politis, particularly those in the periodical *Laografía*. The
easy adaptation of formulas to different dialects (as well as to a variety
of contexts, as we saw in Chapter 3) shows that the combined demands
of the modern language with its fewer inflections, and of the political

verse, which is far less restrictive than the Homeric hexameter, could not have imposed a comparable linguistic conservatism on singers in the modern tradition.

The language of Greek folk song, with its occasional archaisms but more general tendency not to depart from the contemporary vernacular of each region, is unlikely to provide us with much fossilised historical information. The precise significance of such archaisms as exist, and a more exact definition of the language of the songs as compared to normal dialect usage would require a more detailed linguistic study than has been possible here; and one of the greatest problems for such a study would be the lack of song material transcribed with absolute faithfulness to oral performance.

This is not to say that the language of the songs is in all respects identical to that of everyday speech. The language of song or poetry is probably never quite that of conversation, and it may be part of the normal stylisation of poetic language that certain archaic words or forms are retained although long separated from their origins in normal usage. The position as now understood is best summarised by Ruth Finnegan in her world-wide survey of oral poetry:

> Whatever the exact truth, it is clear that the once-held model of 'oral tradition' as necessarily involving the preservation of older strata of language and culture has to be rejected (and *this* implication at least of 'archaism' rejected with it) in favour of a view of poetic conventions where certain established forms fit the *currently accepted* view of the literary language appropriate to particular genres. Poetic selection and development is involved rather than passive acceptance of earlier forms. (Finnegan, 1977, p. 111)

C. SONGS OF THE FALL OF CITIES

Aside from the songs of the klefts, several of which refer to historical events of the eighteenth and nineteenth centuries, the only songs of the demotic tradition which contain certain historical references are those relating to the fall of cities and towns. The earliest of these is the fall of Adrianople, which was sacked several times but most dramatically by the Ottomans in 1361. The text of the song, as given by Passow, is as follows:[1]

Κλαίγουν τἀηδόνια τῆς Βλακιᾶς καὶ τὰ πουλιὰ στὴν δύσιν,
Κλαίγουν ἀργὰ, κλαίγουν ταχυὰ, κλαίουν τὸ μεσημέρι,

95

Κλαίγουν τὴν Ἀδριανούπολιν τὴν βαριὰ κουρσευμένη,
Ἀπού τὴν ἐκουρσέψανε τσὴ τρεῖς ἰορταῖς τοῦ χρόνου,
Τοῦ Χριστογέννου γιὰ κηρὶ καὶ τοῦ βαϊοῦ γιὰ βάϊα,
Καὶ τῆς λαμπρῆς τὴν κυριακὴ γιὰ τὸ Χριστὸς ἀνέστη.

(Passow, 1860, p. 145)

The nightingales of Wallachia weep, and the birds in the west,
they weep late, they weep early, they weep at midday,
they weep for Adrianople, so heavily sacked,
that was sacked on the three festivals of the year,
at Christmas for a candle, on Palm Sunday for palm branches,
and on Easter Sunday for the [greeting] 'Christ is risen'.

There is no immediate sign that this song has much to tell us about the sack of Adrianople, or to support the assertion of Professor George Megas that 'as is known, the historical songs almost without exception, are contemporary with the events to which they refer' (in Academy of Athens, 1963, p. 121). Everything in the song, with the exception of the name of the city, is traditional and found with only slight variations in other contexts. The idea with which the song begins, that of the birds lamenting a human misfortune, is commonly found in laments for klefts who lived and died some five hundred years after the fall of Adrianople, and a variation on the same set of formulas as make up the first two lines of this song is found in *mirolóyia*, funeral laments for individuals:

Σένα σέ κλαίει ἡ γι-ἄνοιξη, σέ κλαίει τό καλοκαίρι,
σέ κλαῖν τ' ἀηδόνια στίς φωλιές καί τά πουλιά στούς κάμπους

(*Laografía* 15, 1954, p. 280)

For you spring weeps, and summer weeps for you,
the nightingales in their nests weep for you and the birds in the
    plains

οἱ δυό νά κλαῖνε τήν αὐγή κι οἱ τρεῖς τό μεσημέρι,
τά ἡλιοβασιλέματα νά κλαῖν οἱ πέντ' ἀντάμα.

(Ioannou, 1966, p. 332)

two [of them] to weep at dawn and [the other] three at midday,
and when the sun goes down, all five to weep together.

The sense and imagery of the last two and a half lines of the song are also repeated in these dirges:

96

νὰ μᾶς τοὺς 'φήκη νά 'ρκουνται τὶς τρεῖς φορὲς τὸ χρόνο:
Τὰ Φῶτα, τὰ Χριστούγεννα καὶ τὴ Μεγάλη Πέφτη
καὶ τὴ Μεγάλη Κερεκή, ποὺ λὲν Χριστὸς Ἀνέστη.

(Petropoulos, 1959, p. 218, No. 4)

for [Haros] to let them come to us three times a year:
at Epiphany, at Christmas and on Maundy Thursday
and on Easter Sunday, when they say 'Christ is risen'.

This 'historical' song, then, is entirely constructed, not only according to the same principles as fictional narrative and purely lyrical songs,
but in the same words and imagery. The reference to Easter, which
N. G. Politis took to refer to an earlier attack on Adrianople by the
Bulgars during Holy Week in 1205 (Politis, N. G., 1914, p. 11) loses
all its historical importance when we find that the 'three festivals of the
year' is a common patterned expression found in the song tradition.
The structure of the song too, which is exactly paralleled in songs for
the dead, strongly suggests that in function this song is a *lament*, not a
historical reminiscence.

This may seem an unimportant distinction, but the song's *local*
function is more remarkable. Of the three extant versions, two derive
from Crete (Passow, 1860, p. 145; Academy of Athens, 1963, pp. 122-
3) while the third comes from Corfu (Manousos, 1850, II, p. 119). The
Academy of Athens version, which was recorded in Crete in 1938, has
tagged on to it a rhyming couplet which picks up the Easter reference
of the last line of the song:

Χριστὸς ἀνέστη, κοπελιά, ἔλα νὰ φιληθοῦμε
καὶ βάστα καὶ στὴ χέρα σου κλῆμα νὰ βλοηθοῦμε.

(Academy of Athens, 1963, p. 123 n)

Christ is risen, my girl, come let's kiss,
hold in your hands a vine for our marriage ceremony.

In fact the song is sung, not as part of the Easter festival, but as a wedding song. And it is a common feature of Greek wedding songs that
laments are sung for the bride as she leaves her parents' home, often
closely echoing the laments sung for the dead at funerals (Alexiou,
1974, pp. 120-2). The song's function has clearly been separated from
the one historical reference which it contains and has become allegori-
cal – as a lament for the 'conquest' and resultant loss to her parents of

a bride as she sets out for the wedding. That this is not merely acciden-
tal is suggested by two factors. Firstly, in the version of the song recorded in Corfu, the 'sack of Adrianople' serves as an introduction to a
narrative about a girl who has been sold into slavery and laments the
fact that the man she loves will never be able to ransom her. And a song
in the seventeenth-century manuscript from Mount Athos, which is
clearly a love song or a wedding song, opens with the same formula as
the Corfu version ('The nightingales of the East and the birds of the
West') and ends with the formula of the 'three festivals of the year'
(Bouvier, 1960, p. 87, No. 2).

It must be suggested therefore that the song of Adrianople, although
containing a historical *reference*, has a function quite other than the
recording or commemorating of a historical fact. The real function of
the song seems to be the expression of grief over loss, without any importance being attached to what has nominally been lost. And in Crete
this underlying function of a lament has been adopted to fulfil a more
specific, local function, in the celebration of a wedding.

The importance of the fall of Adrianople for the rural population of
the rest of Greece was probably not very great, even at the time, and it
is understandable in this case that the name of the city should have lost
its historical significance in the song. But when we come to consider a
much larger group of 'fall songs', those referring to the capture of
Constantinople in 1453, the case is quite different. Once again there is
little sign that singers were ever interested in chronicling the events, but
the importance of the loss of the capital of eastern medieval Christen-
dom, as a synchronic condition of life in later centuries, is undoubted
and is clearly reflected in the songs.

These songs can be divided into four main types. The first and best
known describes the last mass in the cathedral of St Sofia, which
according to tradition was interrupted by the final Turkish attack on
the city. Versions of this song begin either with the formula

Πῆραν τὴν Πόλη, πῆραν την, πῆραν τὴ Σαλονίκη

(Fauriel, 1825, p. 340)

They've taken the City [Constantinople], they've taken it, they've
taken Salonica,

linking the fall of the City with the spread of Ottoman power throughout Greek-speaking lands, or with a description of the many bells being
rung from the cathedral of St Sofia (Zambelios, 1852, p. 599; Kriaris,
1920, pp. 200-1). All of these end with the moving depiction of the

icons in St Sofia weeping, and a voice addressing the icon of the Virgin Mary, begging her not to weep,

πάλε μὲ χρόνους, μὲ καιρούς, πάλε δικά σου εἶναι.

once again after years and ages, once again they will be yours.

A second type, found so far as I know only in Pontos, describes how the keys of the City were given up to the attackers through cowardice, and now to open the City again (that is, to the Christians)

Θέλ ἀπ' οὐρανοῦ μάστοραν καὶ ἀπὸ τὴν γῆν ἀργάτεν

(Politis, N. G., 1914, p. 270)

will take a craftsman from heaven and a labourer from earth.

The third type, again made up of Pontic songs, relates the breaking of the news that the City has fallen – by means of a bird, the sun, or a friend met on the road (Petropoulos, 1958, pp. 154–6).[2] One of the songs printed in modern anthologies, which seems to belong to this type, is that in which a ship arrives off the island of Tenedos and tells, with striking imagery, of the destruction of the City. There is no evidence, however, that this song ever existed in oral tradition, as the versions of Petropoulos (1958, p. 154, No. 4D), Ioannou (1966, p. 93) and Academy of Athens (1963, p. 126) all derive from a literary text of the fifteenth century, the *Anakálima tis Konstantinópolis* (Kriaras, 1965). The lines have been taken quite arbitrarily from the longer text by modern editors, presumably because they bear a strong resemblance to the *style* of folk songs, but this procedure gives no grounds for regarding them as an integral folk song dating from the time of the events.

And the final type, of which only one example is known to me, uses the traditional device of the *adýnaton* (paradox) to express the unnaturalness of the event in the eyes of the singer: a nun is frying fish, and a voice from heaven tells her to stop, as the City (Constantinople) will shortly 'turn Turk'. The nun tartly replies with the *adýnaton*: 'When the fish jump out of the frying pan and come to life again, then the City may turn Turk.' The song laconically tells that the fish did indeed jump out of the frying pan and the Emir (the Sultan) entered the City on horseback (Zambelios, 1852, p. 600, No. 2).

With the exception of one feature, which I will return to shortly, none of these types is unique in the song tradition. Similar structural patterns and the same themes may be used by singers to create a song referring to a quite different set of historical circumstances. In the case of the first type, the same opening formulas and a similar tone of lamentation are employed in a song which tells of the sack of the Turkish-controlled city of Tripolitsá by *Greeks* in 1821. The situation is the reverse of that lamented in the case of Constantinople and the hero of the song was the wealthiest Turkish landowner in the Peloponnese at the time:

Πῆραν τὰ κάστρα πῆραν τα, πῆραν καὶ τὰ ντερβένια,
πῆραν καὶ τὴν Τριπολιτσά, τὴν ξακουσμένη χώρα.
Κλαίουν στοὺς δρόμους Τούρκισσες, κλαίουν ἐμιροποῦλες,
κλαίει καὶ μιὰ χανούμισσα τό δόλιο τὸν Κιαμήλη:
– Ἄχ, ποῦ 'σαι καὶ δὲ φαίνεσαι, καμαρωμέν' ἀφέντη,
πού 'σουν κολόνα στὸ Μοριὰ καὶ φλάμπουρο στὴν Κόρθο,
ἤσουν καὶ στὴν Τριπολιτσὰ θεμελιωμένος πύργος;
Στὴν Κόρθο πλιὰ δὲ φαίνεσαι, οὐδὲ μέσ' στὰ σαράια,
ἕνας παπὰς σοῦ τά 'καψε τὰ ἔρμα τὰ παλάτια.
Κλαίουν τ' ἀχούρια γι' ἄλογα καὶ τὰ τζαμιὰ γι' ἀγάδες,
κλαίει καὶ ἡ Κιαμήλαινα τό δόλιο της τὸν ἄντρα:
– Σκλάβος ραϊάδων ἔπεσε καὶ ζῆ ραϊὰς ραϊάδων.

(Petropoulos, 1958, p. 168, No. 27)

They've taken the castle, they've taken it, they've taken the
    passes,
and they've taken Tripolitsá, the famous town.
Turkish women weep in the streets, the daughters of emirs
    weep,
and one Turkish girl weeps for wretched Kiamil:
'Ah, where are you that no one sees you, our pride and lord,
who were a pillar in the Morea, a pennon in Corinth,
and in Tripolitsá a mighty tower of strength?
You're no longer to be seen in Corinth, nor in the Seray,
a Greek priest has burnt down your poor old palaces.'
The stables weep for horses and the mosques for Agas,
and Kiamil's wife weeps for her unhappy husband:
'He is now the slave of rayahs, and lives – a rayah's rayah.'

That the same opening formula and a similar style should be used in two songs commemorating such different events suggests that the content of each is determined less by the historical facts in the case than by an underlying attitude to a certain type of event.

A similar conclusion is suggested by the fate of the other types of song relating to the fall of Constantinople in the tradition. The second type, with its theme of the keys, recurs with subtle variations in songs purporting to tell of the sieges of Rhodes in 1520, Malta in 1565, Methoni in the south-west Peloponnese from 1685 to 1687, Nafplion in 1715, Berati in Epiros in 1810 and in the fictional ballads of the 'Castle of Beauty'.[3] The principal theme of the third type, that of the super- natural messenger bringing news of the disaster, is found in a wide range of narrative songs in the tradition, and, in a fairly stereotyped form, is used in songs on the historical battle of Dervenakia in 1822, the des- truction of the island of Kasos by the Turks in 1824 and the siege of Mesolonghi in 1825-6.[4] And the fourth type, the *adýnaton*, is widely encountered in Greek songs and proverbs.

The conclusion to be drawn seems to be that the same themes, for- mulas and sometimes images (such as the keys) may be used in tradi- tional songs purporting to describe a wide range of historical events. This can only be understood in terms of a synchronic function of the songs – which is not to report history but to uphold cultural values, and to lament those historical events which threaten them, without making any strong distinction between different events whose cultural significance is the same.

This role of the songs is further emphasised by the one unique fea- ture shared by some, but not all, of the songs of the fall of Constanti- nople. This is the hope or conviction expressed in several of them that 'once again they will be yours' and that 'Romanía [the Byzantine Empire] even if it has passed away will flower and bring forth another', and in the prophetic ending of the song about the keys. A comparable assurance of return to life is never given in laments for the dead, which these songs otherwise resemble. Mourners often beg the dead to return, but it is never finally asserted that they will, nor is such a statement found in any of the songs relating to the fall of other cities, or in writ- ten laments for Constantinople which were composed shortly after the event. This fact was noted by N. G. Politis, who commented that the songs, alone among other commemorations of the City's capture 'express with deep simplicity the emotion of perseverance in the face of great national suffering and affirm the hope of the enslaved race for freedom and regeneration' (1914, p. 12).

None of the emotions Politis describes is actually mentioned in the songs, and his interpretation assumes that singers before 1821 saw the continuity of their culture in terms of nineteenth-century nationalism. But he was right to regard this attitude, that even if Constantinople is lost it will be Christian once again, as the core of the singers' reponse to the event. It was evidently in order to express this hope or conviction that these particular songs were sung.

If part of the songs' function is to deny the finality of a historical event, this tells us something further about the attitude, whether conscious or not, of singers to history. The function of these songs is not in fact to record events for posterity, nor is it to compare the past glories of the City with a state of subjection. The firm authoritative statement that what has been lost cannot be lost for good confirms the view that the songs express the lasting belief of singers in the values of their culture, to which the historical loss of the capital, and the *actual* possibility of its future recovery, are but details of secondary importance. The loss of a city which occupies the key role in the stability of the culture, both political and religious, within which the tradition flourishes, necessitates drastic and undesirable changes at all levels of life. It is in the nature of such a *synchronic* tradition, reflecting cultural values and attitudes, to cry out against this change, to express the conviction that even such a catastrophe cannot alter the fundamental attitudes which comprise the culture. And even though the historian tells us that aspects of Greek culture did change in the centuries following the fall of Constantinople, and even though many elements of Ottoman culture were assimilated during the years of Turkish domination, this conviction is not thereby altered. This helps to explain how the songs of the fall of Constantinople have remained part of the tradition, and were sung at least up until the beginning of this century – not as a slogan for a political ideal, nor out of nostalgia for a lost golden age, but as an affirmation of the changelessness of *current* attitudes and values.

D. THE SONGS OF THE KLEFTS

The klefts (κλέφτες) were a species of social bandit whose activities, so far as they have been documented, were conspicuous during the eighteenth and nineteenth centuries, chiefly in the northern mainland of Greece. They have achieved a lasting place in modern Greek history thanks to their role in the Greek War of Independence (1821–30), but many of those who have been commemorated in songs lived long before this. Most modern accounts of the klefts and their activities are agreed that these men were not primarily motivated by any form of national consciousness (Dakin, 1972, p. 19; Politis, A., 1973, p. li) but, for a variety of reasons, became the hard core of armed resistance to the Ottoman state once the uprising of 1821 had broken out. But the more traditional view, that the klefts before 1821 had been engaged in some form of national preparation, still finds support (Romaios, 1968, p. 192).

During the years of Ottoman rule, local governors recruited armed bands to protect property and to help maintain a centralised authority over their regions. These groups of law-enforcers were called *armatolíkia* and the men who served in them were known as *armatolí*. The existence of these bands, which we know were well established throughout the central and northern provinces of the Greek mainland by the end of the seventeenth century, presupposes that brigandage in those regions was already a problem, and it may be suspected that the *armatolíkia* were often recruited from the footloose fringes of Greek peasant society from which the klefts must also have been drawn. Certainly by the late eighteenth century, the terms *armatolós* and *kléftis* had become almost interchangeable, and well before this time many organised bands of *armatolí* had begun abusing their power and position to embark on acts of brigandage. So much so that in 1720 the *armatolíkia* were effectively abolished in certain provinces, and may well have lost their official standing throughout the rest of Greece (Vasdravellis, 1952, p. 158). By the early nineteenth century, when folk songs began to be collected, there was little practical difference between the *armatolí* and the klefts. Both groups were made up of armed insurgents proscribed by the authorities, and in the songs are often treated as synonymous.

By far the greatest number of kleftic songs referring to people and events before 1821 come from areas where *armatolíkia* were active, although brigands existed throughout Greece at this time, and it has been suggested that the history of brigand songs in Greece is closely bound up with the history of the *armatolíkia* (Politis, A., 1973, pp. xxxvi-xxxvii). Some writers maintain that this institution goes back to Byzantine times (Dakin, 1972, p. 18) or to the fifteenth century (Vakalopoulos, 1964, p. 216), but the earliest certain reference to *armatolíkia* tells us merely that they were flourishing in Macedonia by 1627 (Politis, A., 1973, p. xx). Had brigandage not been a serious problem at this time there would have been no need to recruit and maintain these forces, so it may be assumed that the institution of social banditry, as exemplified by the klefts, was at least two hundred years old when their songs first came to be recorded. It is quite possible that banditry of this sort has a much longer history in certain parts of the

Greek mainland, but this cannot be ascertained. One historian even cites a reference to the word *kléptis*, allegedly in the sense of the later 'kleft', dating from the beginning of Ottoman rule in northern Greece, and suggests that these 'freedom fighters' became established immediately upon the Ottoman conquest (Zakythinos, 1976, p. 76). This may well prove too good to be true.

We do not know for certain whether the songs were composed and sung by the klefts and *armatolí* themselves or at a safe distance by their admirers in the towns and villages (Politis, A., 1973, p. xl). But when we consider that social banditry is almost universally a part-time activity, the bandits being drawn from the surplus rural population and active only at certain times of the year (Hobsbawm, 1972, pp. 30–40), this distinction really disappears. One constant fact to emerge from Professor Eric Hobsbawm's study of social banditry is that the bandit, whether admired or feared or both, remains *within* the local peasant society – it is precisely this that makes a him a *social* bandit as distinct from a criminal. Thus the songs must be regarded as the common property of the klefts and *armatolí* (both of which groups could be classed as social bandits by the second half of the eighteenth century) *and* of the village communities from which the bandits originated. This is confirmed by Fauriel: 'The mountain people have regard only for the kleftic songs insofar as they tell of the lives of these wild men or of shepherds' (1824, pp. cxiii–cxiv), and their contempt for the songs of the towns, according to Fauriel's account, was indicated by the term *tragoúdia poústika* by which they described them. This solidarity of the mountain communities was also reported by William Martin-Leake, whose delicate gloss on the term *poústika* deserves to be quoted:

> These last, in the most vulgar language of that part of the country are often called πουστικά, a word, highly characteristic of the manners of those who have adopted it, and derived from a Turkish word, for which we have happily no corresponding term in the English language. (Martin-Leake, 1814, p. 159)

The songs known as *kléftika* belong structurally to the demotic tradition, although the earlier collections also contain a number of semi-professional minstrel songs similar to those found predominantly in Crete and Cyprus. These latter songs deal mostly with events around the time of the 1821 uprising and often reflect a growing national and political awareness which belongs to the climate of the time. The traditional *kléftika*, however, do not differ from other songs of the demotic tradition in style and structure: but the preponderance in them of named individuals, most of whom are known to history, and of actual events, whether historically verifiable or not, enables us to define part at least of their function in the way in which real people and events are treated in them.

It was clear to Yannis Apostolakis, one of the most independent-minded of writers on the subject, that this function was not a historical one:

> Kleftic song is not history, nor is it a display of emotions or a dra-matic representation, but something deeper and more fundamental: it is the awakening of the individual to the boundless power which nestles within him deeper than his heart and mind. (Apostolakis, 1950, p. 121)

Apostolakis' individualism and rather impressionistic approach to folk song often led him to excess, both in his ideas and in their expression. But he was right to see in the songs a representation of something, not necessarily more fundamental than historical fact, but significantly different. And more recently Alexis Politis has restated the core of Apostolakis' proposition in less poetic terms: 'The chief characteristic of the kleftic songs . . . is their spirit; that is to say their attitude to life. Of all the good things of life only one has any interest for the poet: freedom' (Politis, A., 1973, p. li). In order to understand the function of these songs we must be careful to define the 'awakening to boundless power' or 'freedom' which these commentators regard as fundamental to the kleftic songs.

The kleftic songs are normally brief, and consist of the narration of a single event or perhaps a brief series of events. These are not usually connected as a narrative sequence, but as in the longer narrative songs on mythical or fictional themes, are presented vividly as a succession of images, often rather like 'stills' from a film. The most common such events are battles or encounters between klefts and their personal enemies, and the death of an individual kleft. With the exception of the more spectacular events of the War of Independence and the years which led up to it, such as the campaigns of Ali Pasha of Ioannina against the Souliots, and the decision of Despo Botsari and the belea-guered Souliot women to blow themselves up rather than submit (Passow, 1860, pp. 150–65), most of the battles recounted in these songs had little military or political significance.

The nature of these skirmishes, in which both klefts and Turks were limited by the use of old-fashioned, inaccurate firearms and poor-quality gunpowder, has been vividly described by a historian of the philhellenes in the War of Independence:

Firing their weapons was a lengthy process and often as dangerous to themselves [the klefts] as to the enemy. They invariably fired from the hip and turned their back to the enemy as they pulled the trigger ... Much of their effort during a skirmish was devoted to undermining the enemy's confidence by vigorous shouting of abuse and taunts from behind cover. We hear of Greeks being shot in the bottom while making obscene gestures at the Turks ... Casualties were almost always light on both sides. Sometimes a battle went on for many hours with hundreds of men engaged but without anyone being killed. If someone *was* killed then it became a matter of pride to try to capture and strip the body. After a battle the heads of the dead were invariably cut off and taken in triumph to be piled into pyramids as a trophy. (St Clair, 1972, pp. 37–8)

If this description by a historian is superimposed on the ballad of Yiftakis, there are no actual inconsistencies. One's credulity is not strained to believe that the same event is being described, but the difference in deliberate intention between the historian and the folk singer is abundantly clear.

Διψοῦν οἱ κάμποι γιὰ νερὰ καὶ τὰ βουνὰ γιὰ χιόνια
καὶ τὰ γεράκια γιὰ πουλιὰ κι οἱ Τοῦρκοι γιὰ κεφάλια.
Τάχα τὸ τί νὰ γένηκεν ἡ μάνα τοῦ Γυφτάκη,
ποὺ ἔχασε τὰ δυὸ παιδιά, τὸν ἀδερφό της τρία,
καὶ τώρα παλαβώθηκε καὶ περπατεῖ καὶ κλαίει;
Μήτε στοὺς κάμπους φαίνεται, μήτε στὰ κορφοβούνια.
Μᾶς εἶπαν πέρα πέρασε, πέρα στὰ Βλαχοχώρια·
κι ἐκεῖ ντουφέκια πέφτανε καὶ θλιβερὰ βροντοῦσαν,
μήτε σὲ γάμους πέφτανε, μήτε σὲ πανηγύρια,
μόνο τὸ Γύφτη λάβωσαν στὸ γόνα καὶ στὸ χέρι.
Σὰ δέντρον ἐραγίστηκε, σὰν κυπαρίσσι πέφτει·
ψιλὴ φωνούλαν ἔβγαλε, σὰν παλικάρι ὁπού 'ταν:
– Ποῦ εἶσαι καλέ μου ἀδερφὲ καὶ πολυαγαπημένε,
γύρισε πίσω πάρε με, πάρε μου τὸ κεφάλι,
νὰ μὴν τὸ πάρη ἡ παγανιὰ καὶ ὁ Γιουσοὺφ ἀράπης,
καὶ μοῦ τὸ πάη στὰ Γιάννινα, τ' Ἀλῆ πασᾶ τοῦ σκύλου.

(Fauriel, 1824, p. 20)

The plains thirst for water and the mountains for snow,
falcons for prey and the Turks for heads.
What ever can have happened to Yiftakis' mother,
who lost two children, and her brother made three,
and now has gone out of her mind and wanders and weeps?
She hasn't been seen on the plains, nor in the mountain peaks.
They told us she had gone away, over to the Vlach villages;
rifles were firing there and thundering dismally,
they weren't firing for weddings or festivals,
but wounded Yiftakis in the knee and hand.
He was cut down like a tree, he fell like a cypress;
he gave a shrill cry, like the *pallikári* he was:
'Where are you, brother, my dearly beloved brother,
come back and take me, take off my head,
don't let the pursuit get hold of it and Yusuf the Arab,
to take it to Ioannina, to Ali Pasha the dog.'

The skirmish in which Yiftakis lost his life is not otherwise known to history, and all we know about Yiftakis himself is that he was related to the energetic Boukouvalas family of bandits and probably died close to the beginning of the nineteenth century. The event has not been recorded, and this song tells us nothing about it. Clearly it was not intended to – the song is about the impact of Yiftakis' death on his mother and, by implication, on the rest of the community from which he came. But it is not quite a dirge: Yiftakis has become a local hero and deserves praise as much as lamentation. This song, like a great many of the *kléftika*, belongs to a restricted, intimate social setting and functions as an assertion of a common ideal held by the group. The grief of the hero's mother is weighed against the praise which Yiftakis, dead, has won for himself, so that the song upholds a way of life in which life itself is precarious, by its implied assertion that mere living must be subordinated to the ideals of the kleft, or 'freedom'.

What sort of freedom is it that can outweigh the fact of Yiftakis' death and the touching human grief of his mother? In this song one could be forgiven for supposing that it is the freedom for which the traditional patriot dies, freedom for all from oppression and arbitrary acts of violence. But this is not so. The crux of the matter was pointed out by Alexis Politis: 'What is sung in the *kléftika* is individual bravery: nowhere will we find either national or social consciousness' (1973, p. li). And the emphasis here must be placed on *individual*, since the 'bravery' of the klefts could take a variety of forms.

107

The songs and history

Zaharias, who is known both historically and through the songs about him to have terrorised and robbed the Greek population of the Mani is described:

Μ' αὐτὸς Τούρκους δὲ σκιάζεται, Ρωμιοὺς δὲν προσκυνάει
(Petropoulos, 1958, p. 198, No. 32B)

But he cares nothing for Turks, nor bows to Greeks

Papathymios has no qualms about the use of guile in an attempt to break into the Varlaam Monastery in the Meteora (Apostolakis, 1929, p. 86), and a number of songs also celebrate the corresponding perfidy on the part of monks who informed the authorities if they knew where klefts were hiding. Nor are the songs exclusively dedicated to individuals who fought against the Turks. Stournaris, father and son, were hereditary chiefs of an *armatolíki* in central Greece and between them pursued a pro-Turkish policy for over thirty years, but one, or more likely both of them, are commemorated in a song whose style and apparent motivation are no different from those of more 'heroic' songs (Politis, A., 1973, pp. 30-1). And the fine song of Katsoudas relates how the hero went to Ali Pasha and suggested that the two of them should join forces, using the money which Katsoudas had robbed from the Pasha, to crush a rival *armatolíki*:

Κύριέ μου, τί νὰ γίνηκαν οἱ μαῦροι οἱ Κατσουδαῖοι;
Κι οὐδὲ στὴν Πάτρα φαίνονται, κι οὐδὲ στὸν Ἅγι Σώστη.
Ὁ Φλῶρος ὁ περήφανος, ὁ κάλεσιος Κατσούδας,
πού 'ταν στοὺς κάμπους φλάμπουρα, καὶ στὰ βουνὰ μπαϊράκια.
Κατσούδας πάει στὰ Γιάννινα, πάει νὰ προσκυνήσῃ.
- Πολλὰ τὰ ἔτη ντουβλετή. - Καλῶς τον τὸν Κατσούδα.
Κατσούδα, κάτσε καταγῆς, κάτσε νὰ σὲ ρωτήσω·
πολλὰ σκαέτια μοῦ 'ρθανε 'π' ὅλα τὰ βιλαέτια,
ἀπ' Ἄγραφα καὶ Πατρινὸ κι ἀπὸ τὸ Καρπενίσι.
- Ἀλήθεια, ἀφέντη μ', σοῦ 'ρθανε, καὶ νὰ μὲ συμπαθήσῃς,
χίλια φλουριὰ καξάντησα, τώρα νὰ στὰ μετρήσω·
νὰ διώξουμε τοὺς Βαλτινούς, καὶ τοὺς Κοντογιανναίους.
Κι Ἀλὴ πασιὰς δεν ἤκουσε, τοῦ 'κοψε τὸ κεφάλι.
(Tommaseo, 1842, p. 385)

My God, what can have happened to the unhappy Katsoudas family?
They haven't been seen in Patras or in Ayios Sostis,

The songs of the klefts

Floros the proud and handsome Katsoudas,
who were [like] pennons on the plains, and banners in the
  mountains.
Katsoudas has gone to Ioannina, has gone to pay homage.
'Long life to you, *devletli.*' 'You're welcome, Katsoudas.
Katsoudas, sit down on the floor, sit down and answer me this:
I've had many complaints from all the outlying districts,
from Agrafa and Patrino and from Karpenisi.'
'Quite right, *effendi*, so you have, but look at it my way,
I've made a thousand florins, I'll count them out for you now;
and let's go and rout the men of Valtos, the Kontoyannis family.'
Ali Pasha didn't heed him, but cut off his head.

Finally, the almost narcissistic nature of such absolute individualism
can be seen in the songs (which cannot be regarded as flippant or satirical) in which the klefts groom themselves and admire themselves in
the mirror:

Οἱ κλέφτες μπαρμπερίζουνται καί στρίβουν τό μουστάκι·
κι ἕνας τόν ἄλλον ἔλεε, κι ἕνας τόν ἄλλο λέει:
- Μόρφα κεφάλια πὄχουμε καί μαῦρα 'ν' τά μαλλιά μας,
καί δέν μᾶς πρέπει κόψιμο, μουϊδέ καί χαρμαγκιόλα,
μόνο μᾶς πρέπουν ἄρματα, σοφίλια καί ντουκάδες.

(Spandonidi, 1939, p. 35)

The klefts are grooming themselves, and twirling their moustaches;
and one to another was saying, and one to another says:
'Fine heads we've got, and our hair is black,
not right for cutting, not right for the guillotine,
but right for arms, doubloons and ducats.'

Κάθουνται οἱ κλέφτες, κάθουνται στόν πλάτανο ἀπό κάτου.
Λούζουνται, μπαρμπερίζουνται καί στό γυαλί κοιτιοῦνται.
Κοιτᾶν τήν ἐμορφάδα τους, κοιτᾶν τή λεβεντιά τους.
Κοιτιέται ὁ Δῆμος μιά φορά, τά παλικάρια πέντε,
κι ὁ Κώστας ὁ περήφανος κοιτιέται δεκαπέντε.
Κοιτάει τήν ἐμορφάδα του, κοιτάει τή λεβεντιά του.
Κι ἀπό τήν περηφάνεια του, κι ἀπό τή λεβεντιά του,
δέν πάει τό βράδυ σπίτι του, δέν πάει στή φαμελιά του,
μά 'κατσε ἀπάνου στά βουνά καί στίς ψηλές ραχοῦλες.

(Ioannou, 1965, p. 1)

109

The klefts are sitting, sitting beneath the planetree.
They wash, they groom themselves and look at themselves in
    the glass.
They observe their fine features, they observe their *leventiá*.
Dimos takes one look, the *pallikária* five,
and Kostas the proud looks fifteen times.
He observes his fine features, he observes his *leventiá*.
And out of his pride and out of his *leventiá*,
he doesn't go home in the evening, he doesn't go back to his
    family,
but stayed up in the mountains and high ridges.

The first of these reveals a grim humour, while the second is a more explicit account of the psychology of the Greek bandit. The reason that Kostas takes to the mountains is his own pride – in himself and his *leventiá*, an untranslatable term which combines the ideas of youth, beauty, strength and daring.

In the light of these examples we can define the klefts' idea of freedom as little short of absolute individual self-sufficiency, the complete freedom of self-assertion, whether in the relatively harmless case of Kostas taking to the mountains because he has looked in the mirror and seen that he is too good for the life of the plains, or more seriously in the case of the brutal Zaharias, who cared nothing for Greek and Turk alike. Freedom so understood may well lead to acts apparently less introverted, as happened with Yiftakis, or with Despo Botsari blowing up herself and the rest of the women of Souli rather than fall into Turkish hands. But even here one feels that the freedom invoked in these 'heroic' acts of self-sacrifice is not motivated by political or religious allegiance but by the same self-regarding determination of the kleft to recognise no authority but his own. The logical conclusion of this ideal of freedom is the point where even life, dearly prized as it is in the kleftic songs, must be discarded if continuing to live will force the kleft to submit to another's authority.

The kleft as he portrays himself in the songs is in no sense a revolutionary, but a solitary rebel, refusing all allegiance and obligations. Hobsbawm's sociological study of banditry, as well as common sense, tell us that this cannot quite have been the case in real life. The dependence of social bandits on the local community is well known, and, while the idealised self-sufficiency of the kleftic songs may, as a goal to be achieved, have determined the behaviour of real klefts in action, it cannot have been a *social reality* among them. Thus the kleftic songs do not merely reflect current cultural or social values, which was the furthest we could go in defining the function of the song tradition from the evidence of the historical songs of the fall of cities. To this we must now add the function reflecting cultural *aspirations*. The kleftic songs do not reflect the lives and attitudes of the klefts precisely as they were, but as the klefts would have liked them to be, as they appeared to their own imaginations.

This function is probably not confined to the songs of the klefts – it will account admirably for the historical songs, in particular those in which the return of Constantinople to the Christians is prophesied. And further corroboration is found in the case of love songs in the revealing remark of a Sarakatsan shepherd quoted by J. K. Campbell. Discussing the rigid code of sexual morality practised by these nomads of north-western Greece, this shepherd dismissed the romantic ideals of the love songs sung in his community with the words, 'The songs tell lies' (Campbell, 1964, p. 124). So long as they are not interpreted literally, lies such as this can tell us much. The songs of the klefts are not after all mendacious, but neither was it ever their purpose to be true to historical fact.

7. The Songs as Myth

The discussion of function in Greek folk poetry in the last chapter led us to the generalised conclusion that this was the synchronic reflection of cultural values, attitudes and aspirations. We saw that neither in the historical nor in the kleftic songs are events either placed in time or sequentially related. Neither is historical detail often found in the tradition. The whole barrage of facts and contingencies which clearly separate, say, the siege of Rhodes and the siege of Paros in the mind of the historian is absent from the songs. We find songs referring to the loss of cities, to the death, betrayals and acts of defiance of klefts: from a mass of contingency, only those features which have been frequently repeated on different historical occasions have found their way into the tradition. History (not the facts but the telling of facts) when it repeats itself belongs with other stories which are characterised by their 'timelessness', namely myths. The tale of a captured city, be it Constantinople, Rhodes, or Malta, shorn of the historical contingencies which, for the historian, make the event unique, is no longer a piece of history, but has taken on the character of myth.

No distinction is to be drawn, therefore, between narrative songs on 'mythical' and 'historical' subjects, and the importance of 'myth', understood in this way, will be evident as we come to consider two problems which have traditionally been of concern to folklorists and anthropologists. These have to do with diffusion (how does oral tradition travel?) and with meaning (does a folk song or narrative *mean* anything, and if so how can we interpret it?).

A. DIFFUSION OF SONGS WITHIN GREECE

The problem of 'diffusion' is essentially the problem of 'variants' which was discussed in Chapter 2, viewed from a different angle. As a phenomenon it has been extensively studied and a degree of mystery has

112

grown up around it which is not entirely deserved. Partly this is because the early 'diffusionist' scholars of folklore adapted to the study of oral texts certain assumptions which had been current among the most plodding of nineteenth-century literary scholars (Wilgus, 1959, p. 65). When the same story is found in the work of more than one *writer*, working within the same European literary tradition, it is perfectly possible to trace the evolution of the story through successive 'borrowings'. Since written works, or those at least of sufficient merit to influence succeeding generations of writers, are relatively few and most of the corpus was accessible to practitioners all over Europe from the middle ages onwards, there is no particular difficulty in saying, for example, that Shakespeare took part of the plot of *Cymbeline* from a story of Boccaccio. The evolution of a story can be traced when we possess the earlier stages from which later departures were made: but only when we can be certain that they really are earlier, and also that these are the same early versions as were known to the creators of the later ones. The assumption that this is also true of oral narrative is central to the work of the 'historical–geographical' or 'Finnish' school of folklorists, whose methods have been influential in the study of Greek folk poetry.

This view of diffusion assumed that each narrative started from a single original or archetype, which was then transmitted over an ever-widening area. By comparing variants from the entire area (in some cases the whole world) and interpreting the characteristics of each according to this model of historical and geographical diffusion, it was thought that the folklorist could reconstruct the archetypal form and estimate the approximate time and place of its genesis (Thompson, 1946, p. 440; Finnegan, 1977, pp. 41–4). Most of the followers of this school were concerned with tales rather than with songs, and the relative neglect of songs was probably inevitable in a school which tended to ignore questions of style. The 'tale' was the thing – and it was also inevitable that this meticulous but often unimaginative application of a method of literary research to the study of oral material should have kept its distance from the complementary disciplines of anthropology and sociology. As Dorson, one of the most recent apologists of the 'school', comments, 'where the Finnish method seeks to establish the oldest narrative traits of an international tale, the anthropologist searches for dominant psychological attitudes projected into a tribal tale' (Dorson, 1964, p. 103).

Recent developments have rather altered this picture. Lévi-Strauss' application of the methods of structural linguistics to the study of myth has brought about a resurgence of interest among anthropologists in myths, which are really the folk tales of the Finnish school under a different name. And in a parallel development the disciplines of literature and sociology are coming closer together in the examination of the 'sociology of literature', in which oral or folk material is now seen to play an important part.

The usefulness of these developments will probably not be to provide solutions to problems that have concerned folklorists in the past, so much as to change the fundamental assumptions which gave rise to the problems in the first place. Once it is realised, in the light of Lévi-Strauss' work on transformations in myth and of Parry's and Lord's conclusions on the composition of oral narrative poetry in Yugoslavia, that the myth or the song is not necessarily a separate entity derived by a simple progression from a single archetype, then the need to discover or to reconstruct archetypal forms disappears. And along with archetypes the idea of 'diffusion' may also have to be discarded or at least seriously modified.

The first serious attempt to chart and interpret the diffusion of songs in the Greek-speaking world was made by Professor Samuel Baud-Bovy. A musician and musicologist by training, Baud-Bovy visited the Dodecanese in 1930–3 as part of a project launched by Melpo Merlier to record music and songs from all over Greece. Baud-Bovy's collection of texts and music, the latter transcribed in notation during actual performances, is one of the fullest and most meticulous of all Greek folk song publications. When he published the first volume of his *Chansons du Dodécanèse* (1935) Baud-Bovy was already well advanced on his doctoral thesis – an analysis of the texts he had collected and a detailed comparison of characteristic versions of songs from the Dodecanese with those of other areas (Baud-Bovy, 1936). Both the aim and method of this research are clearly derived from the folk tale studies of the 'historical–geographical' school in Europe and America. Baud-Bovy 's aim, he states, was to 'examiner parallèlement le plus grand nombre possible de versions d'une chanson afin de déterminer sa forme originale et, si possible, le lieu et la date de sa création' (1936, p. 125). In the pages which follow Baud-Bovy examines the characteristic differences between groups of variants of some of the most widely diffused narrative songs in Greece, and ascribes priority to those which omit details of narrative that in other versions show the widest inconsistency. This procedure is justified by the principle that those elements of a song

114

which belong to the archetype will be transmitted more faithfully than those which are accretions. The original form of the song must therefore be that on which the maximum number of versions agree, while its geographical origin must be the area in which the versions closest to the consensus version are still sung.

The flaws in this procedure are clear to see. Baud-Bovy was unable to justify the assumption that a song can be traced back to an archetype and an origin in time and place, and, as regards his method, the omission in a song of the details most susceptible to variation may be considered merely as another case of variation, without special significance. Baud-Bovy's conclusion, that the oldest Greek ballads were composed in Asia Minor in the ninth or tenth centuries and transmitted westwards with the decline of Byzantine power, is consistent with the argument used, but can no longer be accepted without careful reassessment of the method.

Both Baud-Bovy's method and his conclusions have, however, been accepted as solid fact by Entwistle in his authoritative survey of European balladry (1939, pp. 237ff.), more recently by Gareth Morgan (1960, p. 11), and G. Megas (1971), and again by Bertrand Bouvier, a pupil of Baud-Bovy, in his otherwise admirable study of the 'Virgin's Lament' in popular tradition (1976).

An interesting exception to this trend is the work of G. Saunier (1972), who examines the narrative of Diyenis' combat with Death in terms of 'myth', which he then divides into 'themes', and analyses according to a sophisticated version of the 'historical–geographical' method. According to Saunier the themes which comprise the myth gradually change in transmission, so that in time one theme gives rise to another. Where it can be determined that a theme in a certain song is derived from one or more themes found elsewhere, it must follow that the derived form is later. Saunier concludes that from all the existing songs which express this myth, four 'original' themes or forms of the myth can be isolated, each of which has a separate geographical origin. Saunier's analysis is cogent and subtle, but there is an inherent danger in seeking *original* forms within a *myth*, since the two terms normally belong to diametrically opposed methods of approach. One cannot escape feeling, with Saunier himself, that 'Le choix des formes originelles pourra, il est vrai, paraître arbitraire', without being wholly convinced that 'il suffit que la suite de l'analyse le justifie' (1972, p. 124).

B. DIFFUSION BEYOND GREECE

For all its evident hazards, the work of the diffusionist scholar within the confines of a single culture or language-area is relatively uncomplicated. But the enormously wide distribution of so many of the folk tale 'motifs' with which he is pledged to deal requires him to separate the 'motif' not merely from the style, structure and function which govern its expression, but also from the place which it occupies in many different regional cultures. This is from many points of view undesirable as well as difficult; and, in the case of Greek folk songs and those of the neighbouring Balkan countries, immediately gives rise to questions of the national ownership of ballads.

One of the most important questions for the folklorists of the 'historical–geographical' school is how tales and motifs cross cultural and linguistic boundaries. But here problems of method arise which have never been satisfactorily solved. If one believes, with the exponents of the classic 'historical–geographical' method, that the folk tale is somehow a self-generating entity governed by its own laws which can be scientifically studied, and to this extent detachable from the environment in which it is found, then it is indeed possible to isolate the same trait in different cultures and chart its diffusion without reference to the various cultural contexts of which it is a part. But what then is the correct reply to the Greek scholar who maintained that the pan-European ballad 'The Dead Brother' must have been diffused across Europe from Greece, because the Greek versions are perfectly adapted to specifically *Greek* cultural attitudes (Politis, N. G., 1885)?

Such an appeal to the perfect integration of the international 'tale' into a particular culture should not go unheeded. It is here that the greatest weakness of the classic 'historical–geographical' approach is apparent. It is sometimes possible for a single scholar to collect and compare all the world-wide manifestations of a particular 'tale', although this in itself may easily be more than a life's work (Dorson, 1964, p. 94). But it is quite impossible for one person to know intimately more than one or two of the cultures in which this tale occurs, so that in only one or two of many hundreds of cases will he be aware of the degree of integration of the tale he is studying into its surrounding culture. Thus any conclusion reached by an application of the method must be open to challenge from anyone closely acquainted with any of the cultures which effectively have been ignored in the exclusive analysis of a single trait.

This problem was appreciated early on in the 'historical–geographical' debate by the Swedish scholar C. W. von Sydow (Thompson, 1946, pp. 440–1), whose division of an international tale into local 'oikotypes' showed an awareness of the problem but failed to restate it in more manageable terms. The concentration by von Sydow and his followers on local or national 'types', and the failure of the classic 'historical–geographical' school to take into account the place of a tale in the cultures in which it is found have given rise, in the study of Greek and Balkan folk material, to an exceptionally, and unnecessarily, confused situation.

There is no lack of Greek narrative songs which clearly bear some relation to counterparts in other areas of Europe, notably the Balkans. The most widely examined of these are the ballads known as 'The Dead Brother', which has counterparts as far away as Suffolk and Russia, and 'The Bridge of Arta' which will be discussed below.[1] Almost all of these 'diffusionist' or comparative studies are concerned with motifs or elements of the narrative, and not with stylistic features, so that they really concern the *content* of the ballads and not the songs themselves. The assumptions from which such studies begin are invariably those of the 'historical–geographical' school concerning origins and diffusion, yoked with a nationalism or partisanship which is often fostered by each contestant's being most familiar with only one of the national languages and cultures under discussion. Under these circumstances it is hardly surprising that the debate should degenerate into a squabble between national and political allegiances, which is all the more incongruous as so often in the Balkans national boundaries do not correspond with cultural groupings.

In a discussion of 'motifs' without regard to structure or to the place of the song in its own cultural tradition, one-sidedness and distortion are only to be expected, and the avowed methods of research logically deficient. The Hungarian scholar Lajos Vargyas, whose study of the Balkan distribution of the ballad 'The Walled-up Wife' (or 'Bridge of Arta' in Greece) is in many ways useful and informative, puts forward a detailed case for the Hungarian origin of the song. Concluding a discussion of one particular motif, Vargyas says, 'I think the examples shown make it clear on the uniform evidence of several details that the Hungarian formulation shows the purest form: in stylised form all together conform completely to the requirements of ballad style' (Vargyas, 1967, p. 222). This sort of conclusion is only natural if one is comparing material from one's own culture and language with that of other cultures and languages which are less well known or known only through translations, divorced from their context. Vargyas' conclusion is really based on an aesthetic judgement, which need not be challenged so far as it concerns only the songs in Hungarian. But the comparison with other non-Hungarian versions has been made without the linguistic knowledge to appreciate them at the same level and without the detailed understanding of the place of these rival versions in the cultures to which they belong.

The corresponding weakness of Professor Megas' argument, from the Greek side, is no less easy to perceive. The dogmatism of his final comment is forced on him by the 'historical–geographical' assumption reiterated in the first:

> All attempts so far to establish the view of 'polygenesis' for the origin of the song of the walled-up wife lack stability, insofar as we are dealing with a poetic rendition of a folk tale (*parádosi*), whose central theme in the variants of all the peoples of SE Europe is single and for this reason must have a single origin. This origin, for the reasons set out, must be located on Greek soil and in the early Byzantine period. (Megas, 1971, p. 190)[2]

The question is not so much whether all these songs have a single origin but whether, if they did, the modern versions have been derived from it by a process of lineal descent. A less one-sided examination of oral tradition suggests that the interaction of variants and their relation to other songs in the linguistic tradition as well as to cultural factors render it naive to suppose that a single traceable cause has resulted in the distribution of these versions about the Balkans, or that 'diffusion' has taken place in only one direction.

Another important fact is that this wide 'diffusion' is not confined to narrative details or 'motifs'. It is not uncommon to find identical structural patterns recurring in cultures quite remote from one another. Of the two songs which follow, the first is a Greek song lamenting the fate of a loved one in exile, the second is part of an oral poem composed by a Polynesian poet for a friend:

(1) Τί νὰ σοῦ στείλω, ξένε μου, τί νὰ σοῦ προβοδίσω;
   Νὰ στείλω μῆλο, σέπεται, κυδώνι, μαραγκιάζει,
   νὰ στείλω μοσκοστάφυλο κι ἐκεῖνο σταφιδιάζει,
   νὰ στείλω κἂν τὰ δάκρυα μου σ' ἕνα ψιλὸ μαντῆλι,

118

τὰ δάκρυα μού 'ναι καυτερὰ καὶ καίγουν τὸ μαντῆλι.
Τί νὰ σοῦ στείλω, ξένε μου, τί νὰ σοῦ προβοδίσω;

(Passow, 1860, p. 247)

What can I send you, my exiled one, how can I keep you
company?
If I send an apple, it will rot, a quince, it will shrivel,
if I send a muscat grape, that too will dry out,
even should I send my tears on a fine kerchief,
my tears are burning hot and would burn the kerchief.
What can I send you, my exiled one, how can I keep you
company?

(2) If I give a mat it will rot,
If I give cloth it will be torn,
The poem is bad, yet take it,
That it be to thee boat and house. . .

(Finnegan, 1977, p. 204)

Allowing for the disadvantages of translation we can see a common
structural pattern employed by both poets – not in precisely the same
way, but arguably for a very similar reason, to dramatise the love or
respect of the singer for the person addressed through contrast with
the inadequacy of conventional gifts to express his feelings. The device
is both formal and spontaneous (in that it seems to evoke a genuine and
personal emotion); but what is most conspicuous about parallels of this
kind is that neither the pattern itself nor the idea it expresses seems
important or striking enough to merit 'diffusion', even where this is
conceivable.

Similarities between traditions in imagery and even wording are also
as deserving of study as the similarities between the motifs of tales. The
minor role of the expression would seem to rule out diffusion as the
cause of similarity between the Greek,

Βαν' ἀσημένια πέταλα μαλαματένιες λόθρες   (Megas, 1961, p. 488)

He put on silver horseshoes and nails of gold

and the Scottish,

The horse Fair Annet rode upon,
He amblit like the wind;
Wi siller he was shod before
Wi burning gowd behind.

(Child, 1957, No. 73)

119

And in the same way the ending of songs in Greek tradition where two lovers die and a cypress and lemon grow out of the graves of each and intertwine has a significant counterpart in the British tradition where the rose and briar fulfil a comparable role. This is not sufficiently important to the story in either case to be considered as a 'motif', and the chances of diffusion having played a part seem slight. Rather this example suggests that the imagination of singers in more than one culture may respond to a given situation in parallel ways, and that some analogy may exist between the requirements of expression characteristic of different traditions.

C. THE BALLAD 'THE BRIDGE OF ARTA'

This is one of the best known of all Greek narrative songs, and versions of it have been collected from all parts of the Greek-speaking world, as well as from Bulgaria, Albania, Serbia, Romania and Hungary. As a result of the song's popularity and wide distribution it has been a subject for studies of 'diffusion' for close on a hundred years. Scholars have been unable to reach agreement, however, on the song's country of origin (although the majority opinion favours Greece) or, if the song *is* indigenous to Greece, on which of the regional variants is closest to the original.

The broad outlines of the story are these. A master-builder, with a varying number of craftsmen and apprentices, is engaged on a building. In all of the Greek versions this is a bridge, although elsewhere in the Balkans it may be a castle or a monastery. What the masons build by day, however, falls down by night, and the master-builder is in despair until it is revealed to him by a supernatural agent that the bridge will not stand firm unless a human sacrifice is built into the foundations. In most of the Greek versions it is spelt out to him that the sacrifice must be his own wife, although the selection of the victim (always the master-builder's wife) may be made in a number of ways. The master-builder sends for his wife who, to his chagrin, comes all too quickly to the site. In most of the Greek versions the wife is tricked into descending into the foundations, usually on the pretext of recovering a ring which the master-builder has accidentally dropped, and once she is there the masons begin to immure her. As she is being walled up the woman vainly appeals to her husband's sense of pity, then curses the bridge, often lamenting the fact that she is the last of three sisters to die in this way. The master-builder reminds her that she has a brother or son still living who will one day have to cross the bridge and so persuades her to revoke her curse and bless the bridge instead.

No less than sixteen 'historical–geographical' studies of this ballad are summarised and discussed by Megas (1971), whose own approach shows little advance upon that of his predecessors. The essential weakness in all these arguments is the assumption that certain variants of the song must be derived from others (according to varying sets of criteria) and that, depending on the criteria selected, the evolution of the song through a series of variant-types can be traced. The truth is, however, that every oral variant is of equal validity, and has an equal claim to be regarded as 'original' (cf. Lord, 1960, pp. 99–123). The song does not evolve according to a mysterious Darwinian principle, beyond the control of individual singers, but is created anew every time it is sung, the resulting version being determined by the capabilities of each singer and his free artistic choice within the narrow structural conventions of his tradition.

Once these premises are granted, the question 'Which is the original version?' loses most of its meaning, to be replaced by the question 'What is the myth expressed?' Since it is in the nature of myth to undergo certain transformations between one culture and another, there is no reason to insist that the myth expressed is precisely the same in all the languages and cultures in which the song is found. There may be significant, and consistent, differences between the myth as expressed by the Bulgarian, Hungarian and Greek ballads, and this would be a proof not of historical diffusion but of cultural adaptation. This is perhaps why 'The Bridge of Arta' so often seems native to the region and people whose versions are best known to each commentator.

Speaking now only of the Greek versions of the ballad, there are two important features which give a clue to the nature of the myth expressed. The first is the name given to the bridge in different versions. The most common of these is the Bridge of Arta, although other local names are sometimes substituted, such as the Bridge of Adana in Cappadocia and of Larisa in Thessaly, and the improbable location 'on the shore' in the islands of Evia and the Sporades. Otherwise the bridge is not geographically located but instead is given a mythical significance. The next most common name after the 'Bridge of Arta' is the mythical 'Bridge of Hair' (τῆς Τρίχας τὸ γιοφύρι), and there may be a similar mythical intent in the Cypriot and Asia Minor versions which place the bridge 'Down at the edge of the world' (Megas, 1971, pp. 92–3).[3]

Scholars following the methods of the 'historical–geographical' school have devoted much attention to the real monuments mentioned in the song: according to Baud-Bovy the Bridge of Adana is the oldest monument referred to, and therefore the song must have originated in Cappadocia with the building of that bridge in the reign of the Emperor Justinian (Baud-Bovy, 1936, p. 170); while Megas on statistical grounds attaches the song to the bridge of Arta, although that bridge was almost certainly not built until some centuries after the time when he believes the song originated.[4]

Such theories are only credible if one believes that the song relates a historical fact associated with the building of one of these bridges. But the ease with which the song evidently attaches itself to any local monument of sufficient importance (by far the greatest number of 'Arta' variants come from the Greek mainland, although not from Arta itself) is shown by the predominance of unusually imposing monuments in the song (the bridges of Arta and Adana in Greek versions, the castle of Shkodër (Skutari) in Albanian, etc.) and by the large number of such monuments with which it has become associated throughout the Balkans. Since the song is not historical there is no need to believe that any of the actual monuments named is an essential part of the myth.

With the 'Bridge of Hair' we are on quite different ground. In our attempt to isolate the mythical core of the song, we are justified in rewriting the name of any *real* bridge as 'Once upon a time a bridge...' The name Arta or Adana or Larisa would be introduced by singers in order to add verisimilitude and a degree of local immediacy to a fictional story, just as many realist novelists have introduced historical events and even characters into their fictions in order to strengthen the illusion of reality for their readers. But rewritten in the same way, *tis Tríhas to yofýri* becomes 'once upon a time a bridge *of hair*...'. Since this is the only *mythical* description of the bridge, much greater importance must be attached to the 'Bridge of Hair' than might have been expected from a statistical count of its occurrences (17.41 per cent according to Megas, as against 33 per cent for 'Arta'), and this is further borne out by its exceptionally wide distribution.[5]

The mythical significance of the 'Bridge of Hair' is not hard to find. In Greek popular usage the phrase is recorded as meaning figuratively any exceedingly long-drawn out task, but the usage 'He crossed the bridge of hair', meaning that someone has successfully negotiated great difficulties or danger (Politis, N. G., 1901, pp. 621–2), suggests that no distinction is to be drawn between the 'Bridge of Hair' (τῆς Τρίχας τὸ γιοφύρι) and the 'Hair Bridge' (τὸ Τρίχινο γεφύρι).[6] The latter, according to a popular belief attested in many parts of Greece, connects the world of the living with that of the dead:

> In the underworld the souls have to cross a bridge, the Hair Bridge. This is as slender as a hair and is most unsteady. Whatever soul is unable to cross falls into the river which runs beneath and is lost. (Politis, N. G., 1904, I, p. 612, No. 983).

And in a Thracian popular tradition this bridge is actually called the 'Bridge of Hair' as it is in the song:

> In the mouth of the dead man they would put a coin for him to give to the angel and cross the bridge. Whoever had been a just man would easily cross the Bridge of Hair (*τῆς Τρίχας τὸ γιοφύρι*) and whoever was a sinner would fall into the Touna. (*Thrakiká* 11, 1939, p. 197)

The reference to the river Touna, or Danube, which is frequently mentioned in versions of the song, further strengthens the link between this tradition and 'The Bridge of Arta'.

It is possible that this belief and the myth on which the song is based are connected with the Islamic *Sirat* which is described in the Ma'rifet-nāme as 'narrow as the edge of a sword' (Gill, 1953, p. 81) and in the Mulla 'Ali Qārī as 'finer than a hair and sharper than a sword' (Hughes, 1885, p. 595). According to the Islamic sources this bridge connects the earth with Paradise, and while the righteous cross it in a moment, the souls of the guilty fall off it into Hell which gapes below. This belief was presumably known to the Turks and it would be interesting to know whether there are Turkish songs or popular accounts in any way comparable to the Greek.[7]

But the belief and its attendant myths are by no means confined to Islamic culture. The idea that the other world is connected to this by a bridge supernaturally difficult to cross is found in Celtic, Icelandic, Indian, Indonesian, Melanesian, Eskimo and American Indian traditions (Thompson, 1955–8, F 152). Against this background it would be quite reasonable to suppose that the song 'The Bridge of Arta' is connected in some way with myths concerning the passage from life to death.

The second main feature which supports this analysis of the song is found in those versions where the master-builder's wife is persuaded to go down into the foundations of the bridge, generally on the pretext of recovering a ring. At this point the wife may call to her husband above to say that she has found nothing or he may reveal the ruse, telling her that he has the ring and never lost it; but by far the most telling are those versions in which the wife, searching for the ring in the foundations of the arch comes upon the apparently severed hand of a man or monster, or discovers snakes and vipers knotted together. This description, when it occurs, is too consistent to be gratuitous, and it may be supposed that those singers who included or added it did so with a definite purpose. Descriptions of severed limbs and in particular the formulaic evocation of snakes and vipers are a sure indication that the world of the dead is being described. These images only make sense if the bridge represents a crossing from this world to the next. By including these details the singers were able to emphasise the supernatural character of the bridge and incidentally, in doing so, to heighten the dramatic effect: even before she is killed by the masons throwing down rocks and lime on top of her, we know that the master-builder's wife has already entered Hades, from which there is no return.

According to Megas this whole episode of the ring is an intrusion from another song (in fact a series of songs or widely diverging variants), in which a young man is enticed by a beautiful woman to go down a well and recover a ring for her; but the woman turns out to be a spirit and refuses to hold the rope for him to ascend. In many of these songs too, the hero becomes aware of his fate by the discovery of knotted snakes at the bottom of the well (Megas, 1971, pp. 113–19). There is no reason, however, to believe that this theme was ever restricted to a single form and to the context of the 'haunted well', and it is perfectly in accord with the structural principles of the tradition that the theme, with the roles of the protagonists inverted, should form an equally integral part of songs which tell the story of the 'Bridge of Hair'.

A final feature which tends to confirm this approach to the song is the reason for which the dying wife is persuaded to revoke the curse which she has put upon the bridge, and which often includes a specific wish that travellers who attempt to cross the bridge should fall off. In a number of versions the master-builder prevails upon her to take back this curse and bless the bridge instead, by reminding her that she has a brother or a son who will one day cross it. If the bridge is the perilous hair bridge which the souls of the living must cross after death, then it is easy to see why this argument might have such force.

D. THE QUESTION OF MEANING

With the substitution of the question 'What is the myth expressed?' for
the diffusionist 'Which is the original version?' the emphasis in the fore-
going discussion was seen to shift from the diffusion of the ballad to
its meaning. But it will be noticed that I have not been able to give a
more conclusive answer to the latter question than to the former. The
truth is that the kind of answers to these questions expected by the
folklorists of the 'historical–geographical' school must always prove
elusive.

It will be helpful here to take account of the difference not only of
basic assumptions but of *intention* between these scholars and modern
structural anthropologists. The task of the diffusionist, according to
Stith Thompson, 'has not been unlike that of the student of Indo-
European languages who has worked out the theoretical Indo-European
form for a word'. Having first posited a primitive form for all the main
branches of the Indo-European family of languages, 'he arrives at a
hypothetical word which could serve as the common ancestor of them
all. This method of working back to primitive local forms and from
them to an ultimate archetype is applicable not only to language but
also to traditional narrative' (Thompson, 1946, p. 435). The structuralist
approach to 'traditional narrative' or myth was also directly inspired by
developments in the science of linguistics, but developments in quite a
different direction – away from seeking *explanations* for phenomena in
terms of simple cause and effect, towards the attempt to *describe* their
operation by means of more complex models (Lévi-Strauss, 1968;
Chomsky, 1964, pp. 7–27).

When it comes to the analysis of myths or folk tales this difference
is perhaps most apparent, and fundamental, in the treatment of transformations. For Aarne (in Thompson, 1946) and Thompson, the transformations which a tale may undergo in transmission are like the gradual
corrosion of a mineral ore: by reversing the process the scientist may
recover the original untarnished metal. These scholars, like the linguistic
researchers to whom Thompson compared them, regarded the transformations in folk tales as a diachronic progression separable from the
tale itself: thus, a series of *accidents* to which the tale is subjected
(Thompson, 1946, p. 436). Although Aarne even listed types of transformation which tales characteristically undergo, the significance of
these was not noticed either by him or by Thompson. This is that, as
Dan Sperber recently put it,

the differences between two versions are no less systematic than are the similarities. In other words . . . the borrowing of a myth is not simply a departure which, with time, arbitrarily becomes more distant from its model, but rather it is a set of rule-governed transformations. (Sperber, 1975, pp. 76–7)

Two possible consequences follow from Lévi-Strauss' structural analysis of myth. The question of meaning can be transferred to the plane of metaphysics, where the true 'meaning of meaning' can be contemplated (Paz, 1971, pp. 16, 19, 95–6); or one is forced to conclude, with Sperber, that myths are not composed of signs which signify (as is language) and therefore do not *mean* at all (Sperber, 1975, p. 83). According to the second alternative, every interpretation of a myth is merely a rearrangement of its constituent elements and must itself be accounted as a version of the same myth in a subsequent interpretation. As Sperber has said of symbolism, 'exegetical and psycho-analytical attempts seem to obey a cultural plan – in appearance, to interpret symbolism; in fact, to recreate it. For all keys to symbols are part of symbolism itself' (1975, p. 50). This was all but admitted by Lévi-Strauss when, in emphasising the need to consider all versions of the Oedipus myth in order to interpret it, he wrote that 'our *interpretation* may take into account the Freudian *use*' of the myth (my italics). The difference between 'interpretation' and 'use' here is one of perspective only. Lévi-Strauss' own interpretation of the Oedipus myth, or, in his own words, 'what it means' is this:

The myth has to do with the inability, for a culture which holds the belief that mankind is autochthonous . . . to find a satisfactory transition between this theory and the knowledge that human beings are actually born from the union of man and woman. (Lévi-Strauss, 1968, p. 216)

This is no more a meaning and no less a rearrangement of the myth itself than the 'Freudian use'. Lévi-Strauss' structural analysis does not tell us what myths mean but what they *do*, and this is the value of the method. In the case of the Oedipus myth: 'Although experience contradicts theory, social life validates cosmology by its similar structure. Hence cosmology is true' (1968, p. 216).

In a similar manner Sperber in his analysis of symbolism does not attempt to define the meaning of symbols so much as to describe the 'symbolic mechanism'. Sperber, if I have understood him correctly, maintains that symbols are conceptual representations which, having failed to achieve their object, are not valid representations *of* anything, but can still become the subject of further representations as the 'conceptual mechanism' attempts to validate them. It would not then be too wide of the mark to suggest that myth is a conceptual *system* in which, again, the conceptual mechanism carries out its task of organising the data presented to it – data, however, consisting not of information which has been understood and assimilated but of the conceptual representations residual after the *failure* to understand and assimilate (Sperber, 1975, pp. 110–13). Thus myths and their constituent symbols have no meaning: symbols lack the signifying power of the signs that make up language and other codes.

But Sperber's insistence that symbolism is not a semiological system (as Lévi-Strauss had maintained) perhaps does not pay sufficient attention to the fact that symbols behave like signs *in everything except the ability to signify*. True, this is the most important characteristic of a sign, that it stands unambiguously as a representation of something else. But it follows from Sperber's analysis, as I understand it, that myth is an attempt to organise symbols *as if they were signs* and that the organisation is itself an attempt to give values to these supposed 'signs' – in other words to interpret them. If every new 'interpretation' of a myth is merely another version of the myth, to be taken into account in subsequent 'interpretations', then it would not be unreasonable to suppose that each formulation of a myth is conversely an attempt at its interpretation.

This would help to account for the curious fact that myths, although without the real meaning of semiological systems, can in fact support a multiplicity of possible meanings. Let us suppose that a myth, such as that retold in the ballad 'The Bridge of Arta', comprises a systematic arrangement of signs of which we do not know the meaning. The problem facing us is precisely that confronting the student of linguistics coming upon a statement in an unknown language. As with linguistic signs, the 'signs' of the myth are arbitrary, containing in themselves no clue as to their meaning. But the student of linguistics knows that the signs confronting him will have acquired specific meanings through use in combination with other signs. To decipher his text, he must first have a large enough sample of the language in front of him to be able to detect how the signs are used in it. Now, if 'myth' is to be compared to 'language' as a semiological system, what is the mythical analogy for *'languages'*? Surely not 'myths', which would be closer to 'sentences'.

The mythical equivalent for the individual language must be the *mythology* of a cultural tradition, and it is by comparing the usage of the symbols in 'The Bridge of Arta' and in other myths of the same tradition that we can discover how the signs are used in this 'language', and hence what they 'mean'.

Myth, if it is not a semiological system, functions exactly like one, to the extent that within the mythology of one cultural tradition symbols are employed with the same consistency as real signs, thus acquiring specific associations which become their 'meanings' for the people of that culture. An 'interpretation' of 'The Bridge of Arta' ballads sung in Greece need not therefore be inconsistent with the view that myths have no intrinsic meaning. The features which I noted in the previous section as being significant and relating the ballad to myths about the passage from life to death provide at best a partial interpretation of the myth as formulated by Greeks, through the allusions in the ballad to other parts of the same cultural tradition. Two further points can now be made about that analysis. Firstly, that the symbols regularly used in versions of the ballad (the bridge of hair, the snakes and vipers) although devoid of intrinsic meaning, signify quite specific things in modern Greek mythology – respectively the bridge to the underworld and the underworld itself. And secondly, that these associations, linking the story of the walled-up wife to beliefs about the afterlife, are almost certainly restricted to the Greek ballads on the subject. These particular allusions are precluded, or at least greatly reduced in importance, in the other Balkan versions where the building is only rarely a bridge. But there can be no doubt that other allusions of a different sort are made in each of these traditions, and could usefully be contrasted with the Greek. It is by allusion, above all, that a myth is given a place and a semblance of meaning in a cultural tradition, and consequently it is in terms of such allusions that the transformations of myth from one culture to another can most helpfully be understood.

E. 'MIKROKOSTANTINOS'

The meaning of this ballad (quoted in full on pp. 13–15) does not seem to present a problem to those who sing it as part of the Anastenaria ritual. According to them 'Little Constantine is none other than St Constantine when he was young' (Mihail-Dede, 1973, p. 60), and 'This song too shows that St Constantine rid the whole world of slavery' (Megas, 1961, p. 481). It is all too easy to dismiss as naive the interpretations of their myths by those who ought to know them best; so before doing so let us clarify what is meant by this 'meaning'.

The interpretation would go something like this. 'Little Constantine' is equivalent to 'St Constantine' as a traditional saint–martyr, the apparently weak hero who vanquishes the big battalions by moral or supernatural strength. The young saint is called away to war and, given that he *is* a saint and that we know he is going to rid the world of slavery, this departure for war must be counted as a 'positive' sign in the interpretation: it must be a war on the side of the good, and his departure is in line with Christ's teaching that whoever follows Him must be prepared to abandon father and mother. But while Constantine is away ridding the world of slavery this very evil is rife within his own family. His mother reduces his wife to the level of a slave and sets her menial tasks. The moral victory of the wife exactly parallels that of Constantine over his enemies at war, as she accepts her fate with humility, accepting and fulfilling her role as a shepherd or as a monk (pastoral cares both). This is perhaps made deliberately explicit in the line, included so far as I know only in versions sung by the Anastenarides, in which the wife is forbidden to take her flocks to drink in the *River Jordan*. She does so and it is at the site of the first Christian baptism that she meets the victorious Constantine returning. Slavery has been eliminated from the world, with the exception of the saint's own home. The opposition which has been latent throughout the myth between the values of blood relationship and of good and evil is resolved firmly in favour of the latter, with Constantine making the most extreme sacrifice of family loyalty (killing his mother) in order to punish evil (the imposition of slavery) in its most monstrous form (within the family).

This is of course nothing but a flight of fancy. And yet it is a legitimate 'interpretation' of the whole myth which follows from the 'meaning' ascribed to it by those who sing it. Not only is it legitimate, but it could easily be set out in a structural diagram in which the constituent elements of the myth are tabulated under the headings of 'freedom (=good)/slavery (=evil)' and 'kinship/socio-religious order'. But for all this there is clearly something wrong with it.

What is wrong with it is a failing to which even the most sophisticated and objective methods of structural analysis are not immune – namely that it assumes a value for certain 'signs' which (since the system is quasi-semiological) automatically imparts values to other signs in the system.[8] The singer here has added two pieces of information to the myth: that Little Constantine is to be identified with Saint

Constantine, and that he 'rid the world of slavery'. Thus values are given to the 'signs' or constituent elements of the myth 'Little Constantine' and 'he rode off to war', which are not intrinsic either to the elements themselves or to the structured sequence in which they appear. In the attempt at interpretation these elements are arbitrarily motivated, that is to say *made into signs*. The identifications are not implicit in the text of the ballad, read as ordinary language, but are external to it. As a result, the equations which have made the symbols into signs have added new content to the myth, and this in turn must alter its structure.

So what is really wrong with the 'meaning' given by the Anastenarides to their song is that it alters the structure of the myth – and this is easily seen, in this particular case, not just by the gratuitous addition of content it entails but equally by the fact that this 'meaning' is flatly contradicted by a line often still included in the song. In some versions sung by the Anastenarides Little Constantine is described:

Σὰν Ἅϊ Γιώργης πήδηξε, σὰν Ἅϊ Κωνσταντίνος

(Mihail-Dede, 1973, p. 44)

Just like St George did he leap, just like St Constantine

Clearly he is *not* the saint of the same name, and hence the interpretation requires this line to be ignored and ultimately, one would suppose, dropped out altogether. So the 'meaning' is not a meaning at all, but a new version of the myth in which certain simple structural transformations have taken place.

The development and rearrangement of myths by the addition of material designed to interpret them is one of the ways in which a culture makes its myths peculiarly its own. It also shows how myths are rarely static, as each interpretative rearrangement requires in turn to be interpreted. This is one kind of 'meaning' which a myth can have as part of a cultural mythology – a meaning consciously brought to the myth by those who repeat and reshape it. Such a meaning is not false (there is no true meaning to be falsified) but there is nothing to limit the number of possible meanings of this type which can be attributed to a myth even in one culture. (The history of religious and ideological persecution aptly underscores the point.) These 'meanings' are conscious attributions, and unstable. By contrast the associations, or allusions, between the constituent elements of myths in the Greek song tradition are unlikely to be conscious attempts at interpretation, but reveal a systematic 'grammar' of their own, whose rules have been just as much internalised by the Greek peasant as those governing the everyday language he speaks.

I wish to illustrate this briefly, using as an example two of the symbols which commonly occur in versions of 'Mikrokostantinos'. First, the name of the hero. It would be natural to question whether the mere name Mikrokostantinos (Little Constantine) is really a symbol at all. Here statistics can come to our aid, in identifying those mythical contexts in which the name seems to fulfil a structural role, without at the same time prejudging the issue by 'interpreting' what this role may be. No special importance is to be attached to Kostantinos as a name, since in a sample of several thousand songs and variants[9] the same name is given to the hero or a major character 199 times in 45 separate contexts. Mikrokostantinos, on the other hand, is found only 56 times and in 20 contexts, almost all of which are shared with Kostantinos. At this point it might be expected that Mikrokostantinos, as a qualified form of the name with about a quarter of the occurrences of Kostantinos, would occur considerably less often than Kostantinos in those contexts which are common to both. There are, however, five contexts in which, out of a significant number of occurrences, the name Mikrokostantinos occurs as often as Kostantinos or more frequently. In these five cases there can be no doubt that the name of the hero operates as a symbol, an effective constituent element in the structure of the myth, and it is by observing the function of the symbol in each of these contexts that we can determine how and what it has come to 'signify'.

The first of these contexts is defined by the themes of departure, return and recognition and includes the song 'Mikrokostantinos' and other ballads which share these themes. Another is a song in which three heroes, of whom two are 'little' and the third is 'brave' or 'great', are robbed of their womenfolk by the enemy and ride out to recover them (Passow, 1860, p. 92; Petropoulos, 1958, pp. 48–50). The 'little' hero may be either successful or unsuccessful. The third is the song of the haunted well, where the youngest of several brothers descends into a well and cannot escape (Jeannaraki, 1876, pp. 116–17). The evil spirit guarding the well is sometimes disguised as a beautiful woman, who beguiles the inexperienced hero into descending so as to win her favour, and then leaves him there (Petropoulos, 1958, pp. 14–15). The fourth tells how a rejected and slighted lover is reduced to the use of magic in the attempt to sleep with his mistress (*Laografía* 2, 1910, pp. 675–7). This story, of which the most famous example has been given the title 'Harzanis and Lioyenniti', may unfold in a number of ways, although the end is usually tragic, but the emphasis on the 'little' hero is not confined to Kostantinos, and we find other names compounded with the adjective *mikró* in the same way. The final context is that of the hero, often alternatively called Porfyris, who allows himself to be tightly bound, either by minions of the king, who fears his prodigious strength and audacity, or by a rival who does so to elope with his wife. In either case the hero frees himself and exacts a bloody vengeance (*Laografía* 2, 1910, pp. 81–2; Sakellarios, 1868, pp. 3–8).

What is common to all of these is not merely the idea of smallness. The hero who departs, returns and is recognised by his wife is deprived of a sexual relationship by going away to war but recovers it on his return. The Mikro Vlahopoulo, in the second context, is deprived of a sexual (or family) relationship by a hostile raid on his home and recovers (or attemps to recover) it by going to war. The hero of the haunted well is sexually tempted and betrayed by magical means. The hero of the 'Harzanis' songs is sexually humiliated and betrays his mistress by magical means. And the hero of the 'Porfyris' songs allows himself to be humiliated and recovers his wife by magical strength.

The consistency with which the name Mikrokostantinos (and other compounds of *mikro-* with a name too) is associated with sexual deficiency or disadvantage, either balanced by an act of corresponding over-assertion or leading straight to the hero's doom, admirably illustrates how, through usage, this symbol has acquired the status of a 'sign', and the different ways in which this sign can be used in the 'language' of Greek popular mythology.

Returning to the ballad 'Mikrokostantinos', the knowledge that this is what the name 'means' enables us to read the opening lines of the song in a new way:

Ὁ Κωσταδῖνος ὁ μικρὸς κι ὁ μικροΚωσταδῖνος
μικρὸ δὸν εἶχ' ἡ μάννα dου, μικρὸ δ' ἀρραβωνιάξει,
μικρὸ δὸν ἦρτε μήνυμα νὰ πάῃ στὸ σεφέρι.

(Megas, 1961, p. 488, ll. 1–3)

Kostantinos the Little, Little Kostantinos
was little in his mother's arms, and little when she betrothed him,
and little when a summons came to him to go to war.

Giving to the name the sign-value which it has acquired by usage, we may rewrite the lines as follows: 'The hero of the song [is] sexually disadvantaged, [because] (1) his mother has kept him close, (2) she has arranged a marriage for him [too?] young, and (3) [capping the first two with the force of the final proposition of the "rule of three"] this already unstable set of circumstances is crucially aggravated by the hero's enforced departure.'

The second symbol whose associations I wish to trace is that of the cutting of hair. In the song which serves as our starting point, we are told that, as soon as Kostantinos has gone, the evil mother-in-law takes the wife,

ἀπὸ τὸ χέρ' τὴν ἄρπαξε, στὸ μπερμπεριὸ τὴν πάει.
Πὰ στὸ σκαμνὶ δὴ γάϑισε κι ἀντρίκεια δὴ ξιουρίζει

(Megas, 1961, p. 489, ll. 18–19)

seized her by the hand and took her to the barber,
made her sit upon a stool and cut her hair like a man's

In these lines and in the description which follows, where the wife is given a man's clothes and a man's job (as a shepherd or monk), there is a clear implication that the wife has in some sense been made to change her sex. This is implicit in the meaning of the words as ordinary language, but is never explained in the song and leaves behind it a sense of something mysterious – of something, in fact, symbolic.

In the song tradition as a whole the symbol is associated with a limited number of contexts, and an examination of these will enable us to define what, in the tradition, the symbol has come to signify. Aside from songs of departure and return, the symbol is used in three kinds of context. First of all, as an accompaniment to the deliberate disguise of either a man or woman as a member of the opposite sex (the verb *xyrízo* may refer equally to the cropping of a woman's hair to disguise her as a man, as to the shaving of a man's beard). The symbol is found in versions of the 'Harzanis' song, where the humiliated lover disguises himself as a woman to gain access to his mistress' bedroom (*Laografía* 5, 1915, pp. 195–8), in a version of the 'Castle of Beauty' where a Turk among the besiegers of the heavily defended castle disguises himself as a pregnant woman and so is allowed to enter (Haviaras, 1910, pp. 573–4), and in a series of songs where a woman tries to join a group of men in an attempt to escape from the world of the dead and offers to cut off the hair which, they warn her, will betray them to Haros, the keeper of the lower world (Passow, 1860, pp. 300–2).

The association with changing sex is now evident enough, but what is to be understood by 'changing sex'? This will become clearer as we

133

examine the other two types of context for the cutting of hair. In two songs where a priest, falling in love, decides to cut off the long hair and beard which in the Orthodox Church are symbolic of his calling, it is clear that the symbol signifies a change of *role* (Tarsouli, 1944, p. 110, No. 154) and this meaning also holds good for the unusual song discussed on p. 32 in which Kostantinos, released at last from slavery on being recognised by his wife, has his excess hair cut off to restore him to his former status (Louloudopoulos, 1903, No. 50). Two other contexts mediate between this and the final type, in which the cutting of hair by a woman is a sign of grief. In the first of these a wife is grossly ill-treated by her husband and the cutting of her hair implies both grief and protest at an enforced change of role, both social and sexual (*Laografía* 4, 1913, p. 106). That all three meanings are closely related is clear from a version of this song in which a well-wisher advises the bullied wife to cut off her hair to use as a rope to help her in her tasks. She refuses in the following terms:

> Σὰν κόψω τὰ μαλλιά μου, τὴν πρώτη μου στολή,
> ὕστερα τί τὴ θέλω στὸν κόσμο τὴ ζωή;

(Baud-Bovy, 1935, pp. 202–3)

If I cut off my hair, my first adornment,
afterwards what will be the use of living in the world?

And the same mediation is found in versions of the song, usually entitled 'The Wife who Came to Grief', in which a husband squanders his wife's dowry so that she is obliged to join him in his man's tasks in order that both may survive (*Laografía* 9, 1926, p. 187). Here too the cutting of hair combines the values of 'expression of grief', 'change of social role' and 'change of sexual role'.

The symbol of hair-cutting may then point to one or more of three quite specific 'meanings', whose significance is further glossed by the allusions set up among them. Once again the 'meaning' is not arbitrary. Although it is not as satisfactory as the one-to-one equation of a sign, the range of meanings is firmly restricted within the tradition and the symbol acquires a further function in its ability to draw these meanings together. When the singer of 'Mikrokostantinos' tells us that the evil mother-in-law cuts the girl's hair, he is consciously or unconsciously alluding to other types of song where the same symbol occurs and by this 'shorthand' method conveys a good deal of information which aids our understanding of the song. 'Cutting of hair' means here that

Kostantinos' wife is forced (1) to change her sexual role (to dress and act like a man), (2) to change her *social* role (to leave the house where, as a wife, she has a protected position, and to work for a living) and (3) to make a formal show of grief at parting from her husband.

If the associations of every constituent element of the song were listed it would be possible to 'rewrite' the entire ballad according to the 'meanings' acquired by its symbols in the Greek tradition. In this sense, I believe, it is possible to interpret what ballads 'mean' in a given cultural context. But the theoretical question of whether these are 'real' meanings must be left unanswered. Within a tradition the symbols of a myth certainly behave like signs and acquire specific values. But do not these values, too, belong to the symbolic world? It begins to look as if symbols, even when they behave as signs, only signify other symbols. The last word belongs to Sperber:

> It is with symbols as it is with spirits. If spirits speak by causing tables to turn, they don't – for all that – have much to say. If symbols mean, what they mean is almost always banal. The existence of spirits and the luxuriance of symbols are more fascinating than are their feeble messages about the weather. (1975, p. 6)

8. One Tradition or Several?

The demotic tradition which we have so far been considering was defined in the first chapter as a body of folk songs sharing a specific and consistent structure and function. But this tradition, although made up of a great variety of songs, is not synonymous with the whole corpus of Greek folk poetry. There is no lack of material in Greek which falls within the more general definitions of folk poetry, or oral tradition, and yet whose structure and function are significantly different from those of the songs we have been discussing up till now. To regard these as belonging to separate traditions is not, I believe, to impose an arbitrary system of classification. It would be naive to suppose that folk poetry need be uniform, any more than literary poetry; and it is possible to see how, despite a degree of assimilation, traditions of different function and structure are decisively separated within one culture.

Once it is recognised that folk poetry need not be homogeneous but may consist of differently motivated traditions, the kind of diachronic analysis which proved to be impracticable *within* a tradition again becomes possible. That is to say, any attempt to date individual songs and account for their derivation in terms of cause and effect is doomed to failure because of the complex system of interrelations which give the demotic tradition its unity and internal consistency, but a tradition as a whole, and the relation between the traditions, may still be treated historically, as was attempted for the demotic tradition in Chapter 5.

A. RITUAL AND FUNCTIONAL SONGS

These are songs whose structure is determined by a specific function, whether religious or secular, and, despite the many differences among them, this fact in itself enables us to draw a distinction between such functionally determined songs and those of the demotic tradition.

Ritual and functional songs

(i) Quête songs

These form an important sub-group of songs which fulfil a ritual function. Their content, like that of other ritual songs, is determined by the occasion to be celebrated and its accompanying religious beliefs, but a further factor is that they are always performed by groups of children whose role, whatever the ritual or festival celebrated, is to importune householders and passers-by with demands for money: a common feature of these songs therefore is the demand for money, often accompanied by playful threats.

This type of song existed in Greece in antiquity and two examples are quoted by Athenaeus (VIII 359d–360d). Functionally there is no difference between the 'Crow' and 'Swallow' songs which he quotes and the *kálanda* sung by children today at most of the major church festivals. But the antiquity of this tradition, even in points of detail, is affirmed by the survival of one ritual seemingly intact from antiquity until the present day. This is the celebration of the arrival of the first swallow, described by Athenaeus, 'There is a sort of collecting the Rhodians call Playing the Swallow (χελιδονίζειν), which occurs in the month of Boedromion [March]. The term "swallowing" (χελιδονίζειν) is used because of the custom of singing in refrain' – and he quotes the song.[1] The modern ritual is described by Kyriakidis: 'These delightful little songs are sung by children and principally by young schoolboys on 1 March going from door to door, holding in their hands a likeness of a swallow' (1965, p. 56).

Since the theme of the song, its structure and method of performance are dictated by the same ritual, it is not altogether surprising that there are close textual similarities between the swallow song quoted by Athenaeus and modern '*helidonísmata*'.[2] No less remarkable are the differences between the *helidonísmata* and songs of the demotic tradition. The ancient song begins with the proclamation of the swallow's arrival,

ἦλθε, ἦλθε χελιδών   the swallow has come, has come,

and of the good weather it is supposed to bring with it. The singers then demand a share of last year's harvest, supporting their claims with playful threats, and the song ends,

ἄνοιγ' ἄνοιγε τὰν θύραν χελιδόνι·
οὐ γὰρ γέροντές ἐσμεν, ἀλλὰ παιδία.

open, open the door to the swallow;
we are not old men, but children.

These themes are also found in modern versions, of which the most striking has an identical opening line to the ancient (Passow, 1860, pp. 227–8), and these are often combined with a reference to the children's teacher, who beats them, and to his teaching:

Ὤρισεν ὁ δάσκαλος,	The teacher made it a rule,
Καὶ ὁ θιὸς ποῦ τἄδωκε,	and so did God who gave us them,
Ν' ἀγοράσωμεν ὀχτώ,	that we should buy for eight,
Νὰ πωλῶμεν δεκοχτώ,	and sell for eighteen,
Νὰ κερδαίνωμεν τριάντα,	and make a profit of thirty,
Διάφορα μεγάλα πάντα	big profits always

(Passow, 1860, pp. 227–8, ll. 26–31)

Quaint though it sounds, this exarsis of the profit-motive can be seen to play its part in a ritual celebrating the return of spring and the promise of gain to come at harvest-time.

A song fulfilling an identical function is also known from the middle ages, if the testimony of Canon Benedict of St Peter's in Rome is to be trusted. The canon's *liber politicus*, written in the twelfth century, contains the text of a *quête* song about the swallow, which, he tells us, was sung at the time by the Greek schoolchildren of Rome (Maas, 1912). This text, written in Latin characters, is extremely garbled and presents many problems of interpretation. Some of the difficulties have been resolved by Baud-Bovy by ingenious references to modern texts (1946), and the success of these efforts confirms that the twelfth-century song belongs to the same tradition as its modern counterpart. The song begins with a greeting to the master of the house, followed later by an invocation to March and to the swallow. The swallow is addressed as 'counsellor of angels' and the final part of the song is full of religious fervour and Byzantine patriotism which are external to the ritual. But references to the schoolmaster are similar to those of the modern songs, and the meaningless line,

πέντε πέντε, ἄλλα πέντε, δέκα πέντε
five [and] five, another five, fifteen,

suggest that the profit-motive was also present in the medieval version.

The excessively garbled nature of this text, which cannot be fully accounted for by normal lapses of memory or by misreading or mishearing of a source, points to another unusual characteristic of the *helidonísmata* not shared by other *quête* songs, but conspicuous in ritual songs where the *ritual* is of great antiquity. If the modern versions of the *helidónisma* are looked at carefully they too seem suspiciously garbled. All of them have an incantatory quality which seems to depend on the rhythm and *sound* of words rather than on their meaning. Structure in the *quête* songs is generally linear and there are no architectonic patterns, but in the *helidonísmata* the linear development is loose to the point of being inconsequential. Consider the words given to the swallow in this, the best known of the modern versions:

Θάλασσαν ἐπέρασα,	*Thálassan epérasa,*
Τὴν στεριὰν δὲν ξέσχασα,	*tin sterián den xéschasa,*
Κύματα κἂν ἔσχισα,	*kýmata kan éschisa,*
Ἔσπειρα, κονόμησα,	*éspira, konómisa,*
Ἔφυγα κι᾽ ἀφῆκα σῦκα,	*éfiga ki afíka síka,*
Καὶ σταυρὸν καὶ θημωνίτσαν,	*ke stavrón ke thimonítsan,*
Κ᾽ ἦρθα τώρα κ᾽ ηὖρα φίτρα,	*k' írtha tóra k' ívra fítra,*
Κ᾽ ηὖρα χόρτα, σπάρτα, βλίτρα,	*k' ívra hórta, spárta, vlítra,*
Βλίτρα, βλίτρα, φίτρα, φίτρα.	*vlítra, vlítra, fítra, fítra.*

(Passow, 1860, pp. 227–8, ll. 11–19)

I crossed the sea, / I did not forget dry land, / I even cut through the waves, / I sowed, I saved, / *I departed and left behind figs,* / and a cross and a haystack, / and now I've come *and found green shoots,* / *and found green vegetables, broom and greens,* / *greens, greens, green shoots, green shoots.*

The meaning of the swallow's words can be disentangled, but it seems most unlikely that whoever was responsible for putting it in this form did so to make this meaning clear. The meaning is contained in the statements, 'I sowed, saved, and left at harvest-time', 'I crossed the sea', and 'I have returned and found green shoots'. An obvious comment would be that they are in the wrong order in the song, but the song, with its theme of the seasons, is itself cyclical: the order of ideas is only very loosely fixed. The lines in italics show a preoccupation with the pure sound of words to which their approximately relevant meaning seems incidental. *Síka* (figs) seems to have been chosen from all the possible symbols for the end of summer for its assonance with *afíka* (I left behind), but this is not all. The same song continues with

139

an address to the lady of the house: Sí kalí ikokyrá, which seems innocuous enough until set alongside a variant of the same line in another version: Síko sí kalí kyrá (get up, good lady of the house) (Passow, 1860, p. 229). The chain of sound-associations could be extended, and the conclusion to be drawn is that considerable portions of these songs have been generated through play on the sound of words which are only loosely connected by their sense. Given a tradition of this sort, in which the elaboration of nonsense plays a part and whose structure resembles a cyclical series of incantations, one need not be too surprised at the chaotic and inconsequential series of lines recorded by Canon Benedict in the twelfth century.

The separation between this functionally determined tradition and that of the folk songs we discussed previously is clear to see. The difference of structure between the *helidonísmata* and the demotic tradition is further emphasised by the persistence in the former of a four-stress metre, alternating between trochaics and iambics and between lines of seven and eight syllables. This metre, which may have been the direct ancestor of the more widespread political verse of folk song (Baud-Bovy, 1973; and p. 76 above) is also found in Byzantine popular acclamations (Maas, 1912) as well as, in rhymed form, in love songs, children's songs and lullabies of the modern demotic tradition. The use of this metre in the *helidonísmata* does not itself distinguish these songs from the demotic tradition, but the exclusion of all other metres of folk poetry in these songs must be suggestive, especially when the twelfth-century version seems to have been based on this same metre, and the line-length in all later *helidonísmata* is almost identical to that of the opening of the ancient song.

Although the case of the *helidonísmata* demonstrates the antiquity of the tradition of *quête* songs in Greece, those which continue to be sung at Christian festivals do not generally have the same unusual features. The *kálanda* (carols) sung on these occasions are recorded in collections of folk songs in the common popular metres and are relatively stereotyped in form, although some ingenuity seems to have been lavished on the praises of householders and ways of asking for gifts (Petropoulos, 1959, pp. 3–13; 21–34). Many of these carols which have been recorded from oral tradition were formerly *written*, and there are instances of *kálanda* which preserve the mixed formal and popular language of ecclesiastical chapbooks despite their oral transmission (Petropoulos, 1959, p. 8, No. 30). These chapbooks would have been read in schools (which under Byzantine and Ottoman rule would have been church schools) and the songs learnt by heart to be sung on the appropriate occasions (Petropoulos, 1959, p. x). Needless to say the liturgical theme of any Christian song in oral tradition is likely to derive ultimately from a written source, and the contrast between the oral demotic tradition and that of songs with a religious content is aptly pointed in the *kálanda* for St Basil's day (New Year). The saint, newly arrived from Caesarea, is questioned about his journey and asked to sing a song. St Basil sanctimoniously replies that the Teacher from whom he comes is not a teacher of songs and offers the alphabet instead (Petropoulos, 1959, pp. 4-6). Similarly in the Byzantine and modern *helidonísmata* it is not impossible that the Mr Thwackum who taught the carollers the theory of financial gain also taught them the song itself from written songsheets.

(ii) The 'Virgin's Lament'

Not all ritual songs are *quête* songs and none presents more complex problems than the popular laments of the Virgin Mary, which combine features of functionally determined ritual songs with the narrative techniques and structure of secular ballads. In common with some of the *kálanda*, these songs do not belong to a purely oral tradition, although the oral element is certainly predominant (Alexiou, 1975, p. 135; Bouvier, 1976, pp. 49-51). To complicate matters further there was also a well-established *literary* tradition of laments on the same theme, of which the sixth-century *kontákion* of Romanos, 'Mary at the Cross', is the earliest datable example (Alexiou, 1974, p. 63; 1975, pp. 113-16). The modern oral laments have several themes in common with these literary versions, and of course the characters and background of the crucifixion, against which the substance of the laments is projected, all derive more or less directly from written sources in the Gospels and the teaching of the Church. For this reason it is impossible fully to separate the oral from the literary and popular religious traditions which together have played a part in shaping the laments. On the other hand, there is evidence of demotic formula-types associated with the theme from as early as the fifteenth century (Bouvier, 1976, pp. 67-71), and there is no doubt that the laments are constructed according to the patterns of structure and of thought with which we are familiar from the demotic tradition.[3]

Many versions of the lament begin with a brief invocation, frequently the well-worn demotic formula,

Σήμερα μαῦρος οὐρανός, σήμερα μαύρη μέρα

(Baud-Bovy, 1935, pp. 51–2)

Today the sky is black, today is a black (unhappy) day

This may be followed by the scene of Jesus' betrayal and capture and then, almost invariably, the news is brought to Mary his mother. The Virgin immediately falls to the ground in a dead faint – in some versions the action is punctuated by repeated swoons – and has to be revived. Gathering her women friends and relatives together she then sets out, and passes on the way the gypsy blacksmith who has forged the nails for the Cross. He had been asked by the Jews to make three nails, but from excess of zeal or simply by mistake has made five, adding the gruesome instruction that the fifth ('and fatal') nail is destined for Jesus' heart. (Here also a familiar demotic formula-type is used.) The Virgin curses the gypsy to eternal vagrancy and goes to Pilate's court-yard. At first she fails to recognise her son soaked in blood with the crown of thorns on his head, but John takes her aside and gently points him out. The formal question and answer between Mary and John (often erroneously called the Baptist in the songs) follows a pattern frequently found in the demotic tradition:

– Ἄι μου Γιάννη Πρόδρομε καὶ βαπτιστὰ τοῦ γιοῦ μου,
μὴν εἶδες μὲ τὸ τέκνο μου, καὶ σὲ τὸ δάσκαλό σου;
– Δὲν ἔχω στόμα νὰ σοῦ πῶ, γλῶσσα νὰ σοῦ μιλήσω,
δὲν ἔχω χεροπάλαμο, διὰ νὰ σοῦ τὸ δείξω.
Βλέπεις ἐκεῖνο τὸ γυμνό, τὸ παραπονεμένο,
ὁποὺ φορεῖ πουκάμισο στὸ αἷμα βουτισμένο;
Ἐκεῖνο 'ναι τὸ τέκνο σου καὶ μέν' ὁ δάσκαλός μου.

(Baud-Bovy, 1935, pp. 51–2)

'My Saint John the Baptist and baptist of my son,
by any chance have you seen my child, your teacher?'
'I have no mouth to tell you, no tongue to address you,
I have no outstretched hand to show him to you.
Do you see that man there, naked and suffering,
who wears a shirt all soaked in blood?
That man is your child and my teacher.'[4]

There is no transition from here to the scene at the foot of the Cross, and the impression is often given that the Crucifixion actually takes place in Pilate's courtyard. The Virgin approaches the cross and addres-ses her son,

142

Δὲν μοῦ μιλᾶς, παιδάκι μου, δὲν μοῦ μιλᾶς παιδί μου;

Won't you speak to me, my little child, won't you speak to me, my child?

In some versions she continues by expressing a wish to die since life will now be unbearable for her, for which Jesus reprimands her, 'If you die the whole world will follow suit.' Otherwise he replies that nothing he can say now will lessen her grief, but goes on cryptically to announce the Resurrection: at midnight on Easter Saturday the *church bells will ring*. In these laments the Resurrection is seen not as a real event of momentous significance (as in the learned tradition) but as a recurring *ritual*. The effect of anachronisms such as the church bells ringing is to confer ritual status on the death and Resurrection of Christ rather than to treat it realistically as a historical event. The mourners in the Good Friday procession are not commemorating a distant historical happening but lamenting an annual death.

In other versions Jesus tells his mother to go home and to prepare the funeral meal. This injunction in the song has given rise to the popular belief that the ritual of the funeral feast which is still practised when someone dies in the villages, first began in this way; but as often happens in such cases the ritual is a good deal older than the myth by which it is explained. The modern *parigoriá* (funeral feast) is in fact a survival from pre-Christian times (Alexiou, 1974, pp. 71–2; Bouvier, 1976, pp. 257–8, 283–4).

The final episode of the lament, which is found in a small number of versions, tells how the obscure personage Ayia Kali (St Kali, or Beautiful) passes by the door as the funeral meal is in progress and taunts Mary for sitting down to eat while her son is on the Cross. The Virgin, who is portrayed throughout as a Greek village mother, immediately curses the busybody and the episode and the whole song close with the curious wish that this saint should never be venerated or have a church built in her name except in the most remote and inhospitable places, on the mountains or in the middle of the sea. The significance of this episode has never been satisfactorily explained but there is little doubt that Ayia Kali is the direct descendant of a pre-Christian deity (Alexiou, 1974, pp. 75–6; Bouvier, 1976, pp. 276–84).

Although the form of ritual with which these songs have been associated in modern times is not always the same, it is significant that they are never sung on any occasion other than Good Friday. To do so, according to several women singers, would be impious and even dangerous. There are signs that the popular ritual of the Good Friday

143

lament has been modified through the influence of the Church even in quite recent times, and this probably accounts for some of the diversity both in practice and in the texts of the accompanying songs. In its traditional form the Good Friday ritual closely resembled that still observed on the death of a real person. There are accounts of the laments of the Virgin being sung by women at an all-night wake, gathered round a likeness of Christ's tomb covered with spring flowers, and also on Good Friday evening when this is carried in procession round the parish. The grief of the women as they sing the lament in chorus is very real: as they lament they *become* the Virgin and the women at the foot of the Cross. It is as if, in the words of one, 'Christ were my own child' (Alexiou, 1974, p. 77; 1975, p. 135; Bouvier, 1976, pp. 28–46, 52–5).

This ritual, with its echoes of ancient Greek cults, in particular that of Adonis, seems to be chiefly responsible for the laments of the Virgin that we know today. It would be a simplification to suggest that this Good Friday ritual, which is not part of the official liturgy, was wholly a pagan survival and that the modern laments are of pre-Christian origin. As we have seen, the songs have been shaped over a considerable period of time during which several influences have been brought to bear. But the evident survival of pagan elements in the songs, together with the ultimately pagan origin of the ritual to which they belong, indicates that the tradition of such songs has been a very long one. The ritual itself has changed far more than that of the *helidónisma*, as it has gradually been brought closer to official liturgical practice, and as a result the songs have been exposed to a greater degree of compromise with other traditions. It would be possible to imagine a time, if this part of the Good Friday ritual were to disappear altogether, when the laments might lose their ritual function entirely and be sung for entertainment. And it would be a likely prediction, if this were ever to happen, that they would quickly become indistinguishable from other songs of the demotic tradition, adopting new themes and having a wider range of variants than their present ritual context allows.

(iii) 'Pagan' songs

The ancient origin of a song in oral tradition can never conclusively be proved, even if it contains features which seem ultimately to be of pagan derivation. But the survival of ritual practices and observances over a long period is often difficult to deny, particularly in Greece where classical and Hellenistic evidence can be compared with modern. Certain practices and beliefs, such as those surrounding death and burial, undoubtedly represent an unbroken although not entirely static tradition (Alexiou, 1974, *passim*), and it may well be true more generally that rituals of this kind are more resistant to change than other cultural traits. Songs which are merely associated with a seemingly ancient ritual, such as the 'Mikrokostantinos' ballads in the Anastenaria, cannot be assigned to such an ancient tradition, since these songs are more integrally related to their variants which elsewhere fulfil a range of different functions than to one particular ritual. But songs whose text not only reflects a given ritual but is determined by the actions to be performed, and whose performance is restricted to the ritual context, can and indeed must be assigned to a separate tradition, in which transmission is governed by the extreme conservatism and emphasis on exact repetition which is part of the nature of ritual.

We have already seen that the *helidonismata* and elements of the Virgin's lament show signs of such a long and conservative transmission, and this was confirmed in both cases by evidence of long continuity in the rituals to which they belong. To these must now be added two songs which serve a similar function in local rituals of seemingly pagan content. The song and ritual of Lidinos in a single village on the island of Aegina, and of Zafiris in the Zagori region of Epiros both celebrate seasonal rituals. The former, lamenting the 'death' of summer, is celebrated in September; the latter, whose theme seems to be the resurrection of spring, takes place in early May. The song of Lidinos, in regular trochaic octosyllables with only a few rhymes, has a formal archaic character which immediately distinguishes it from the more personal laments of the demotic tradition, while that of Zafiris (at least in its present form) is not stylistically distinct from it. But what is most significant in both cases is that the laments are addressed to an effigy (Lidinos) or to one of the participants *pretending* to be dead; in both cases it is understood (and stated in the song) that the death which is now lamented will be followed immediately afterwards by a resurrection. This represents an important structural difference between these songs and the laments of the demotic tradition in which the return of the dead is never promised, and this difference is directly brought about by the difference in function between the two traditions.

Once again, this separation between traditions cannot be taken as absolute. The Zafiris song, in particular, includes formulas and imagery from demotic laments and other lyrical songs, and neither contains linguistic archaisms. Nothing can be said concerning the antiquity of

the texts as we now know them, but the undoubted antiquity of the
ritual in each case suggests that they come of a tradition which may be
much older than that of other folk songs in Greek (Kyriakidis, 1965,
pp. 59–61; Alexiou, 1974, pp. 78–82, including English translations of
the songs).

(iv) Work songs

No kind of folk song is more closely bound up with the function it
serves than the songs chanted by groups of men or women as a rhythmi-
cal accompaniment to a set task. The visible proof of this is the rapid
disappearance of these songs as soon as the kind of work they accompany is superseded, as has tended to happen in Europe and America in
the last hundred years. Work songs, strictly defined, are not just songs
sung by people at work. There are several Greek songs recorded which
were sung by women at the loom or by shepherds out on the mountains
with their sheep, which refer to these occupations in a lyrical manner
but which are not therefore work songs (Politis, N. G., 1914, pp. 241–
3; Petropoulos, 1959, pp. 174–80). The distinction of the work song
proper is that the rhythm and the sound of the words are determined
by the nature of the work on hand and actually assist the singers in
their task. For this reason they are rarely solo performances, but are
chanted by a group, usually with a leader who may give the time and
lead off with a solo line which is then taken up by the others. The
waulking songs of the Hebrides, British sea-shanties and the songs of
American negro work gangs all belong to this type.

It has sometimes been supposed that because of its highly functional
nature and consequent lack of development in other directions, this
type of song represents the earliest and most primitive form of folk
song, from which all others have gradually evolved (Kyriakidis, 1965,
p. 52; Lloyd, 1975, p. 270). But the study of music in supposedly
'primitive' or undeveloped societies suggests that this is not in fact the
case. In such societies the range of different types of song has been
found to be surprisingly wide, and as for their work songs, 'Most of the
so-called working-songs are . . . intended for amusement; only a few
show any direct connexion with the rhythm of labour' (Schneider,
1957, p. 38).

Only certain types of work are likely to generate work songs in the
strict sense, and while it is possible that these songs might remain unchanged over a very long period, this conservatism probably reflects no

more than an unchanging pattern of work. Although work songs can be assigned to a tradition, it is a tradition which has almost no existence apart from the activity to which it belongs. Far from being primitive survivals, work songs may suddenly and unexpectedly spring into being whenever they are required by working conditions, and as suddenly disappear again.

Greek folk poetry, or such as has been recorded, is not rich in work songs. At least two songs sung by women to accompany the action of grinding flour by handmill are known from different parts of Greece, and bear a striking resemblance in their opening words to a similarly functional song recorded from antiquity:

Ancient: ἄλει, μύλα, ἄλει   (Plutarch, *Moralia*, 157E)

            Grind, mill, grind

Modern: Ἄλεθε, μύλο μου, ἄλεθε
                            (Politis, N. G., 1914, p. 241, No. 234)

            Grind, my mill, grind

            Ἄλεσε, μύλε μ᾽, ἄλεσε σιτάριν καὶ κριθάριν
                            (Petropoulos, 1959, p. 173)

            Grind, my mill, grind wheat and barley

It would be rash to deduce from this evidence a continuous *song* tradition from antiquity to the present day, although one need not doubt that the grinding of flour has always been done in much the same way. The dependence of the song on its function is such that, if the custom of singing an accompaniment to the milling of flour had at some time fallen into disuse, and then been resumed after a long interval, these almost identical words could quite naturally have been readopted for the purpose, even though no oral tradition had preserved them in the meantime.

With other work songs in Greek we have no information about the possible length of tradition involved. Kyriakidis quotes a fire-lighting song from the Mani and a rowing song from Karpathos in the Dodecanese which admirably highlight the functional character of these songs (1965, pp. 52-5). Songs such as these must have had a long currency but this is not a necessary characteristic of work songs. The tradition of British sea-shanties lasted for little more than fifty years (Lloyd, 1975, pp. 271-8), while that of Greek milling songs may scarcely have changed over two millenia.

147

B. RHYMING DISTICHS

It is a general though not an invariable rule that songs of the demotic tradition do not use rhyme. The single consistent exception is the distich known variously as *mantináda* (Crete, Dodecanese), *patináda* (Hios), *tshiáttisma* (Cyprus), *amanés* (Asia Minor), *kotsáki* (Cyclades) or, generally, *lianotrágoudo* (Kyriakidis, 1947). These couplets, which are sung and improvised today in all parts of the Greek-speaking world, share most of the characteristics of the demotic tradition, and it would be pedantic to assign them to a separate tradition merely on account of their rhyme. The rhymes are, however, an important distinguishing feature, since it is rhyme that gives the punch to the epigrammatic statement, and largely determines the structure of what precedes it. Although the balancing and patterning of half-lines is retained in these couplets, the overall structure of only four half-lines limits the extent of these patterns and throws greater emphasis on the balance or antithesis between the two rhyming lines.

These distichs are especially popular today in Crete, the Dodecanese and Cyprus, where the art of spontaneous improvisation in this form is highly prized and (in Cyrpus) even organised into contests. The subjects suitable for expression in these couplets are almost limitless. The praise of a girl's beauty, innuendo directed at another person, direct insult (especially in the competitions), obscenity, and even political satire are all commonly found in these topical, social songs. A more lugubrious note is sounded in the *amanédes* of Asia Minor which, whether in Greek or Turkish, lament the futility and transience of earthly life with a passionate world-weariness that seems to have been common to all the inhabitants of the cosmopolitan cities of the late Ottoman Empire; and the couplet form is also frequently used by the women in the villages who improvise laments to the dead.

These distichs, with their integral use of rhyme, can be distinguished from the rest of the demotic tradition by their structure, as the ritual and work songs we have been discussing were distinguished by their function. Although in the case of distichs the distinction is not sufficient for them to be assigned to a tradition of their own, an understanding of the origin and development of their peculiar structure is essential in dealing with the rhymed epic-style songs of the 'historical tradition' which will be the subject of the next chapter.

Rhyme was never systematically used by the ancient Greeks, or in any of the literary forms which flourished under the Byzantine Empire. Its appearance in the Greek world came late, and through the medium of western European *literature* (Baud-Bovy, 1936, pp. 129–30; 1956; Dimaras, 1974, p. 72). The use of rhyme therefore spread from those areas under French or Italian rule in the fifteenth and sixteenth centuries, and from the literary poet who had read foreign originals to the non-literate villagers or poorer townspeople who could only have heard him recite. By the early nineteenth century, we know from Fauriel, rhyme was general in the songs of the towns and islands (1824, p. cxx), the most common of which appear to have been distichs (1825, p. 267), but was unknown on the rural mainland. The association of rhyme with the 'Franks', or westerners, and with literature, both equally effete in the eyes of the rural mainlander, was preserved, even in Fauriel's day, in the contemptuous dismissal of rhymed songs by the highland Greeks as proof of sexual deviancy (see p. 104 above).

It has been suggested that the couplet form predates the use of rhyme, and examples have been quoted of two-line epigrams from ancient and Byzantine sources (Soyter, 1921, pp. 386–91). Of course, the occasional sense-unit of exactly two lines is quite likely to occur in any non-rhymed poetry, but cannot be regarded as significant unless it is systematically employed. The adoption of rhyme or assonance as a regular principle makes this possible, and there is in fact no *systematic* use of the couplet form in Greek before the introduction of rhyme. The earliest datable manuscripts in which rhyme appears are of the fifteenth century, and by 1500 at the latest the rhymed couplet had become standardised in Crete (Morgan, 1960, pp. 78–81).[5] It is quite possible that these early rhymed poems were composed to be sung (Morgan, 1960, pp. 75–5, 77–8), but no less certain that men like the Cretan Sahlikis and the Rhodian Georgillas (Politis, L., 1973, pp. 40–1, 39) had a first-hand knowledge of literature and were themselves educated, writing poets.

Two manuscripts which include distichs in popular style have been dated to the second half of the fifteenth and the beginning of the sixteenth centuries respectively (Hesseling and Pernot, 1913; Pernot, 1931). The first, entitled *Erotopaignia* by its editors, contains only twenty-three distichs, most of them unrhymed. The second has a greater number of distichs, of which some are unrhymed, others rhymed, and others again employ assonance or half-rhyme which their editor considered to be 'embryonic' (Pernot, 1931, p. 12). Both of these manuscripts contain material in the style of the demotic tradition, and

Baud-Bovy has noted interesting examples of non-rhymed couplets and larger groupings in the *Erotopaignia* which seem to have been normalised as rhyming couplets in modern oral tradition (Baud-Bovy, 1936, pp. 372–5); but as with other early rhyming poems in Greek there can be little doubt that both collections were the work of writing poets. Many of the poems are even in the form of love *letters*.

The evidence of these two manuscripts and of the early works of the Cretan literary renaissance seems to indicate that the strict couplet form became stabilised after a period of experiment in which the mutual dependence of rhyme and the couplet form was discovered by trial and error. The impetus for these experiments must have been the influence of western literature, predominantly French and Italian, and their vernacular character can also, in part at least, be attributed to the same source. In Italy, Dante Alighieri had espoused the cause of the vernacular in his *De Vulgari Eloquentia* (shortly after 1300) and throughout western Europe in the late middle ages there had developed a taste for refined poetry *in the vernacular*, as opposed to Latin. Sahlikis, Georgillas and the anonymous writers of the love poems would naturally enough, as men of the western Renaissance, have turned to their own vulgar tongue for inspiration. And it is equally natural that as a result their poems should both resemble folk songs and in turn have exerted an important influence upon the latter's subsequent development. It was in this way, with the recitation or even singing of written poems among which the new form of the rhyming distich quickly became stabilised, that rhyme and the distich entered into Greek folk poetry.

9. The Historical Tradition

There is a tendency, among admirers of folk poetry, to equate the 'folk' or 'true folk' with what is 'good'. As a result, understandably little attention is paid to types of folk poetry which from an aesthetic point of view are more often mediocre or bad. One may chuckle at the lack of dexterity shown by the English broadside balladist in the lines,

> A handkerchief she said she tyed
> About his head, and that they tryed;
> The sexton they did speak unto
> That he the grave would then undo   (Child, 1957, No. 272)

or at the incongruity of the Cypriot farmer, who on his own admission could neither read nor write, including in a song of Diyenis the line,

> Γράφουν το τὰ βιβλία μας, δὲν εἶναι παραμύθι
> > (Notopoulos, 1959, p. 17 and gramophone record)
> It's written in our books, it's not a folk tale

These absurdities, together with an irritating exactitude about dates and a tendency to moralise, are found in certain Greek songs, as in British broadside ballads, and a number of prominent scholars, such as Francis Child for the British and Stilpon Kyriakidis for the Greek, have in effect refused these songs recognition as part of the folk traditions in which they are found (Child, letter to Grundtvig, in Hustvedt, 1930, p. 254; Kyriakidis, 1965, pp. 107–11). But the mere existence (and persistence) of these incongruous and irritating tendencies in such a wealth of material as the British broadside and the Greek *rímes*, as they are sometimes called, deserves attention. Both types of song belong unquestionably to folk poetry, if that term is to have any meaning at all. Yet there is an immediately perceptible difference between the broadside 'Suffolk Miracle' and, say, 'Lord Randal' or 'Edward', which is oddly difficult to define. Similarly, Greek scholars have generally recognised that the rhymed and often topical narrative poems of Crete and Cyprus seem not to be quite 'folk' on internal grounds (Petropoulos, 1954, p. 374), but, naturally enough, have been unable to suggest what else they might be. With the Greek *rímes* a number of important questions come into being which are also posed by the broadside tradition in Britain. What, for example, is the status of a tradition of 'folk' or popular poetry which makes some use of writing, is topical and sensational and yet uses the forms and some of the clichés of 'traditional' poetry? Does this kind of song represent an intermediate stage between the oral and the written? Why is it inferior to 'traditional' folk poetry? And how is it to be defined in relation to the 'traditional' poetry of the demotic tradition?

A. THE POET

It is often said that the traditional folk poetry is by its nature anonymous. As it happens this holds true for the Greek songs of the demotic tradition as well as for traditional British balladry. In neither type of song is an author ever alluded to nor is there any other kind of evidence which would enable us to name a song's originator. But it is not true of oral traditions in general. Ruth Finnegan cites examples of poets whose names are known to us and who are nonetheless both oral and traditional, and points out that the supposed anonymity of a poem 'is sometimes a mere function of *our* ignorance (rather than that of the people themselves) or of the theoretical assumptions of researchers who felt it inappropriate with oral art to enquire about the names of the poets' (1977, p. 202). A. L. Lloyd has gone further, with the assertion that the identity of the lower-class singer has tended to be ignored for social reasons, and so that 'the famous anonymity of folk song is, in the main, an economic and social accident' (1975, p. 24).

The true reason for the anonymity of the singer in the Greek demotic tradition is simpler. In an important sense he is not anonymous at all: his audience all know him personally and he has no need to recommend himself to them. A good singer in a Greek village is respected as a member of the community, one of themselves to whom people will listen. He is in no sense a professional, although bank notes will quite often be slapped on his forehead or stuffed down his shirt front, and it is a mark of honour to be seen to appreciate a performer in this way. What is more, like the Yugoslav bards (some of whose names we know only because they happened to be recorded by Parry and Lord) he will never claim that the song is his own invention; nor would it occur to his audience that a new performance or version of a well-known song could be the creation of the performer. Although *we* know that the singer does play an important part in shaping the song, recomposing it in a way which may diverge considerably from those of other singers, we also saw (in Chapter 4) that neither he nor his audience recognises the importance of this fact. There is no reason therefore for the singer's name to be especially remembered. The 'anonymity' of this tradition consists merely in the fact that the singer never draws attention to himself *in the song* – and that for the simple reason that he has no cause to do so.

If a singer mentions himself in his song, either begging indulgence, and perhaps money, for his performance or claiming that the song is his own composition, then he is not addressing his audience on an equal footing. He may be a courtly poet–musician enjoying some social standing and protection in an aristocratic house or he may be a blind beggar at a fair. Whatever the case his relationship with his audience depends on his being able to entertain them. In this sense he is a professional,[1] and in marked contrast to the singer of demotic songs, whose talents may increase his social standing among his peers but who is not dependent upon them for social recognition. The professional poet, whether bard or beggar, stands in a different relation to his audience and this affects the content of his songs. First of all he must entertain and, as an outsider, he will not do this by merely repeating songs which his audience already know and would rather hear sung by 'one of their own'. His surest course is therefore to avoid the themes of traditional song and compose or adapt pieces of topical and current interest. And secondly, he must make sure that he is adequately rewarded. To this end he may flatter his audience and their locality, invoke God's blessing on them, and commend himself to them as deserving his reward.[2]

The status of this kind of poet is liable to be precarious. In the middle ages patronage guaranteed many minstrels some stability and these conditions are probably reflected in the high quality, for example, of much *trouvère* and *troubadour* poetry. And in present-day Cyprus the *pyitáris* enjoys considerable popularity, especially in the rural districts (Petropoulos, 1954). But the profession is more at the mercy of circumstances than most. These poets have never gained a secure position on the mainland of Greece, although we hear of the temporary success of a few who were adopted by kleftic chiefs to sing of their campaigns during the War of Independence, and some *rímes* recorded at the time are probably their work. Otherwise the minstrel without a regular audience and without the benefits of patronage became a target for contempt and abuse, and was obliged, at any artistic sacrifice, to ingratiate himself with his audience.

An early Greek example of the contempt in which the cheapjack professional could be held is the remark of Bishop Arethas of Caesarea in the tenth century, quoted on p. 77, and wrongly supposed by many scholars to refer to singers of the *demotic* tradition. The remark may be compared to that of an English bishop, John Earle, writing some seven hundred years later, who described

> a man and a fiddle out of case: and he in worse case than his fiddle. One that rubs two sticks together (as the Indians strike fire) and rubs a poor living out of it: Partly from this, and partly from your charity, which is more in the hearing, then giving him, For he sells nothing dearer then to be gone: He is just so many strings above a beggar, though he have but two: and yet he begs too, only not in the downright *For God's sake, but with a shrugging God bless you* ... A good feast shall draw him five miles by the nose and you shall track him again by the scent. His other pilgrimages are fairs, and good houses where his devotion is great to the Christmas: and no man loves good times better. (Quoted in Woodfill, 1953, p. 128)

Fauriel claimed that the only professional itinerant singers in Greece were beggars, and since begging was an ignoble occupation for a healthy man, he further inferred that all Greek beggars were blind (1824, p. xc). On this evidence Fauriel considered that many topical, historical songs were the work of these blind beggars, or 'rhapsodes' as he preferred to call them, after the ancient tradition. The notion that this class of performer is exclusively made up of the handicapped and decrepit, for whom no other employment can be found, has a specious attractiveness,[3] and might help to account for the hack quality of so many of the *rímes*. But in reality almost anyone could become a singer–composer of this kind. The Homeric scholar James Notopoulos described the Cretan *lyráris* as one who 'is usually poor, old, disabled and goes from one village to the other singing his verses during religious festivals' (1952, p. 238). But Professor D. Petropoulos, who accompanied Notopoulos on a collecting trip to Crete and Cyprus the following year, described singers of greater vigour if not youth, and pointed to the high esteem in which they are held, especially in Cyprus (1954).

There is considerable variety among professional singers, and the only characteristics which seem generally to be shared in Greece and Cyprus are poverty, talent and a very elementary education. If he was slightly more affluent or had a wealthy patron, and had been better educated, such a singer probably became a writer in the 'art' tradition of his time. Given even less schooling and a position in a traditional community, there would have been no need for his repertoire to extend beyond the more conservative demotic tradition. In addition to their professional status, only one other generalisation can really be made about the singer–composers of the *rímes*: that they were *semi-educated*, with just enough education to aspire to personal composition and to have acquired the taste for novelty, but falling well short of the sophistication demanded by readers of written ('art') literature.

B. 'DASKALOYANNIS' AND THE SONGS OF THE CRETAN *RIMADORI*

In 1770 the Cretans of Sfakiá, in the mountainous south-west of the island, rose against their Ottoman rulers. The rebellion seems largely to have been prompted by promises of Russian aid, and when this failed to materialise it became evident that the Sfakiots, under the leadership of Daskaloyannis, were bound to be beaten. To avoid greater losses Daskaloyannis accepted a treacherous invitation from the Pasha to go to Kastro (modern Iraklion) to discuss terms, and was flayed alive for his pains. The story is told in an epic of 1,034 lines, in rhyming couplets, which was written down shortly afterwards from the dictation of one Barba-Pantzelios, a cheese-maker of Sfakiá. In an epilogue to the poem, the amanuensis describes the recitation:

’Εγὼ ’Αναγνώστης τοῦ Παπᾶ ὁ Σήφης τοῦ Σκορδίλη,
αὐτὰ ποὺ σᾶς διηγήθηκα μὲ γράμμα, μὲ κοντίλι.
’Αρχίνηξα καὶ τά ’γραφα λιγάκι κάθε μέρα
κ’ εἰς τὴ Παπούρα κάθουμουν στὸ Γκίβερτ’ ἀπὸ πέρα.
Εἰς τὴ Παπούρα κάθουμουν, γιατ’ ἤμουν γκαλονόμος,
καὶ μὲ τὸν μπάρμπα-Παντζελιό, ἀπού ’τον τυροκόμος.
’Εγὼ ἐκράθιουν τὸ χαρτὶ κι ἐκράθιουν καὶ τὴ μπένα,
κι ἐκεῖνος μοῦ δηγάτονε καὶ τά γραφα ἕνα-ἕνα.
Τὰ μάθια του δακρύζουσι, σὰν τὸ ἀναθιβάλει,
ὄντες μοῦ τὸ δηγάτονε τοῦ Δάσκαλου τὸ χάλι.
‘Η γι-ὁμιλιά του κόβγεται, συλλογιασμοὶ τὸν πιάνου

καὶ μαύρους ἀναστεναμοὺς τὰ σωθικά του βγάνου. . .
Τραγουδιχτὰ μοῦ τά 'λεγε, γιατ' εἶναι ριμαδόρος,
γιατὶ ἔχει κι ἀποὺ τὸ Θεὸ τὸ πλιὰ μεγάλο δῶρος.
Ὅσα δὲν εἶδε ἐκάτεχε, κι ὅσα εἶδε δὲν τὰ ξέχνα,
γιατὶ ἔχει καὶ θυμητικὸ πλιότερ' ἀπὸ κιανένα.

(Laourdas, 1947, pp. 48–9, ll. 991–1002; 1009–12)

I, Sifis, the Lector, son of the priest Skordilis,
have told you the tale, in letters and in writing.
I began to write it a little every day
while I was living at Papoura beyond Givert.
I was living at Papoura minding milk-sheep,
and with me was Barba-Pantzelios the cheese-maker.
It was I who held the paper and held the pen,
while he told the story and I wrote down every word.
His eyes were full of tears as he related it,
as he told me of Daskaloyannis' pitiable state.
His voice would break off, he would be lost in thought,
and heave up unhappy sighs from the bottom of his heart. . .
He told it me in song, because he is a *rimadóros*,
because he has of all God's gifts the greatest.
Whatever he hadn't seen himself he knew about, and what he had
    he doesn't forget,
because his memory is better than any man's.

The humble occupations of both men should be noticed. Barba-Pantzelios himself was presumably illiterate, and Sifis would only have learnt to write because his father was a priest. The recording of the poem was probably a laborious business, if it was done 'a little every day' and the fact that it was done at all under these conditions is a sure indication that with 'Daskaloyannis' we are dealing with something very different from the songs of the demotic tradition. Barba-Pantzelios, unlike the Yugoslav epic singers to whom Notopoulos compared him (1952), is known to us by name not through an accident of collecting but *because he wished to be*. In the recording of 'Daskaloyannis' in 1786 we have the first hint of a sense of copyright, of authorship as the creation of something new which belongs to the creator, a sense summed up by the Greek expression *pnevmatikí idioktisía* (spiritual property). Not only that, but Sifis' praise of Barba-Pantzelios' talents is a form of discreet advertisement for his version of the story as the most authentic and emotionally affecting.

There are other features which the song of Daskaloyannis shares with shorter and more recent compositions by *rimadóri*.[4] These are the pious beginning and the statement, in the first person, of the intention of singing about a particular person or event; the generally bald, often pedantic narration of events; and, in the epilogue, the insistence on versifying the date on which they took place:

Στὰ χίλια ἐφτακόσια ὀγδοήκοντα ἔξε ἔτος,
'ποὺ τοῦ Δασκάλου τὸν καιρὸ δεκάξε χρόνια ὀφέτος

(Laourdas, 1947, p. 49, ll. 1017–18)

In the year seventeen hundred and eighty six,
sixteen years this year from the time of Daskaloyannis. . .

As one might expect, the language and style of 'Daskaloyannis' are significantly different from those of the demotic tradition; and yet we have the evidence of Sifis that 'Daskaloyannis' was orally composed. There is no reason to believe that the demotic tradition ever ran to songs of this length, and the kind of formulaic composition which we analysed in the second chapter would clearly have been of little help to Barba-Pantzelios. In 'Daskaloyannis' we encounter oral composition of a different kind.

The key to this is to be found in the invariable use by Cretan *rima-dóri* of the rhymed couplet. In 'Daskaloyannis' the use of rhyme is far more than a stylistic device. Every couplet is a completely self-contained statement, ending with a full stop or with the possibility of one. The poem is in effect nothing but a series of distichs. The importance of this is clear when we examine its structure, and the ways in which these self-contained distichs are linked to form a narrative.

Πιάνει, βουλώνει μιὰ γραφὴ πέμπει τη στὸ Σουλτάνο
γῆ νὰ σηκώσει τὴν Τουρκιὰ ἀπού τὴν Κρήτ' ἀπάνω,
γῆ νὰ σηκώσει τὴν Τουρκιὰ ἀπού τὰ τρία Κάστρη
γῆ θὰ τοῦ κάμει πόλεμο κι οὖλα θὰ τὰ χαλάσει.

(Laourdas, 1947, p. 19, ll. 119–22)

He writes and seals a letter and sends it to the Sultan:
either he takes his Turks away and leaves Crete alone,
either he takes his Turks away and gives up the three Castles
or [Daskaloyannis] will make war on him and lay everything waste.

Πόλεμον ἐσηκώσασι τσοὶ Τούρκους νὰ ξυγώξου
σταυρὸ νὰ προσκυνήσουσι, γῆ οὖλους νὰ τσοὶ σκοτώσου.

Πόλεμον ἐσηκώσασι, κεφάλι τσ᾽ ἀφεδιᾶς σου,
νὰ πάρουσι τσοὶ τόπους σου, νὰ διώξου τὰ παιδιά σου.

(Laourdas, 1947, p. 20, ll. 131–4)

They have risen in arms to bring the Turks to heel,
to make them worship the cross and if not, to kill them all.
They have risen in arms, O [Sultan] our master,
to take from you your lands and drive your children into exile.

Each couplet consists of two main statements, contained in the first half of the line, and two subsidiary statements, including the rhyme-words, in the second half-line. In the first case, the sense of the first couplet has been carried over and elaborated in the second by the repetition of the second main statement of the *first* couplet as the first main statement of the second. And in the second case two couplets have been devoted to the theme of rising up in arms by the restatement, in the second, of the first main statement of the first.

This is not the most inevitable way of building up a sustained narrative, and would certainly not have been necessary had the epic been composed at leisure, on the page. But more interesting still is the fact that these at first sight curious structural devices are precisely those used in the traditional genre of improvising *mantinádes*. Both structures are used to connect this modern series of *mantinádes*, in which the repeated main statement is underlinded:

Ἀλάργο μ᾽ ἐξορίσανε ὀγιὰ νὰ σοῦ ξεχάσω,
<u>καλλιὰ νὰ φάω μπαλωθιά,</u> παρὰ νὰ τὸ λογιάσω.
<u>Καλλιὰ νὰ φάω μπαλωθιά</u> ᾽πὸ ᾽ναν καλὸ παιγνιώτη,
παρὰ νὰ τὴν ἀπαρνηθῶ τὴν ἀκριβή σου νιότη.
<u>Καλλιὰ νὰ φάω μπαλωθιά,</u> καλλιὰ νὰ φάω μπάλα,
παρὰ νὰ τ᾽ ἀρνηθῶ ποτὲ τὰ μάθια σου τὰ μαῦρα.

(Lioudaki, 1936, p. 200, No. 115)

They've sent me into exile far away, so that I'll forget about you.
I'd sooner be shot than think of it.
I'd sooner be shot by a good marksman,
than renounce your precious youth.
I'd sooner be shot, I'd sooner be shot dead,
than ever give up those black eyes of yours.

In the last chapter we saw that the art of improvising *mantinádes* is highly prized in Crete, and no one who has heard a dialogue built up between two skilled improvisors could doubt that a narrative of over a thousand lines could be composed in this way, given the talent and the urge to do so. While *mantinádes* are still improvised in large numbers, many are also traditional, and a particularly well-turned *mantináda* is valued and remembered for several generations. The rhymes serve a mnemonic function, and many Cretans today remember dozens, perhaps even hundreds of these couplets which they have heard. Some even bear a surprising resemblance to couplets written down in the late fifteenth century (Baud-Bovy, 1936, pp. 342, 270–9).

If the poem is seen as a series of self-contained *mantinádes*, the singer's task of remembering his composition will not then seem impossibly demanding, as he can omit or add distichs at will, and all he need remember is what he wishes to say and the pair of rhyme-words he used last time, to reproduce a passably similar version. That such compositions were actually transmitted in this way can be demonstrated in practice. In Barba-Pantzelios' version of 'Daskaloyannis', the hero's escort to the Pasha is described:

Ἐσέρνασίν τονε πολλοί, πεζοὶ καὶ γι-ἀτιλῆδες,
στὸ δρόμο τῶν ἐπρότεινε νὰ γίνουν ριτζατζῆδες.

(Laourdas, 1947, p. 37, ll. 691–2)

Many people dragged him along the way, men on foot and horsemen,
and as they went he asked them if they would plead his cause.

And in a nineteenth-century version, in which the whole story has been compressed into only thirty-eight lines, we find the same idea and the same unusual rhyme-words, although the rest of the distich has been completely re-formed:

Τὸ Δάσκαρον τριγύρισαν σαρανταπέντ᾿ ἀτλῆδες,
κι αὐτὸ τὸ κακορίζικο ἔβανε ριτζατζῆδες:

(Jeannaraki, 1876, pp. 24–5, ll. 17–18)

Daskaloyannis was surrounded by forty-five horsemen,
and he, ill-fated man, set them to plead his cause.

In another version the departure from the written text is greater, but the same point in the story is told with the same rhyme-*sound*, and one of the rhyme-words is again a Turkish loan-word of slightly unusual character:

'Ομπρὸς ὀμπρὸς τόνε λαλοῦν σαράντα μπεξελῆδες,
κ' ἔχουν καὶ τὰ σπαθιὰ γδυμνὰ καὶ φαίνουντ' οἱ λεμπίδες.
(Academy of Athens, 1963, pp. 142–3, ll. 35–6

Right in front of him were gossiping forty gaolers,
and their swords were drawn and you could see the blades.

Part at least of the inspiration for this practice of composing and memorising texts in the form of rhyming couplets must derive from the popularity of *Erotokritos* and other literary works written in this form in the fifteenth to seventeenth centuries. The same motive, as well as the same method, for relatively accurate transmission is surely responsible for the preservation of several of these renaissance works in contemporary oral tradition. Not only are sections of *Erotokritos* still performed in Crete as folk songs, but many Cretans whose formal education has been minimal and who have certainly never read the text of the poem can recall several thousands of lines from it with considerable accuracy. Nor is this phenomenon confined to *Erotokritos*: sections of the sixteenth-century tragedy *Erofili* have been preserved by oral tradition, in a mixture of rhyming couplets and prose summary, as has the pastoral poem *Voskopoula*, which was written about 1600 (Doulyerakis, 1956). These works clearly entered the oral tradition through being sung or recited, and it was natural enough that the more ambitious of an emergent class of professional composers should have imitated their technique and style, as well as aspiring, by as accurate a means as possible, to confer on their own oral compositions the permanence of the written text.

Perhaps because of this there has always been a clear separation in Crete between the *rímes*, with their ill-assimilated borrowings from literature and persistent hankerings after the written word, and the demotic tradition. The latter has survived in Crete only in the conservative *rizítika* tradition of the mountainous west of the island, and in the art of extempore composition in *mantinádes*. In the *rizítika* the universally popular rhyme is unknown; and as the professional compositions of *rimadóri* have courted length and a discursive style, these traditional songs have become extremely brief and lyrically concentrated. The average length of a *rizítiko* song is only about ten lines.

These two traditions of folk poetry, clearly separable in their main characteristics, have flourished side by side in Crete for something like four hundred years. They have not done so in mutual isolation, and the signs of a long period of coexistence are easy to see. Although there seems never to have been much professional influence on the *rizítika*, the *rimadóri* were content to adopt demotic formulas and use them in their own way. Returning to 'Daskaloyannis', for instance, we find traditional formulas depicting defiance against Turkish authority, which are more familiar from the songs of the mainland klefts that were being sung at about this time, than from the Cretan *rizítika*; and in any case, in the text of 'Daskaloyannis' they have quite a different structural role, functioning as little more than clichés. But in the course of transmission 'Daskaloyannis' has become more like a song of the demotic tradition, with greater use of demotic formula systems. In this version I have underlined the half-lines which belong to formula systems commonly used in the demotic tradition:

Στὴ στράτα τὸς ἐπάντηξε ὁ Δάσκαλος ὁ Γιάννης,
ὁ καπετάνιος τῶ Σφακιῶ, τσῆ Κρήτης τὸ λιοντάρι.
Σύρνει τὸ μαχαιράκι του ἀπ' ἀργυρὸ φουκάρι,
καὶ μέσα τὸς ἐμπῆκεν-ε γιουροῦσι τός-ε κάνει.
Στὸ ἔμπα χίλιους ἤκοψε, στὸ ἔβγα δυὸ χιλιάδες,
καὶ στὄμορφον του γύρισμα ἐξηνταδυὸ πασᾶδες.

(Mango, 1954, p. 51)

On their way they were met by Daskaloyannis,
the *kapetánios* of Sfakiá, the lion of Crete.
He drew his dagger from a silver sheath,
and went among them and attacked them.
As he went in he cut down a thousand, and as he came out two thousand,
and on his fine return, *sixty two pashas.*

In other versions the assimilation is less advanced, but all show a tendency to abbreviate the epic expansiveness of Barba-Pantzelios in conformity with the taste in the demotic tradition for brief, more effectively concentrated pieces.

The tradition of which Barba-Pantzelios is the earliest known exponent has continued to thrive well into the twentieth century, with the singers being known nowadays simply as 'poets' (*pyités*). The functions of these professional singers have gradually been usurped by other forms of popular entertainment – newspapers, comic strips, the cinema and most recently television. But as late as during the Second World War the tradition of the *rimadóri* was as active as ever, and when Notopoulos and Petropoulos visited Crete in 1953, in what has probably been the only systematic attempt to collect songs of this kind,[5] they recorded no less than fifty compositions in which episodes of the German occupation of the island were recounted (Petropoulos, 1954, p. 393 n). One of these, which the collectors heard performed orally by its composer, amounted to 'about 480 lines', that is, almost half the length of 'Daskaloyannis' (Petropoulos, 1954a, p. 231). And the song of Anoyia, the village on Mount Psiloritis destroyed in reprisal for the abduction of General Kreipe, was composed by two women of the village, reportedly improvising alternate *mantinádes*:

Λουλούδια μὴν ἀνθίζετε πουλιὰ μὴν κηλαϊδῆτε,
τ' Ἀνώγεια μας ἐκάψανε καὶ νὰ τὰ λυπηθῆτε.
Μιὰν Κυργιακή, μιὰ ταχυνή, ὥρα ποὺ λειτουργοῦσι,
μπῆκαν στ' Ἀνώγεια γερμανοὶ τσ' ἀντάρτες καὶ ζητοῦσι.
Ἀντάρτες δὲν εὑρήκανε καὶ κάμανε τὸ κόμμα
γέρους καὶ γυναικόπαιδα κάτω τὰ 'κάμαν ὅλα.
Μαῦρα φοροῦνε τὰ βουνὰ κι' ὁ γέρω Ψηλορείτης
πενθοῦν τ' Ἀνώγεια τὸ Χωργιὸ καὶ τσ- ἥρωες τσῆ Κρήτης...
Τ' Ἀγούστου εἰς τὶς δέκα τρεῖς, καταραμένη ὥρα,
μιὰ συφορὰ μᾶς πλάκωσε καὶ μιὰ μεγάλη μπόρα...

(Frangakis, 1950, p. 772)

Flowers, do not bloom and birds, do not sing,
they have burnt down Anoyia, our village, so be sad.
One Sunday morning as mass was being said,
the Germans came to Anoyia looking for partisans.
They found no partisans, and started slaughtering people,
old men, women and children, they slaughtered them down below.
The mountains wear black, even old Psiloritis,
and mourn the village of Anoyia and the heroes of Crete...
On the thirteenth day of August, an accursed hour,
a disaster fell on us and a great cataclysm...

C. THE CYPRIOT *PYITARIDES*

The custom of composing rhymed songs in an epic manner upon events of topical interest is even more widespread in Cyprus, although there too the art seems to have declined rapidly in recent years and for much the same reasons. The professional poet–singer in Cyprus is the *pyitáris,* a term which seems to cover as wide a range of diverse individuals as the corresponding Cretan *rimadóros*. Of his professional and specialised status, however, there can be little doubt. The suffix *-áris* in the

Cypriot dialect denotes the production of or trade in a commodity (Papadopoullos, 1967, p. 4), so that the *pyitáris* literally is a 'purveyor of poems'. A vivid description of a performance by one of these poets is given by Konstantinos Yangoullis:

> I remember him, when I was still at primary school, coming to my village every Sunday to cry his wares. He would take up a position where he could be seen and from there would begin the recitation of his poems. Around him a crowd of people would listen with bated breath to the murder, love affair or disaster sung by the *pyitáris* Aristotelis to a long-drawn-out melody. When the recitation was over he would sell his poems to the audience, and then go on to another café and do the same all over again. And this he would repeat every Sunday and in every village. In this way the *pyitáris* became famous throughout the district and people took to calling him 'old Aristotelis' or 'the poet'. (Yangoullis, 1970, p. 35)

Aristotelis Nikolaou was about seventy at this time but, as in Crete, the dearth of young poets today is probably due to comparatively recent circumstances. Certainly, around the turn of the century, there were young *pyitárides* as well as old (Menardos, 1921, p. 181).

Although the songs of these *pyitárides*, like those of the *rimadóri* in Crete, are the work of semi-educated poets to some extent emulating literary texts, there is no single group of poems or plays comparable to those of Kornaros and Hortatzis in Crete which could have inspired them. The most likely source of inspiration for the *pyitárides* would probably have been the popularising chronicles of late Byzantine literature, but even so an important question is left unanswered. This has to do with the relation between the two folk traditions in Cyprus.

In Crete the development of the *rímes* into something like an epic tradition was counterbalanced by an opposite trend in the traditional folk songs which became exaggeratedly brief and concentrated. But while the professional, topical compositions of the Cypriot *pyitárides* cultivate the style and dimensions of epic, it is also in Cyprus that many of the traditional panhellenic ballads achieve their most extended form. Ballads of such mythical heroes as Diyenis, Kostantas and Porfyris in Cyprus acquire epic characteristics which are matched nowhere else in the Greek-speaking world, and for this reason are often regarded as earlier versions from which the shorter Greek ballads derived. On the other hand the historical compositions of *pyitárides* share many of the same epic characteristics, but their origins are less romantic and much less remote in time.[6] Is there, then, only one tradition, and do all Cypriot narrative songs belong to an oral epic tradition perhaps going back, as some would have it, to the early middle ages? Part of the answer to this question is to be found in the role of the *pyitárides*.

These poets have been relatively little documented in comparison with the work that has been done in publishing and studying their songs, with the result that agreement has still not been reached among scholars on who may and may not be termed a *pyitáris*.[7] The most important question which has still to be resolved is whether these professional singers also sing and transmit *traditional* songs. It was categorically stated by N. G. Politis that they did (1915, p. 506) and equally categorically asserted by Kyriakidis that they did not (1915, p. 650). The first authoritative account of these poets offered a kind of compromise, showing that the term *pyitáris* has a broad range of meaning covering three distinct classes of singer: those who sing traditional songs, those who sing their own compositions, and those who compose and sing distichs (Pantelidis, 1923) and this seems to have been confirmed in a general way more recently (Petropoulos, 1954). Since then, however, Yangoullis (1965) has returned to the proposition that the *pyitárides* are exclusively composers of their own songs and a new compromise has been offered by Theodoros Papadopoullos (1967): that the classes of *pyitáris* are not distinct and that the topical, historical type of song was a development of the demotic tradition which grew up in the nineteenth century with the introduction of printing into Cyprus.

Scholarly confusion here probably reflects a real confusion. Whether or not a *pyitáris*, strictly defined as a composer of his own songs on topical subjects, may also perform songs on traditional themes, there is no doubt both that professional *pyitárides* do handle traditional material, adapting it according to their own requirements, and that non-professionals such as women, when they sing traditional songs, do so after the manner of these professional singer–composers. A version of 'The Death of Diyenis' which Notopoulos recorded from a *non-professional* 'shows that the singer is following closely the tradition of these itinerant bards in the island [the *pyitárides*]' (1959, pp. 15–21). Notopoulos' singer had learnt his version of the traditional ballad either from hearing a professional *pyitáris* or from a broadsheet; and, to confuse the issue still more, this oral version by a non-professional can be traced back to a broadsheet published in 1906, itself a hybrid 'composition', mixing traditional lines with the characteristic style of the *pyitáris* (Papadopoullos, 1967, pp. 20–4).

The Cypriot pyitárides

That *pyitárides* have been aware of the different types of material in their repertoire can be seen in the different formulas they tend to use for 'signing off'. The formula,

Ἐκεῖνος ὅπου τό 'βγαλεν σὰν ποιητὴς λογᾶται,
κείνου πρέπει συγχώρεση κι ἐμένανε σπολλάτε
(Petropoulos, 1954, p. 380)

He who composed the song is regarded as a poet,
he deserves your indulgence and I your good wishes,

directs the audience's attention to the performer and reminds them that he hopes to be rewarded. But he askes no more than his fair share: he is not the composer of the song, merely the singer. This disclaimer is so common in Cypriot songs that one might suspect it has become as conventional and meaningless as the appeals to non-existent sources in western medieval romances. But it is noteworthy that this formula occurs much more frequently appended to songs whose themes are traditional than to evidently personal compositions. In another type of formula the singer may either leave out all mention of the composer of the song and merely seek his audience's indulgence on his own behalf,

ἂν ἔχετε λλίγον κρασίν, πρέπει νὰ μᾶς κερνᾶτε,
τ' ἀγίου πρέπει δόξασι καὶ ἐμέναν τ' ὡς πολλά 'τε
(Papadopoullos, 1975, pp. 23–4, ll. 50–1)

if you have a little wine, you ought to let us have some,
give praise to the saint and to me your good wishes;

or he may indicate that he is himself the author:

Ἰδοὺ τὸ τέλος ἔκαμα, γιὰ νὰ βεβαιωθῆτε,
καὶ ὅσοι τὸ ἀκούσετε χρόνους πολλοὺς νὰ ζῆτε.
(Papadopoullos, 1975, pp. 115–23, ll. 315–16)

See, I have made an end, so that you know what happened,
and to all who have listened [I wish] a long life.

These formulas, in contrast to the first type, are used with greater frequency in songs which appear to be personal compositions of *pyitárides*, showing that a real distinction, although naturally not an absolute one, exists in the minds of these poets between original and received material.

The academic confusion arises because the roles of different types of singer are not clearly defined; in other words, in Cyprus, in contrast to what happens in Crete, the transmission and development of the demotic tradition are largely in the hands of the same professional singers who have created and developed the topical, historical tradition, and of their non-professional admirers.

It would seem from this that the epic length of traditional songs in Cyprus is due not to the preservation of a medieval epic tradition lost in the rest of the Greek-speaking world, but to the influence of the *pyitárides* and the development of narrative as a means of professional entertainment. As a result we find that the Cypriot traditional songs, although much longer than their mainland counterparts, contain little or no more actual information, the greater length being achieved by a variety of devices such as excessive repetition, prevarication, and the inexpert tacking together of self-contained episodes. One of the most glaring instances of repetition used for this purpose is in the two Cypriot variants of 'Mikrokostantinos' mentioned in Chapter 2 (examples 7–8), where the recognition is effected by the wife's repeating the entire song, word for word, up to the penultimate scene. On a smaller scale, the desire to gain length by repetitions which hold up the action and hopefully create a mood of suspense in an audience can be seen in the use in very many traditional songs of stereotyped formula sequences such as this:

Πρῶτα διᾶ τους μουστουνιὰν τζαὶ ὕστερα ρωτᾶ τους:
– Πέτε μου, βρὲ Κατσίγγανοι, εἶντά 'ν' ποὺ ἐξηᾶστε;
Τζαὶ πέτε μου τζαὶ τὸ ποίημαν στὴν ἀφκοποταμοῦσαν.
– Χαμμάζομέσ' σε, Διενή, τὰ λόγια ποὺ μᾶς λέεις.
Πρῶτα διᾶς μας μουστουνιὰν τζαὶ ὕστερα ρωτᾶς μας.
Ἔπαρ' μας λλίην 'πομονήν, λλίην καρτερωσύνην,
νὰ φέρουν φῶς τὰ μμάδκια μας τζαὶ νοῦν ἡ τζεφαλή μας
τζαὶ λοῖσμὸν τὰ μήλη μας τζαὶ μεῖς νὰ σοῦ τὸ ποῦμεν.
Παίρνει τους λλίην πομονήν, λλίην καρτερωσύνην,
ἐφέραφ φῶς τὰ μμάδκια τους τζαὶ νοῦν ἡ τζεφαλή τους
τζαὶ λοῖσμὸν τὰ μήλη τους, σταθῆκαν νὰ τοῦ ποῦσιν:

(Kyriakidis, 1926, pp. 140–9, ll. 24–34)

First he gave them a slap in the face and then he asked them:
'Tell me, Katsingani, what's that you're talking about?
And tell me this poem of yours here by the river's edge.'
'You amaze us, Dienis, speaking such words.
First you give us a slap in the face and then you ask us.
Have a little patience with us, wait a little,

while our eyes find light and our heads good sense,
and our limbs find reason, and then we'll tell you.'
He had a little patience with them, waited a little,
while their eyes found light and their heads good sense
and their limbs found reason, and then they stopped and told him:

This looks like a parody of an oral style, especially when the same sequence is trotted out time and again whenever a question has to be asked.

There are other ways too by which the Cypriot singer may prevaricate and lend the appearance of epic length to the material of traditional ballads. In one song in which Kostantas' bride is stolen and he rides out on his supernaturally swift horse to recapture her, the action is suspended at the crucial moment by twenty-three lines describing a clowning interchange between the hero and his talking horse (Sakellarios, 1868, pp. 3–8, ll. 97–119). This is a piece of invention inspired by the single line in a number of ballads where the horse asks its rider not to use his spurs. Another such case of prevarication is found in one of the songs where Diyenis carries off his chosen bride, who was supposed to be marrying someone else at the time. In this song his old mentor Filopappos is at first unwilling to help him and a trivial argument ensues in which the old man's objections are overcome. Once again the singer creates an atmosphere of suspense by throwing a trivial obstacle in his hero's way, and more exciting things must wait until it has been surmounted (Sakellarios, 1868, pp. 11–13).

Another means of obtaining the required narrative interest was to juxtapose loosely connected episodes. This is a perfectly valid means of traditional composition, but some of the Cypriot examples of 'composite' songs fail to make any rational connection between their component stories. A song in which three different versions of Diyenis' death are told consecutively clearly illustrates this (*Kypriaké Spoudé* 37, 1973, pp. 15–18). Even more revealing is the song of Kostantas already mentioned. The first part of this song tells of the rival Fteropoullos' resolution to abduct the hero's wife, his asking his parents' blessing in the enterprise and their attempts to dissuade him. This rather trivial introduction is an addition to the traditional theme, as in most other versions the singer has preferred to concentrate on Kostantas' passivity in the face of a brash wife-stealer, and his correspondingly merciless efficacy in recovering his wife and punishing the abductor. In this introductory part of the story the text is highly confused: there are several unattached half-lines and a predominant but inconsistent use of rhyme.

Once the introduction is over and the story proper commences, the singer seems to have got into his stride. The rhymes practically disappear and there are no loose half-lines. In this song a *pyitáris* (or an amateur entertainer influenced by the craft of these poets) has combined a retelling of an unrhymed traditional song with a composition in his own style, based on the couplet form, in order to give it epic dimensions.

That *pyitárides* actually did this was confirmed by Pantelidis:

> Often one comes upon lines wholly foreign to the narrative, which the *pyitárides* have introduced themselves for the sake of a rhyme for the following line of the narration; but they admit that 'these are our own, to make the song fit'. (1923, p. 117)

There are numerous examples of songs in a mixture of rhyming couplets and unrhymed lines which show how the *pyitárides* have 'stretched' the traditional material to make it suitable for audiences attuned to the style of their own compositions.

Sometimes it is difficult even to tell to which tradition a song belongs. What are we to say of the song of Arodafnousa, which in its many versions has become almost a Cypriot national epic? The tale of royal jealousy seems to have had its origin in a real event of the fourteenth century (Petropoulos, 1958, p. 98), but the historical names have all disappeared, as have all the trappings of professional composition – the dates and circumstantial details. Most of the versions can now only be ascribed to the demotic tradition, although the song may well have started out in life as a professional piece of journalism.

D. PROFESSIONAL COMPOSITION IN MAINLAND GREECE

On the mainland of Greece no comparable proliferation of professional, personally composed songs has been recorded. In the early nineteenth century, however, during the period of the War of Independence from the Ottomans, we know that bards in some respects similar to the *rimadóri* and *pyitárides* of Crete and Cyprus existed and composed songs inspired by the events of the times. Probably the earliest of these poets known to us is Panayotis Kalas (Tsopanakos) of Dimitsana in the Peloponnese. Born in 1789, Tsopanakos was a hunchbacked dwarf gifted with a fine voice and a talent for improvising verses. In this capacity he attached himself to the chieftain Nikitaras, for whom he composed many songs, frequently humorous or satirical, until his death in 1824 from an overdose of unripe plums (Politis, N. G., 1915, pp. 501–4).

Fauriel, in describing the 'blind rhapsodes' he had heard about from his expatriate informants, painted a vividly accurate picture of the modern Cypriot *pyitáris*:

> Toujours par voies et par chemins, toujours en quête de ce qui peut émouvoir leur imagination ou satisfaire leur curiosité, aucun bruit ne leur échappe de ce qui se passe dans les villes, dans les villages et dans les campagnes. Ils tiennent note de tout, chantent sur tout; et avec leurs chansons se répand peu à peu dans la Grèce entière la renommée des aventures et des hommes qui en font le sujet. (1824, p. xcii)

But if these professional singers were at any time so numerous on the mainland of Greece, the songs and the fame of almost all have proved remarkably transitory. Fauriel's insistence on universal blindness among these singers, his use of the ancient term 'rhapsodes' to describe them, and his mistaken description of the modern *lýra* which they played as the lyre of the ancients, all suggest that his account may have been exaggerated by an enthusiastic confusion of ancient and modern in Greek affairs which was all too common in the last century. We are probably on safer ground with his description of Gavoyannis, a blind singer and improvisor who lived in Thessaly and, unlike the 'wandering rhapsodes', spent all his life in his native village. This man became rich and famous in the district for his songs describing the activities of the klefts, and would receive visits from chieftains or adventurers seeking poems to commemorate their deeds. Such was his success, from a professional point of view, that

> Les Albanais à la solde des pachas qui ne trouvaient pas aisément des panégyristes de leurs exploits parmi les rhapsodes des Klephtes, et qui, dans leur humeur fanfaronne, voulaient cependant être aussi chantés, avaient souvent recours à ce vieux Gavoyannis pour obtenir de lui des vers à leur louange, qu'ils lui payaient bien. (Fauriel, 1824, p. xciv)

It appears that 'rhapsodes of the klefts' did exist, although little reliable information has been recorded about them. Two accounts describe ancient, blind and decrepit singers, long after the War of Independence was over, begging in the streets and singing the songs they claimed to have composed for their guerrilla chiefs in the days of their

169

prime (Politis, N. G., 1915, p. 509; Vlahoyannis, 1938, pp. 167–8). But it is now generally agreed that, with very few exceptions, the surviving songs of the klefts are non-professional compositions and there is no evidence to suggest that the patronage of professional singers by leaders of the klefts was either a widespread or a long-lived practice (Politis, A., 1973, pp. xl–xlii). The most that can be said is that the events of the War of Independence gave a probably brief stimulus to professional singers whose status, both before and after, was in general much lower than that of their counterparts in Crete and Cyprus.

Few songs survive which can certainly be attributed to professional singers. Most are appalling, and all of them are much more closely derivative from the demotic tradition than are the Cretan and Cypriot equivalents, suggesting that they come of a less developed tradition. In 1828 a series of thirteen songs was recorded from a blind *lýra*-player in the south-west Peloponnese, Yannos Panayis (Melahrinos, 1946, pp. 3–13). They are bald, inexpert narrations of the deeds of minor heroes of the War of Independence, full of formulas borrowed from the demotic tradition, but tacked together with none of the dexterity and tight construction of traditional Greek song. The extent to which they are derivative is revealed by the first song, about the rising in Crete, whose opening formula and rhyming structure indicate clearly that Panayis had learnt it from a Cretan *rimadóros*. None of his other songs employs rhyme, and most of his opening formulas are demotic in origin. But, derivative and plodding though they are, these songs seem not to have been memorized word for word but have been re-composed by Panayis. The extreme monotony of the twelve texts other than the Cretan can be attributed, on examination, to poor-quality oral composition. The events in each of the songs are almost exactly the same, the sentiments are identical, and all are built up from a very restricted number of formulas which hardly vary, and which probably represent the singer's entire repertoire.

Somewhat different from these are two songs commemorating the kleft Kitzio Andonis (Katsandonis) recorded by Martin-Leake, probably about 1810 (Marshall, 1935, pp. 42–5; English translations in Clogg, 1976, pp. 70–1). The first describes, at slightly greater length than is common in the demotic tradition, how the Turkish authorities and Greek village notables resent the depredations of Andonis, and an expedition is mounted against him. The result is a single combat between Andonis and Veli Gekas, an Albanian *derbendağa* (captain of the passes) known for his courage and cruelty. Andonis shoots the Albanian, mortally wounding him, and Veli Gekas cries out to his comrades to cut off his head so that it won't fall into the hands of the klefts. The second song describes the capture and death of Andonis, whose arms and legs Ali Pasha commanded to be crushed with heavy hammers.

The first of these events took place in 1806, and the second a year or so later,[8] so that the songs Martin-Leake recorded must have been composed very shortly afterwards. There are a number of reasons for supposing that these were professional compositions. The first song, in particular, is long and rather circumstantial, and while its second part, describing the meeting of Kitzio Andonis and Veli Gekas, is paralleled in traditional versions, the first twenty-four lines resemble a professional singer's preamble, designed to hold back the action and catch an audience's attention. This song also begins with the pedantic detail,

στὲς δεκαφτὰ τοῦ ἀλωναργιοῦ, στὲς τέσσαρες Αὐγούστου

(Marshall, 1935, p. 43)

On the fifteenth of Alonaris, on the fourth of August.

The month of Alonaris is normally July, but here refers to the Revolutionary Fructidor which began on 19 July. To specify the date of an event with reference to two different calendars is surely the act of a singer determined to show that he has been to school. And the second song, although in many respects a traditional lament for the death of a kleft, is distinguished from all the demotic versions of the death of Katsandonis in that it relates the true manner of his execution. Of the demotic songs, some tell only of an ambush and the kleft's determination to die fighting, while others describe him being shot down, using the type of formula which also described the death of Veli Gekas (Passow, 1860, pp. 76–82).

There are signs that at the courts of ambitious, practically independent local rulers, such as the Greek beys of the Mani, of whom the last, Petrobey Mavromichalis, is the most famous, and the Albanian Ali Pasha in Ioannina, some form of professional epic-style poetry was encouraged. It is possible that these songs of Kitzio Andonis, which reflect exasperation more than admiration for the kleft's heroic activities, were in fact composed at the court of Ali, who had him put to death, rather than among his fellow klefts.

There are other indications too that professional composition was more prized in Ioannina than elsewhere. N. G. Politis mentions an 'Alipashiad', an epic in which the notorious pasha's exploits are extolled, by an Albanian Moslem, Hadzi Serket, interestingly enough in

Greek (1915, p. 513). Two other poems from the court of Ali are unusual for their use of rhyme: a banal account of his revolt against the Sublime Porte in 1820 said to have been composed by one of his sons (Fauriel, 1825, pp. 347–53), and the famous lament for Kyra Frosyni, the Greek mistress of another son of the Pasha, who was put to death in 1801 (Petropoulos, 1958, p. 165); and although these poems are very different in style, the fact that in Ioannina almost alone on the Greek mainland at this time, rhyme was used in songs on historical subjects, suggests that a class of professional singers, comparable to those of Crete, may have begun to emerge for a brief period under the patronage of Ali Pasha.

A tradition of the same sort may also have floursihed for a time at the court of the powerful beys of the Mani. When Dimo and Nicolò Stephanopoli, Corsicans of Maniot descent, visited Mani on a diplomatic mission from Napoleon, they recorded a song in eighty-seven political lines to which they gave the title 'The Complaint of Roumeli' (1800, II, pp. 74–83). This was performed by three women, singing in turns, and accompanied by an old man playing 'une espèce de guitare', probably a *tambourás*. The performance seems to have been part of a formal occasion, as it was put on at the bey's command to entertain his diplomatic guests and emissaries from other parts of Greece. In *form* the song owes something to the demotic tradition, and it opens with a theme which we know well from other contexts:

Ὅλος ὁ κόσμος χαίρεται·	All the world is glad;
Ὅλοι βαροῦν παιγνίδια·	and everyone is at play;
Ἡ Ῥούμελη καὶ τὰ νησιὰ	[but] Roumeli and the islands
Στέκουνε πικραμμένα.	are grieving bitterly.
Ῥούμελη, γιὰ δὲν χαίρεσαι,	Roumeli, why are you not glad,
Γιὰ δὲν βαρεῖς παιγνίδια;	why are you not at play?

(Legrand, 1870, p. 9) [9]

In the demotic tradition a series of formulas of this kind is often used to introduce a brief lament for the plight of a city besieged or captured by the enemy. But here these lines serve only as a rhetorical device to introduce a long series of grievances against foreign tyranny, reminiscent of the political pamphlets of the time which were in fact largely inspired by the ideals of the French Revolution. Roumeli, replying at length to the stranger's question, details the miseries of Ottoman yoke with the trite rhetoric familiar from the revolutionary propaganda of the middle classes:

Ὅποιος καὶ ἂν εἶσαι, ἄνοιξε

Τὴν ἱστορίαν, καὶ ἴδε

Τ᾽ ἦτον ἡ Γραίκια μία φορά,

Καὶ ἄκουσε τ᾽ εἶναι τώρα.

Ποῦ ὁ τύραννος μοῦ ἐρήμαξε

Τὸ γένος τῶν Ῥωμαίων.

Ποῦ εἶναι ἡ Ἀθήνα μου,

Ποῦ εἶναι κείνη ἡ Ἀθήνα,

Ποῦ ὁ κόσμος ἐθαμάστηκε,

Καὶ σέβεται ἀκόμη;

Ἐκεῖ ἐπρωτοφάνηκε

Ἡ ἐλευθερία εἰς τὸν κόσμον

Ἐκεῖ διαλάλησε ὁ Σολῶν

Τῶν Ἀθηναίων τοὺς νόμους·

Ἐκεῖ ἔτρεχαν νὰ φωτισθοῦν

Τῆς Εὐρώπης τὰ ἔθνη·

Καὶ, ἀπὸ τὰ πέρατα τῆς γῆς,

Ἔρχουντον στὴν Ἀθήνα

Τῶν βασιλέων τὰ παιδιὰ

Στερηᾶς καὶ τοῦ πελάγου,

Ἄλλα νὰ ἰδοῦν τὰ ἐργόχειρα

Τῶν θαυμαστῶν τεχνήτων·

Ἄλλα νὰ σμίξουν τοὺς σοφούς,

Νὰ μάθουν ἐπιστήμαις·

Ν᾽ ἀκούσουν παραδείγματα

Ἀπὸ τοὺς φιλοσόφους·

Ἐκείνη ἡ Ἀθήνα ποῦ ἀγροικᾶς

Ποῦ ἔλαβε τόσην φήμην,

Τώρα ἡ σκλαβιὰ τὴν ἔφαγε,

Τώρα δὲν εἶναι πλέον.

Τώρα οἱ διαβάταις ποῦ περνοῦν,

Οἱ ξένοι ποῦ διαβαίνουν,

Ἄλλον ἐκει δὲν βρίσκουνε,

Ἄλλον ἐκεῖ δὲν βλέπουν

Παρὰ ἕνα ἔρημον χωριὸν

Κεῖ ποῦ ἦτον ἡ Ἀθήνα·

Καὶ ἕναν φιλάργυρον Ἀγὰν

Στὸν τόπον τοῦ Ἀρεοπάγου.

Whoever you may be, open
the history book, and see
what Greece once was
and hear what she is now:
how the tyrant has laid waste
the Romaic race.
Where is my Athens,
where is that Athens,
that the world once held in awe
and still reveres?
There for the very first time
freedom came into the world;
There did Solon proclaim
his laws to the Athenians;
Thither did the nations of Europe
hasten for enlightenment;
And from the ends of the earth
there came to Athens
the children of kings
by land and sea,
some to see the handiwork
of marvellous craftsmen;
Others to mix with wise men,
and taste of learning;
To hear examples
from the philosophers.
That Athens you hear tell of
that won such fame,
is now engulfed by slavery,
and now exists no more.
Now the travellers who pass through,
the foreigners who travel,
find nothing there,
see nothing there
but a deserted village
where Athens used to stand;
And a money-grubbing Aga
in place of the Areopagus.

(Legrand, 1870, pp. 10–11)

The historical knowledge betrayed here, together with the poet's interest in such things as the classical past and the doings of the 'nations of Europe', clearly reveal that, for all its borrowings from tradition as regards its form, the content of this song precludes it from being in any sense traditional. But neither does it appear to be merely the work of a literary hack. Whether or not it was composed on the page, and the number of literary and historical allusions suggests, although it by no means proves, that it was, the 'Complaint of Roumeli' was evidently intended for oral *performance*, and it is not hard to imagine how composition in this oddly mixed style might have been fostered, at this period, by the arrogant and independent Greek beys of the Mani.

E. THE EMERGENCE OF THE HISTORICAL TRADITION

The songs we have so far been considering, which together comprise what I have called the historical tradition, mostly belong to two main branches, the Cretan and the Cypriot. It would be rash at this stage to speak of the 'origins' of either branch of the tradition, but both have a surprisingly long pedigree for a type of song which might have been taken for a kind of transitional growth between oral and written traditions. There are, in fact, three kinds of evidence that a historical tradition, from which the modern Cretan and Cypriot branches have grown, has flourished since at least the fifteenth century.

First of all we have the evidence of historical songs which narrate, in the detailed and even pedantic manner of this tradition, events of past centuries. Examples are the Cypriot songs of the siege of Malta in 1565 and the fall of Cyprus to the Ottomans in 1570–1 (Sakellarios, 1891, pp. 181, 55), and the song 'The Death of the Emperor Constantine Dragazis' recorded from oral recitation in the island of Kythira in the nineteenth century, which describes the fall of Constantinople (Legrand, 1874, pp. 74–7). Some of the arguments that were used in Chapter 6 against dating demotic songs to the time of the events referred to must obviously apply in these cases also. There is no guarantee, for instance, that a *pyitáris* in the nineteenth century did not merely read of the events in a book and versify them as he would a contemporary 'shock horror' story. Indeed the inclusion in the Constantinople song of the legend that the last Emperor was buried under a laurel surely dates the first composition of the song *in its present form* to at least a hundred years after the event, when according to Legrand, the legend became current. On the other hand, one of the features of the historical tradition which strongly contrasts it with the demotic is the emphasis placed

174

by singers on accuracy in reporting and on the recording of details for posterity.

It is not inconceivable therefore that these nineteenth-century versions derive ultimately from the oral compositions of professional singers in the fifteenth and sixteenth centuries; and we have the evidence of de Lusignan that a song about the siege of Malta was circulating and widely popular in Cyprus within a few years of the event (1580, p. 221). But it is no less likely that all three songs were composed at a later date in imitation of written poems in a popular style. For both of the Cypriot songs there exist written parallels which we know to be roughly contemporary with the events in question (Prousis, 1945, pp. 24–9), and which may even prove to have been the direct originals of the oral narratives. The song of the fall of Constantinople certainly shows signs of a tenacious oral memory, in that the precise date of the event and many details which are left out in the oral demotic laments have been included, but here too it is impossible to hazard a safe guess at its date of composition. Written historical laments on the subject certainly existed in this case too, and as we saw in the case of Cretan renaissance literature, oral transmission in Greece of *written* texts can be strikingly accurate over long periods, perhaps owing to the popular association of the written word with permanence and even pedantry.

The second kind of evidence is more satisfactory. This is to be found in poems of the late middle ages and the two centuries following the fall of Constantinople, which appear to fulfil a closely similar function to that of the professional compositions of the more modern historical tradition. One of the most contentious examples is the fourteenth-century *Chronicle of the Morea*, the enormously long verse narrative which tells, in the vernacular, of the Frankish conquest of the Peloponnese at the end of the century before. A recent study, using computer techniques, has shown that the text of this poem is highly repetitious, and may be the product of formulaic oral composition (Jeffreys, 1973). But, unlike some of the Cretan and Cypriot poems to which it bears a sometimes uncanny similarity of style, it was undoubtedly composed to be *read*, and may even be a translation from French. This confusion of a popular, perhaps oral, style with the role of chronicler, which almost by definition presupposes a man well educated in a written tradition, is also found in the professional compositions of *rimadóri* and *pyitárides*, and it is curious to note that some of the most frequently recurring 'formulas' in the *Chronicle* are still current in the historical tradition.[10]

The opening lines of the poem, with the poet's declaration of intent and computation of the date when his story opens from the beginning of the world, are strikingly similar to more recent examples from Crete:

Θέλω νὰ σὲ ἀφηγηθῶ ἀφήγησιν μεγάλην·
κι ἂν θέλης νὰ μὲ ἀκροαστῆς, ὀλπίζω νὰ σ' ἀρέσῃ.
῞Οταν τὸ ἔτος ἤτονε, ἀπὸ κτίσεως κόσμου,
ἐξάκις χιλιάδες δὲ κ' ἐξάκις ἑκατοντάδες
καὶ δώδεκα ἐνιαυτούς, τόσον καὶ οὐχὶ πλέον

(Schmitt, 1904, p. 3)

I want to tell you a tale, a great tale;
and if you want to hear me, I hope it will please you.
When the year was, from the creation of the world,
six times a thousand and six times a hundred
and twelve years, so much and no more. . .

'Σ τὰ χίλια ὀχτακόσια εἰκοσιοχτώ, μιὰν Τρίτη,
Ἀφρουκαστῆτε νὰ σᾶς πῶ ὀγιὰ τὴ μαύρην Κρήτη.

(Jeannaraki, 1876, p. 66)

In eighteen hundred and twenty eight, on a Tuesday,
listen while I tell you what happened in wretched Crete.

There is one interesting difference, however. While the Cretan poet, like all the Cretan and Cypriot poets who address an audience directly, uses the plural form of the verb, the author of the *Chronicle* tellingly has the singular – he is addressing only one person, the reader.

Other characteristic techniques of more recent professional composers are to be found in two poems dated a century or more after the *Chronicle of the Morea*. These are the 'Plague of Rhodes' by Emmanuel Georgillas (1498) and Manolis Sklavos' 'The Disaster of Crete', a seemingly contemporary account of an earthquake in 1508. Their subject matter is enough to provide an immediate link with the later historical tradition, but the resemblance does not stop there. Both are among the earliest examples of the fully developed couplet form, which as we saw was integral to the composition and transmission of the Cretan and Cypriot poems, and Sklavos twice refers to the fact that his poem is a *series of distichs*. Georgillas, starting off in his first line with the date of the plague, several times refers to himself by name and tells us something of his circumstances and that he was an eyewitness of the events he describes (Wagner, 1874, pp. 32–52). Sklavos' poem begins with a familiar invocation to the deity and continues with the conventional statement of intent, followed by no less than seven lines spelling out the date and time when the earthquake struck. The end, in which the poet declares his identity, also has later Cretan parallels:

Μανόλης Σκλάβος μὲ σπουδὴ καὶ μὲ μεγάλον κόπον
τοῦτα τὰ δίστιχ' ἔβγαλλα διὰ θρῆνον τῶν ἀνθρώπων.

(Wagner, 1974, pp. 53–61, ll. 279–80)

Manolis Sklavos am I who, with study and great pains,
composed these distichs for the lamentation of men.

Υἰὸς τοῦ παππᾶ Ἱερωνύμου, Σετιανὸς Μανόλης,
Χαρκιώτης εἶν' ὁ ποιητὴς τῆς ἱστορίας ὅλης.

(Fauriel, 1825, p. 360)

Son of Ieronimos the priest, Manolis from Sitia,
[surnamed] Harkiotis, is the poet of this whole story.

That these and other techniques were in continuous use from the fifteenth century is suggested by a passage in an eighteenth-century literary work of Kaisarios Dapontes. The second chapter of his 'Garden of Graces' begins,

Ἐλθὼν λοιπὸν αὐτὸς ἐδῶ εἰς χρόνους τοὺς χιλίους
καὶ πέντε καὶ τριάκοντα ἐπὶ ἑπτακοσίους

(Legrand, 1881, p. 11)

Myself, then, arriving here in the year one thousand
and five-and-thirty above seven hundred. . .

Dapontes was a monk and in no sense a folk poet, but his use of this unpoetical device suggests that it may have been a well-known cliché of popular literature in the first half of the eighteenth century; and before the end of that century we find it again in folk poetry, where it is used in all seriousness in the epilogue to 'Daskaloyannis'.

The third piece of evidence for the continuity of the historical tradition is that competitions in improvising rhyming distichs took place in the islands in the sixteenth century (Kyriakidis, 1965, p. 82 n). We do not know whether these competitions were between professionals, as often happens at modern Cypriot festivals. But the Cypriot word *tshiáttisma* (rhyming distich) comes from the Turkish *çatmak*, whose meaning involves the idea of confrontation, suggesting that this may have been among the earliest functions of the distich in Cyprus. This fact, taken together with the importance that Manolis Sklavos evidently gave to composition in distichs, tends to confirm the impression that some of the impetus for the rise and subsequent popularity of the historical tradition came from the success of the couplet form in the fifteenth century.

Inseparable from the rhyming distich, as we saw at the end of the last chapter, is the western literary tradition in which it originated; and the development of a new vernacular literature on western models in Crete and Cyprus coincides with the last period of western rule after the fall of Byzantium, in both islands. It would not therefore be entirely coincidental if the same period had also seen the rise of a new form of folk poetry, inspired by a literary development which had itself approached so closely to the style of popular song. But probably this was not quite the beginning of the historical tradition. Undoubtedly the stature and popularity of poems such as *Erotokritos* and other works of the Cretan literary renaissance had a decisive effect upon the later development of the professional folk poetry of the *rimadóri*. But the epic characteristics of the Cypriot songs can owe little to the refined Petrarchan love poems which were the height of literary achievement on the island in the sixteenth century. Similarly, although the importance of rhyme in the historical tradition cannot be denied, it is probable that in its essentials the tradition predates the introduction of rhyme, in works such as the *Chronicle of the Morea*. And the existence of unryhmed songs in this tradition as late as the nineteenth century in mainland Greece suggests that songs advertising novelty and recording spectacular history could be and have been composed without using rhyme. If the ultimate 'origins' of the historical tradition are to be sought it must be in the chronicles and romances of the fourteenth century and earlier, rather than in the literary renaissance of the Aegean which has shaped its more recent development.

10. Greek Folk Poetry and Writing

A. WRITING AND ORAL TRADITION

There was never ane o' ma songs prentit till ye prentit them yoursel' and ye hae spoilt them a' thegither. They were made for singing and no for reading, but ye hae broken the charm now and they'll never be sung mair. And the warst thing o' a', they're nouther right spell'd, nor right setten down. (Hogg, quoted in Wells, 1950, p. 249)

With these words James Hogg's mother, one of the sources on whom Walter Scott had drawn for his *Minstrelsy of the Scottish border*, dismissed the publication and the well-meaning attempt to preserve oral folk poetry in print. The charge levelled against Scott appears confirmed by subsequent history, to the extent that it is now almost a commonplace that literacy is incompatible with a healthy oral tradition.

In Greece, as elsewhere in Europe, there has been a gradual breakdown of traditional oral poetry, beginning, so far as one can tell, about the time that songs began to be collected and distributed to a reading rather than to a listening public. It seems now to be widely believed that the growth of literacy during this period is predominantly responsible, and in the study of other folk cultures the idea has recently been refined. Albert Lord, in contemplating the visible decline of oral composition in the Yugoslav epic tradition, laid the blame not so much on literacy (which has existed in Yugoslavia for the last thousand years) as on the post-war drive to extend its use throughout all classes of the population. As a result, Lord affirms, oral singers have been confronted with written texts of their own songs, and he concludes, 'an oral tradition may die; not when writing is introduced, but when published song texts are spread among singers' (1960, p. 130). And again, 'It seems clear, then, that it is not literacy *per se* but the idea of fixity that will eventually destroy the oral poet's power to compose oral poetry' (1968, p. 5). This argument was given a further refinement by Jeffreys, who pointed out that in earlier periods (in Anglo-Saxon England and the middle ages in Europe) an oral poet who learned to read and write would almost inevitably do so in the *written language* – Latin in the west and Atticising Greek in the east – so that it is only in principle since the invention of printing and in practice quite recently that this confrontation between the oral singer and mass-produced, fixed texts of vernacular material could have occurred (1973, pp. 168–9).

Lord's conclusions are based on personal observation over many years and one need not doubt the role played by the increase in general literacy in Yugoslavia since the war in the breakdown of oral tradition there. It may be, however, that this happened in subtler and more diverse ways than Lord envisaged. For example, once his erstwhile audience had learnt to read and newspapers and comic strips became popular in the café where he had formerly sung, it may have been immaterial whether the singer himself was greatly affected by the confrontation with printed songsheets. And how easy was it to hold the attention of an audience who had heard of dialectical materialism and Yalta with the old-fashioned heroism and stylised narrative of the Battle of Kossovo?

It is not only literacy that has been able to coexist with a thriving oral tradition without detriment to the latter. In England the introduction of printing, far from destroying the oral tradition, stimulated the enormous broadside ballad industry, producing, alongside a mass of trivia, songs whose career over several centuries seems to have embraced both oral and written transmission, to the extent that it is now often difficult (and perhaps not important) to determine whether particular ballads began in life as traditional (oral) songs or as broadsides (Shepard, 1962, p. 77; Lloyd, 1975, pp. 24–32; Finnegan, 1977, pp. 162–4). The qualitative difference mentioned in the last chapter between traditional and broadside ballads in Britain has still to be kept in mind, but it must not simply be assumed that this distinction arises because the latter were written. Broadside publishers sent out agents into the country to report traditional songs which could either be printed as they stood or cannibalised in the preparation of a new, professional composition; and most broadsides have at the top an indication of the tune to which the ballad is to be sung. The broadsides were often therefore oral in origin, and almost always oral as regards performance: although written and distributed through the medium of print, these ballads were not composed to be read, like a detective story, but to be sung.

It is part of the old romantic approach to 'traditional' song, to which even Lord was not immune, to suppose that *total* orality is a condition of this material and one which marks it off decisively from other kinds. Lord seems to have envisaged the relation between oral and literary traditions as one of transition, as though the one necessarily followed the other in time. This may be one of the reasons for his conclusion that there was no such thing as a 'transitional' text (1960, p. 132), since a truly transitional text would have to have been written by an oral poet while in the process of becoming a literary one. And there is no evidence (*pace* certain Homeric scholars) that this has ever happened. The people who first use writing to record folk poetry are by no means always the poets themselves, but they are *never* oral poets who at the same time are emergent *literary* figures – unless we are to cite Sir Walter Scott as an oral poet. This confusion has to be removed because transitional texts do exist, in the sense of songs not fully oral in the demanding sense extrapolated by Lord from his experience of Yugoslav tradition, but yet not belonging to literature either. The British broadside ballads would seem to be a case in point, as would the historical tradition of Crete and Cyprus, and both have flourished for too long, and alongside both oral and literary traditions, to be described as 'transitional' from one to the other.

One solution would be to distinguish, as does David Buchan, between 'non-literate tradition' which he calls oral, and 'the word-of-mouth tradition of a literate culture', to which he gives the term 'verbal' (1972, p. 2). Applying this distinction to the ballad tradition of the north-east of Scotland, Buchan determined that this tradition was 'oral' up until the mid-eighteenth century, since when, following the spread of literacy in the area, it has been a 'verbal' one. Buchan's book is in large part an attempt to apply Lord's theory of oral composition-in-performance to Scottish balladry, and in this, because his analysis is sensitive and undogmatic, he is largely successful. But as a consequence of following Lord's lead, and adopting his general theory of oral tradition as a package rather than critically, Buchan could not avoid what might be termed the romantic fallacy of oral tradition: that a tradition is oral either totally or not at all.

According to this fallacy, Buchan's excellent analysis of Scottish ballads in terms of formulas, themes and architectonic patterns, required as a precondition the total orality of the poems analysed – and conversely, if successful, would automatically prove it. Buchan's distinction between 'oral' and 'verbal' traditions was a way out of a logical corner but may not, as a generalisation, be really as helpful as it first appeared.

The more recent tradition of the Scottish north-east is in no sense 'totally oral', but it is no easy matter to prove that it ever has been in the past either. How can we be certain that, even when the tradition included a greater degree of, say, re-composition in performance than it does today, it was at any time a truly 'non-literate' tradition? Buchan aptly shows how Mrs Brown, in his opinion the last of the Scottish 'oral' singers, in the eighteenth century, altered the texts of her songs from one singing to the next like the Yugoslav bards, and did not write them down. But, far from being illiterate, Mrs Brown was the daughter of a professor at Aberdeen University, and her letters show that she was a woman of considerable education. Even pure 'traditional' folk poetry does not require illiteracy, or 'total orality', in order to flourish.

Recent work by Professor Jack Goody and others on literacy in traditional societies has tended to confirm this. According to Goody the number of communities anywhere in the world which are entirely without literate influences is much smaller than is often supposed:

> at least during the past 2,000 years, the vast majority of the peoples of the world (most of Eurasia and much of Africa) have lived . . . in cultures which were influenced in some degree by the circulation of the written word, by the presence of groups or individuals who could read and write. They lived on the margins of literacy. (Goody, 1968, p. 5)

The 'margins of literacy' surely accurately describes the greater part of rural Greece (or Scotland) before the nineteenth century, and in discussing the oral folk poetry of either society we must account for the relation between literate and oral traditions in more ways than by the rise of the one at the expense of the other.

The written word has existed in most of Europe for at least two thousand years, in Greece for nearly twice that long. In Greece the interaction between literate and oral traditions (leaving aside the problems associated with Homer) goes back to the time of classical Athenian tragedy, whose stories were for the most part culled from a wide variety of often conflicting oral traditions, and may have become oral once again in the performances of popular pantomimes in a later period. And elsewhere in Europe signs of this complex interaction are beginning to be examined. Peter Dronke, in an excellent study of a medieval Latin ballad, shows how a poem belonging to the literary tradition, besides reflecting identifiable literary influences, seems to derive from earlier forms of surviving folk ballads on the theme of the lover's ghost. Dronke suggests a two-way influence as early as the tenth century if not before: not only, he believes, did literate poets who knew their Ovid and wrote in the learned language, Latin, allow themselves to be influenced by folk poetry, but one of the pervasive influences on all European balladry was the (written) Song of Songs, disseminated through the church (Dronke, 1976). One need not accept all of Dronke's arguments in detail (although I find them persuasive) but there is ample evidence to support his main conclusion that literary and oral traditions in Europe have not grown up in mutual isolation (cf. Finnegan, 1977, pp. 166–7).

Evidence of a different sort, for cheerful competition between the oral bard and the story-teller who used a book, is to be found in the medieval Welsh *Mabinogion*:

> And this story is called the Dream of Rhonabwy. And here is the reason why no one, neither bard nor story-teller, knows the Dream without a book – by reason of the number of colours that were on the horses, and all that variety of rare colours both on the arms and their trappings, and on the precious mantles, and the magic stones. (Jones and Jones, 1974, p. 152)[1]

B. THE DEMOTIC TRADITION AND WRITING

'It is clear', writes Professor Jack Goody (1968, p. 5), 'that even if one's attention is centred only upon village life, there are large areas of the world where the fact of writing and the existence of the book have to be taken into account, even in discussing "traditional" societies.' How this comes about had already been hinted at by R. Redfield: 'If we enter a village within a civilization we see at once that the culture there has been flowing into it from teachers who never saw that village, who did their work in intellectual circles perhaps far away in space and time' (quoted in Goody, 1968, p. 9).

Certainly if we enter a Greek village today, no matter how remote and 'traditional', the signs of this are everywhere to be seen. Many of them, such as the jukebox and the motor car, are of obviously recent importation, but what about the churches (even the tiniest hamlets often have several), the police station and the tax official? These are the representatives of a distant and centralised authority, whether that of the Patriarch, the Byzantine Emperor, the Ottoman Sultan or national government. For more than two thousand years the rural communities where Greek has been spoken have formed part of a civilisation (although not always the same one) in which literacy has been an important instrument of government and medium for culture. When we say, therefore, that the Greek folk songs of the demotic tradition are *oral* what precisely do we mean?

The distinction between 'oral' and 'verbal' will not help us here, since the greater part of all known oral poetry, including the Yugoslav epics, must strictly speaking be assigned to the verbal 'word-of-mouth tradition of a literate culture'. In fact the songs of the Greek demotic tradition, like those of the Yugoslav *guslari*, are oral in the sense that they appear to have been composed, performed and transmitted without being written down and given a fixed form by those who did so. But it would be naive to imagine that the singers of these songs had never come into contact with writing, or with ideas, stories and information disseminated by means of the written word. Certain key concepts that are constantly reiterated in the songs have been shown to be the result of a complex interplay between literary and popular traditions. Such is the figure of Haros, the personification of death (Alexiou, 1978), and many traditional themes and formulas in lamenting the dead seem to have had a similarly mixed background (Alexiou, 1974, *passim*).

Nor is there a lack of references in songs of the demotic tradition to writing, pens and ink, and even schools. In a Karpathian song of Andronikos (often dubiously identified with the ninth-century general Andronikos Doukas), the child prodigy not only learns feats of arms at an unnaturally early age, but goes to school at six and manages to write by the age of nine (Mihailidis-Nouaros, 1928, pp. 273–4). Ballads of child-murder often begin with the child safely out of the way at school learning *kondýli,* that is, his letters, and arriving home unexpectedly to find his mother in bed with a lover. And there is surely conscious irony in the description of Papathymios, at one time 'young at letters, young at his slates', who in his old age has become a leader of klefts and crafty enough to deceive a monastery into opening its gates to his raiders (Petropoulos, 1958, pp. 202–3).

These references are sufficient to remind us that the centuries of Ottoman rule in Greece were not, as one is frequently given to understand, an unrelieved dark age in which the twin lights of literacy and literature were extinguished. Indeed one has only to read a reasonably thorough history of modern Greek literature to realise that, although often poor in quality, the *quantity* of literary production was scarcely abated during these centuries. At no time in its development has the demotic tradition really been isolated from writing, but it is only in the last hundred and fifty years that it has begun to disintegrate. Before attempting to account for this decline we must say something about the historical tradition and the generalisation (after Mrs Hogg) that the use of writing to record and disseminate oral songs is necessarily destructive to oral tradition.

C. THE HISTORICAL TRADITION AND WRITING

The professional *rimadóri* and *pyitárides* of Crete and Cyprus were, as we saw in the last chapter, oral poets: many were and are illiterate or able to read and write only with difficulty. Yet writing and the written text are often prominent in the minds of these oral versifiers. If the poet is unable to write himself, he values – and sometimes envies – the power and permanence of the written word:

Ήθελα νά 'μαι ποιητής, νά ξέρω νά συντάσσω
καὶ τὸ χαμό σας, ἥρωες, εἰς τὰ χαρτιὰ νὰ γράψω

(Petropoulos, 1954, p. 391)

I wish I were a poet, and able to write a story
and your destruction, heroes, I'd write out on paper.

Τὰ γράμματα δὲν ἤξευρα, καὶ νὰ μὴ τὴν ξεχάσω,
Τραγούδι τοῦ τὴν ἔκαμα, καλὰ νὰ τὴν φυλάξω.

(Fauriel, 1825, p. 356)

I couldn't write, and so as not to forget it,
I made it into a song, to hold on to it well.

Often the poems were published or written out on broadsheets which would be declaimed by those who could read them, and there is no doubt that the circulation of these broadsheets has also played a part in the transmission of the songs (Pantelidis, 1923; Petropoulos, 1954a, p. 231). Petropoulos cites an example of the modern transmission of 'Daskaloyannis' which shows the interaction between oral composition and memorisation of a written text:

When in Hora Sfakión last year a descendant of Skordylis [Barba-Pantzelios' amanuensis] wished to sing the song, he sang several lines which he had memorised from a broadsheet. But he would often depart from the initial text, he would modify lines and leave many out in his haste to reach the end, so as to give the dramatic story in its entirety. (Petropoulos, 1954a, p. 232)

If he was able to write, a *rimadóros* would often commit his song to paper, although he might not have the means to publish it. A case in point is the song by Nikolaos Markakis, in an autograph manuscript dated 5 May 1895, commemorating the consecration of the Cathedral of St Minas in Iraklion, which had taken place three weeks before. The poem is 228 lines long and the poet must have worked fast to have had it finished and copied out in the time. What's more, on his own admission he was a villager and his knowledge of writing poor; and according to the editor of the manuscript this was no false modesty but the plain truth, borne out by the poet's painstaking but unpractised calligraphy (Alexiou, L., 1956). It is almost impossible therefore that Markakis could have composed his poem on the page in only three weeks. Also, the poem is in the usual couplets, many of which are structurally connected by the repetitive devices we have learned to associate with improvised *mantinádes*. Clearly Markakis composed his poem orally and then, once it was complete, began the laborious task of putting it down on paper. And we need not seek far to discover the reason for the poet's desire to fix his poem in writing or for the speed with which he did so: he tells us himself that he was in competition with the local newspaper (ll. 225–6).

In Cyprus the *pyitárides* seem to have had, if anything, greater success in circulating texts of their songs, and seem to have advertised them with less diffidence than their Cretan counterparts:

Πό ναν χαρτὶν νὰ πάρετε, κύριοι, νὰ χαρῆτε,
κι' ἃς δώσῃ κάθε ἀδερφὸς τὸ ὅ τι προαιρεῖται.

Πό ναν βιβλίον πάρετε, ἂν θέλετε, πὸ μέναν,
νὰ βλέπετε τὶ γίνεται 'ς τὴν Κύπρο καθημέρα.
Κλεάνθης Σάββας γράφεται τ' ὄνομα τὸ δικόν μου,
'ς τὸν Ἄη Μάμαν, κύριοι, ἒν τὸ γεννητικόν μου.

(Politis, N. G. 1915, pp. 504–5)

Take each a [ballad] sheet, gentlemen, if you please,
and let each brother give what he chooses.

Take each a [ballad] sheet, if you will, from me,
and see what's happening in Cyprus every day.

Kleanthis Savvas is my name and it's written there,
Ayios Mamas, gentlemen, is my birthplace.

We do not know how these broadsheets were originally transcribed –
by the poet himself or by an amanuensis; but it is probable that
many Cypriot *pyitárides* could not themselves read with fluency the
printed copies of their own ballads which they hawked round the
audience after a performance. Printing was not introduced into Cyprus
until 1878 (Papadopoullos, 1967, p. 4), so that large-scale distribution
of song texts would have been impossible before that date. The historical tradition in Cyprus had, of course, been flourishing long before this,
and, as in Crete, seems deliberately to have imitated vernacular literary
texts. Writing was certainly known to the *pyitárides* before 1878, and
the same envy and emulation of the fixed, written text as we observed in Crete can also be detected in Cypriot compositions. But the
introduction of printing and the sudden availability of printed texts in
large numbers, far from sounding the death knell of the oral tradition
or destroying the oral poet's power to compose oral poetry, resulted in
an explosion of *printed oral texts*. According to the bibliography of
N. G. Kyriazis, published in 1935, the first known song text appeared
in 1889, followed by two the next year and no less than fifteen in
1892. After that the number of publications fluctuates slightly, with a
marked decline during the First World War, rising to an average of
nearly forty-five a year for the last five years covered by the bibliography (Papadopoullos, 1967, pp. 42–3). The decline of this tradition,
both in Cyprus and Crete, many years later can hardly be because
'those singers who accept the idea of a fixed text are lost to oral traditional processes' (Lord, 1960, p. 137).

There is another sense, however, in which literacy and the assumption of certain of its consequences are fundamental to the existence of
the historical, oral tradition, and which also serves to distinguish it from
the equally oral demotic tradition. We saw that a primary function of
this tradition was to report and record 'news' for entertainment. Deriving in all probability from the popular chronicles of the late middle
ages, an essential requirement of a song in this tradition is that the
story, although doubtless embellished after the singer's fancy, should
literally have happened. It is news, not fiction; history, not myth. And
'historical consciousness', as Felix Jacoby has argued, 'is not older than
historical literature' (quoted in Goody and Watt, 1968, p. 48 n).
This essential difference between the historical and demotic traditions
is amply illustrated by the use of dates in the former. The synchronic

attitude to time which is found in the Greek demotic tradition, as well as in wholly non-literate traditions, is incompatible with the historical perspective implied by recording the day, month and year of a given event. The man who begins his song,

'Σ τὰ χίλια ὀχτακόσια ἔτος πενῆντα ἔξη

(Jeannaraki, 1876, p. 83)

In the year one thousand eight hundred and fifty six,

is separated by a whole cultural tradition, of which he himself may scarcely be aware, from his compatriot who begins,

Ὁ Διγενὴς ψυχομαχεῖ κι' ἡ γῆ τονε τρομάσσει

(*Laografía* 1, 1909, p. 242)

Diyenis is in the throes of death, and the earth trembles in
  fear of him.

The demotic singer in the second example is unconcerned with *when* Diyenis was in the throes of death. Characters on the scale of Diyenis, Kostantinos and the other recurring heroes of the demotic songs cannot be confined within an age and among real, familiar happenings. They exist as a paradigm in the imagination of singers and audiences, and their existence there belongs to now and always, untouched by historical time. The characters and situations of the historical songs, on the other hand, are always familiar. A conventional Providence is substituted for the miraculous, the location is clearly indicated and usually well-known, and the story of murder, uprising or devastation set against the background of everyday life.

Lord encountered such songs in Yugoslavia and, recognising the significance of their use of dates, assumed that they must have been written and not part of the oral tradition (1960, pp. 132-3). He may be right about the Yugoslav songs, but the singers in Crete, Cyprus and occasionally elsewhere who betray their historical sense by the use of dates cannot be described otherwise than as oral poets. They were, however, oral poets who had once been to school and had had the experience of learning from books. What is more, they had perceived the value for themselves, as professional entertainers, of imitating the texts and the attitudes which had come down to them from a literate – and better off – section of society.

188

D. THE DECLINE OF ORAL TRADITION IN GREECE

Mrs Hogg's objections to writing down and publishing oral folk poetry do not then seem to be fully valid, at least as far as *writing* is concerned. Most attempts to explain the decline of, particularly, the creative component in oral poetry during the last hundred years have concentrated on the act of writing and its effect on the oral poet. But when we consider the oral traditions which have flourished in Greece we find nothing to suggest that confrontation with the technique of writing and with fixed texts of oral poems has any predictable effect on the oral poet. For many hundreds of years singers who composed and sang in the demotic tradition seem to have ignored writing altogether, while the professionals of the historical tradition quickly learnt to exploit its possibilities as an accessory to *oral* composition and performance. Today, however, many young people learn the texts of songs at school, and the effects of this are aptly demonstrated in a recording, made from oral performance, of the ballad 'The Dead Brother' which follows word-for-word the text published by N. G. Politis.[2] Since Politis' version is an academic collage made up from many different oral variants, its existence in oral tradition can only be due to deliberate learning of this text.

The suggestion I wish to make is that a creative oral tradition is adversely affected, not by the impact of writing on singers, but by that of *reading* on their *audiences*. The assumption is often made that a written text presupposes a reading public – for example by Lord: 'Writing as a new medium will mean that the former singer will have a different audience, one that can read' (1960, p. 131). But neither the great majority of British broadsides, nor Skordilis' transcription of 'Daskaloyannis', nor the proliferation of Cypriot broadsheets, were ever intended to be read, silently, alone by the fireside, or still less at a school desk. They were commercially viable because the singer who distributed them could count on the desire of members of his audience to emulate his performance. At no time until very recently would the public for these printed songs have included enough people able or willing merely to *read* them for the business to have been profitable. On the other hand the farm hand in town for the day, who hears a new and enthralling song performed in the market square, will willingly pay the price of a copy and spend an hour over beer with his friends in the effort to construe it, for the pleasure of being able to go home the first, as he hopes, to sing or even just tell the latest story.

Even in western Europe it was not until the nineteenth century that the practice of reading for pleasure became general. Reading, especially among people who had had little opportunity to become proficient at it, was normally a way of learning rather than a means of entertainment. Those who did read for pleasure at the beginning of the nineteenth century were still a class apart, sharply divided from the majority by manners and education. What must have distressed Mrs Hogg about Scott's publication of her ballads was that they would inevitably become the property of people who lived in quite a different world, that they would be *read* by people of refined taste who would judge them by alien standards and despise or patronise them, so that less sophisticated people would be ashamed to sing and take pleasure in them.

In Greece the many volumes of folk songs published in the nineteenth century were intended to appeal to the opposite end of the social spectrum from the peasant audiences for whom they had been sung, and to people whose tastes and interests were remote from theirs. Fauriel in his preface set out the reasons why he thought the songs in his collection should be read (see pp. 6–7 above), thus guaranteeing that those who did so would approach them and respond to them in ways incomprehensible to a Greek villager of the time. This process of alienation went further as the century progressed and the songs were edited and interpreted by the educated in conformity with their own preconceptions. The child at a village school today is taught his own folk culture from books. He learns that Diyenis was the medieval champion of Hellenism and Christianity and that Politis' text of 'The Dead Brother' is the 'correct' one. In these circumstances it is no wonder that traditional singers today have generally lost the ability to re-compose songs as they sing them, since they have been taught that they never had it.

The wheel has now gone full circle. Education, based in part upon a falsification of the oral song tradition by a small reading public, has now enlarged that public to include the villager who had previously relied on the oral tradition for his entertainment. Together with the ability to read, the former audiences for oral poetry have discovered the 'correct' versions and interpretations of the songs they used to hear. Now that they know that 'The Dead Brother' is 'correct' in Politis' version, why should they stop to listen to Barba-Yannis' rendering, when it is full of mistakes?

But this is only part of the reason for the gradual decline of oral folk poetry in Greece. The first sign of decay can be seen in a couplet which seems to have been composed in 1827:

Ὅλα τ᾽ ἄρμενα ἀρμενίζουν μὲ ἀέρα, μὲ κουπιά,
τοῦ Κοκράνη τὸ βαπόρι ἀρμενίζει μὲ φωτιά.

(Kyriakidis, 1965, p. 96)

All the sailing ships sail with wind and oars,
but Kokrani's steamship sails with fire.

The occasion for the couplet was evidently the arrival of the first steamboat, the *Kartería*, to be seen in Greek waters, a move for which Lord Cochrane (Kokrani) was largely responsible. Its main statement, with its naive tautology, is already *quaint*. A sophisticated tradition has been forced into primitivism. The same tendency is more marked in songs composed to mark the arrival of the Bavarian Otto, the first king of Greece, in 1833:

Τώρ᾽ ἔφθασεν ὁ βασιλιᾶς, τώρ᾽ ἔφθασεν ὁ Ὄθων,
κ᾽ ἠ ὁ οὐρανὸς χαμογελᾶ, κ᾽ οἱ κάμποι λουλουδίζουν.
Καπιταναῖοι, φεύγετε, καὶ σεῖς, παλληκαράδες·
δὲν εἶναι πλέον ὁ καιρὸς τοῦ δόλιου μπάρμπα-Γιάννη,
Τώρ᾽ ἔφθασεν ὁ βασιλιᾶς, τώρ᾽ ἔφθασεν ὁ Φράγκος.

(Legrand, 1874, p. 166; cf. Passow, 1860, pp. 234–6)

Now the king has come, now Otto is here;
and the sky is smiling and the plains are flowering.
Kapetánii, flee, and you too, boastful heroes;
the days of poor old Barba-Yannis are over,
now the king has come, now he is here, the Frank.

The traditional form and language of the demotic tradition are here operating under considerable strain – first, because the whole subject matter, the arrival of the foreign king, belongs to the new and unfamiliar world of diplomacy, of a Greek ruling class and its pompous official language. The word *pléon* (l. 4) belongs to *katharévousa*, the 'purifying' form of the language which had just been adopted by the new Greek state, and there may also be a slight uneasiness implicit in the form of the king's name *Othon*, which helpfully fits the metre but lacks the familiarity of the vernacular *Othonas*. The tenor of the song is also new in the tradition, as the singer was obliged to veil his contempt for the 'Frank' (a pejorative term for a westerner) under the form of a panegyric.

An unusually successful example of a song which attempts to reflect a serious reponse to changed conditions is this one from western Greece

191

Greek folk poetry and writing

which laments the fixing by international treaty of the Greek frontier at the town of Arta in Epiros, in 1881:

Σ' οὖλον τὸν κόσμο ξαστεριά, σ' οὖλον τὸν κόσμον ἥλιος,
καὶ στὰ δικά μας τὰ χωριὰ νοῦλο καπνὸς κι ἀντάρα.
Ἡ γι ἀντάρα 'ν' ἀπ' τὰ κλάϋματα κι ἡ καταχνιὰ ἀπ' τὸ ντέρτι.
- Ἀνάθεμά σε, 'πιτροπὴ καὶ σύ, βρὲ βασιλέα,
ποὺ βάνατε τὰ σύνορα στῆς Ἄρτας τὸ γιοφύρι,
στὴν Ἄρτα καὶ στὴν Πρέβεζα, ψηλὰ στὸ Περιστέρι.
Καὶ τὴν καϋμένη Πράμαντα τὴν κόβουνε στὴ μέση.

(Spandonidi, 1939, p. 24, No. 39)

In all the world the sky is clear, in all the world the sun shines,
[but] in our own villages all is smoke and storm.
The storm is made by our tears, the mist by our sadness.
'A curse on you, committee, and on you, old king,
who made the frontier at the bridge of Arta,
at Arta and at Preveza and up at Peristeri.
And wretched Pramanta is cut in half.'

Only one line defeated the traditional formula systems at the singer's disposal – that which includes the word 'committee' and the *katharévousa* ('correct') form of the word 'king'. The structure of the song is substantially that of other laments on a variety of subjects, as even is the *structure* of the offending line: curses are often formulated according to the same pattern.

But a world governed by committees and international treaties cannot convincingly be described or evoked by a conservative system of formulaic patterns and recurring themes. Too many things changed and too quickly in the life of the rural villager, as his village came to be incorporated into the Greek state, for his traditional modes of expression in song to keep pace. With the growth of education the first thing he learns is that he is illiterate, rustic and backward. And the more he learns that is unfamiliar to him, the less adequate is his stock of traditional formulas and themes to express his reponse to it. The result is a gradual fossilisation of the song tradition. Versions of songs which have the approval of the educated come to be accepted as 'authentic' and then, since there is nothing more to be said or done with them, remembered as imperfectly as the rest of what one learns in primary school, and finally perhaps forgotten altogether.

E. THE DEMOTIC TRADITION IN THE TWENTIETH CENTURY

This trend has been observable in Greece throughout the present century, although it would not be true to suggest that as a result oral folk poetry there is now dead. The expropriation of folk song by the educated class in the nineteenth century has also had the positive result that most Greek literary poets of stature owe an enormous debt to folk poetry and many of the themes of the demotic tradition have become staple themes in the works of such different writers as Solomos, Sikelianos, Kazantzakis, Seferis and Elytis. Nor is the survival of the oral tradition confined to its influence on modern literature and culture, which is diverse in the extreme. Parts, at least, of the oral demotic tradition have continued to flourish after the end of the nineteenth century and have adapted successfully to changed circumstances.

(i) Rebétika

If the growth of education and the rise of new values tended to make traditional ways of composing and singing obsolete in the eyes of the villager who saw a new prosperous future dawning in the towns, there was one class of society on which they had quite the opposite effect. This, very broadly, consisted of the urban population who, having moved into the towns and cities, had failed to reap such benefits as were to be had. These were people of limited, but varying, degrees of education and literacy, but who saw no prospect of advancement in adopting the values of the growing middle class. The movement to the towns in Greece had begun in the eighteenth century, and the Greek population of the great commercial centres of the Ottoman Empire, Istanbul and Izmir (Smyrna), had been settled there for much longer. The song tradition of the urban lower classes had had adequate time to develop, although almost nothing is known of it before the beginning of this century. But whatever its beginnings, this urban song tradition was by its nature likely to be immune to the effects of the values and attitudes propagated by the nation state. And for a time it seems that it was.

It is often said that the *rebétika* are songs of the criminal underworld (Petropoulos, I., 1968; Butterworth and Schneider, 1975); and there is no lack of references in the songs to prisons and violence. But hashish-smoking, the one activity most widely extolled in songs of this type, did not really count as a criminal activity before the introduction of new drug laws in 1936, and for all the violence we encounter in the songs, their singers have surprisingly little to say on the subject of organised crime. Many songs recorded from the twenties and thirties appear to have been composed and performed by professional artistes who made a living out of appearances in the *tekédes* (hashish houses) and *café-amán* (oriental coffee houses), where audiences would have included a wide range of people from local shopkeepers and labourers to petty criminals of various sorts. It was not until the 1930s that the police began to gain the upper hand in certain areas of Athens and Piraeus, and when the law was enforced at best on a random basis the dividing line between criminal and non-criminal cannot have been very clear-cut.

The term *rebétika* by which these songs have come to be known has yet to be satisfactorily explained, and occurs relatively rarely in the songs themselves. Opinions differ considerably on the precise nature and delimitations of *rebétika* songs; but many of their structures and themes are taken from the demotic tradition, and the variants of songs found in different recordings strengthen the belief that this was an oral tradition, a natural development of the materials and techniques of the rural demotic songs in response to new circumstances; although at least for the period most fully documented, from about 1920 onwards, it was an oral tradition with a marked emphasis on personal, professional composition.

An event which had an important impact on the urban tradition of *rebétika* was the defeat of the Greek armies in western Turkey in 1922, and the ensuing exchange of populations between the two countries. Constantinople was exempted from the exchange, but a high proportion of the million or so Christians deported from Turkey to Greece came from Smyrna, which had been almost totally destroyed by the advancing army of Kemal Atatürk. Most settled in Piraeus and Salonica, and it is often said that the rise of *rebétika* in Greece dates from the time of this influx of refugees from Smyrna. In the songs commemorating these events it is characteristic that the grief of the refugee is centred upon a purely personal bitterness, the loss of a homeland for which 'Mother Greece' can never be an adequate substitute. Often these refugees were more fluent in Turkish than in Greek; if they came from Smyrna they were used to a sophisticated, cosmopolitan environment compared to which Athens or Salonica at that time must have seemed puritanical and provincial:

194

Τί σὲ μέλει ἐσένανε ἀπό ποῦ εἶμαι ἐγώ,
ἀπ' τὸ Καρατάσι, φῶς μου, ἢ ἀπ' τὸ Κορδελιό;

Τί σὲ μέλει ἐσένανε κι ὅλο μὲ ρωτᾶς
ἀπὸ ποιὸ χωριὸ εἶμαι ἐγώ, ἀφοῦ δὲ μ' ἀγαπᾶς;

'Απ' τὸν τόπο ποὺ εἶμαι ἐγώ, ξεύρουν ν' ἀγαποῦν,
ξεύρουν τὸν καημὸ νὰ κρύβουν, ξεύρουν νὰ γλεντοῦν.

Τί σὲ μέλει ἐσένανε κι ὅλο μὲ ρωτᾶς,
ἀφοῦ δὲ μὲ λυπᾶσαι, φῶς μου, καὶ μὲ τυραγνᾶς;

'Απ' τὴ Σμύρνη ἔρχομαι νὰ βρῶ παρηγοριά,
νὰ βρῶ μέσ' στὴν 'Αθήνα μας ἀγάπη κι ἀγκαλιά.

(Schorelis, 1977, p. 126)

What is it to you where I come from,
from Karatasi, light of my life, or from Kordelió?

What is it to you, that you keep asking me
what village I'm from, since you don't love me?

Where I come from they know how to love,
they know how to hide their sorrow, and how to enjoy themselves.

What is it to you, that you keep asking me,
since you've no pity for me, light of my life, and torment me?

I've come from Smyrna to find some comfort,
to find in this Athens of ours a loving embrace.

Here was a development of the oral demotic tradition capable of expressing the attitudes, values and aspirations of a class of people caught up in situations very far removed from those depicted in the rural songs. Up until the end of the thirties these songs retained their inventiveness and subtlety, even though the advent of sound recording had added an element of commercial competition and a sense of personal ownership of songs. (Composition remained largely an oral process, involving recombining the themes, formulas and lines of other songs – often 'claimed' by other composers.) Then this tradition, too, began to decline. Part of the reason was the gradual removal of the social conditions in which the *rebétika* had flourished, and in particular the drive begun by the Metaxas dictatorship in 1936 to stamp out the use of narcotics and the censorship of all reference to them on gramophone records.[3] (This law was enforced as recently as 1978, to prohibit the reissue of historic *rebétika* recordings.) But undoubtedly another cause had to do with commercial recording. When songs began to be distributed by means of gramophone records the immediate effect on the oral tradition seems to have been comparable to that of the introduction of printing on the historical tradition in Cyprus: the fixity of the recorded text did not in the least inhibit the inventiveness of oral composers. What it did, however, was to introduce the songs to audiences for which they had never been intended. *Rebétika* towards the end of the thirties began to be fashionable.

When in the mid-thirties Markos Vamvakaris, the foremost of a generation of professional *bouzoúki* players in Athens, began playing at Votanikós, a slum district in the suburbs of the city, the scene as he later described it was exaggerated, certainly, but not fictitious:

> It was pandemonium each evening. That meant work, lots of work. All sorts of people would come down there. High society aristocrats as well as *mánges* and bums and they raved it up till morning. All the froth of Athenian society came along. The whole of Kolonaki. They wouldn't dance, though, they just sat there. (Vamvakaris, 1973, p. 175)

And at the same period the *bouzoúki*, from being despised as a symbol of depravity and crime, began to acquire social cachet. Probably without intentional irony, Vamvakaris charted its rise in a song composed about the same time:

Μπουζούκι γλέντι τοῦ ντουνιᾶ
ποὺ γλένταγες τοὺς μάγκες
κι οἱ πλούσιοι σοῦ κάνανε, μπουζούκι μου
μεγάλες ματσαράγκες.
Τώρα σὲ βάλαν σὲ χαλιὰ
καὶ σὲ σαλόνια ἐπάνω
ἀκόμα κι ἀπὸ τὸ βιολί, μπουζούκι μου
δυὸ σκάλες παρὰ πάνω.
Μὲ ἀσανσὲρ ἀνέβηκες·
σὲ πολυκατοικίες
κι ἔπαιξες καὶ γουστάρανε, μπουζούκι μου
ἀνφὰν γκατὲ κυρίες.
Τώρα θ' ἀνέβεις πιὸ ψηλὰ
θὰ φτάσεις καὶ στὸν Ἄρη
καὶ ὁ Ἀπόλλων ὁ Θεός, μπουζούκι μου
κι αὐτὸς θὰ σὲ γουστάρει.

(Vamvakaris, 1973, pp. 130–1)

Bouzoúki, life's delight,
you used to delight the mánges
and the rich, my bouzoúki,
did you down.

Now they've spread out carpets for you
and in their salons placed you higher
even than the violin, my bouzoúki,
by two whole rungs.

You've risen in the lift
to apartment blocks
and played, and enfant gâté ladies, my bouzoúki,
found you to their taste.

Now you're going to rise still higher,
you'll get as far as Mars
and even Apollo the god, my bouzoúki,
will find he likes you really.

After the Second World War singers in the rebétika tradition (which after all was firmly commercial by this time and possibly had always been) directed their compositions more and more towards a middle-class audience. As the prosperity of audiences and singer-composers alike increased, the references to low life, the underworld and dubiously legal activities became distant and conventionalised and, what is more, conventionally shocking. This song of 1949, composed by Vasilis Tsitsanis to words perhaps by a hack writer, seems intended to supply a frisson of horror and disapproval by its portrayal from a safe distance of (conventionally) unconventional behaviour:

Τρέξε, μάγκα, νὰ ρωτήσεις νὰ σοῦ ποῦν ποιὰ εἶμαι γώ·
εἶμαι γὼ γυναίκα φίνα, ντερπεντέρισσα,
ποὺ τοὺς ἄντρες σὰν τὰ ζάρια τοὺς μπεγλέρισα.

Δὲ μὲ συγκινοῦν ἀγάπες φτάνει νὰ καλοπερνῶ·
κάθε βράδι νὰ τραβάω τὸ ποτήρι μου
καὶ νὰ σφάζονται λεβέντες γιὰ χατίρι μου.

Πῶς θὰ γίνω γὼ δική σου, πάψε νὰ τὸ συζητᾶς·
δὲ γουστάρω τὶς παρόλες, σοῦ ξηγήθηκα,
στὶς ταβέρνες καὶ στὰ καμπαρὲ γεννήθηκα.

(Petropoulos, I., 1968, p. 239)

Run, *mángas*, get them to tell you who I am;
I'm a woman of quality, a *derbendérissa*,
and I've played with men as I do with dice.

Love affairs don't move me, it's enough to enjoy myself;
every evening to pick up my glass
and have young men kill each other for my sake.

I'll never be yours – give up talking about it;
I don't like idle talk, I've told you,
I was born in the tavernas and the cabarets.[4]

(ii) Rural songs

Outside the urban centres where the singers of *rebétika* had scant respect for education and authority, the art of recombining traditional themes and formulas in response to new situations seems to have declined rapidly during the twentieth century. Only in those cases where history has continued to repeat itself, have events provoked a response in the traditional manner. This song of the German parachute landings in Crete in 1941 escapes incongruity because its language, form and attitude to the events described are consistent with those of other songs of different periods which evoke similar experiences:

- Παιδιά, κ' εἶντά 'ναι οἱ μπαλλωτές, στὸν κάμπο οἱ καμπάνες,
ἄτζεμπα γάμο κάνουνε ἢ πανηγύρι ἔχουν;
- Οὔτε καὶ γάμο κάνουνε, οὔτε καὶ πανηγύρι,
μόνο ἐπέσαν Γερμανοὶ ἀπὸ τ' ἀεροπλάνα
κι ἀρχίσανε τὸν πόλεμο στὸν κάμπο οἱ καμπῖτες.

(Academy of Athens, 1963, p. 179)

'Lads, what's that shooting, and bells ringing in the plain,
perhaps they're having a wedding or a festival?'
'It's not that they're having a wedding, or a festival either,
but Germans have been landing from the aeroplanes
and the plainsmen have started fighting in the plain.'

And in a similar way the formulaic patterns once regularly applied to the loss of a kleft or his band are effective and moving in this lament for the reprisal killings of the villagers of Dístomo in Roumeli in 1944:

(Ὢρ') ἕνα πουλάκ' ἐλάλησεν πρὸς τῆς Λειβαδιᾶς τὸ ρέμα
καὶ κοίταγε (παιδιά μ') τὸ Δίστομο.

(Ὦρε) μοιρολογοῦσε (παιδιά μ᾿) κι ἔλεγεν, (ὦρ᾿) μοιρολογεῖ καὶ
  λέει·
- Στὸ Δίστομο (παιδά μ᾿) σκοτώνουνε. . .

(McNeish, 1965, side 1, track 4)

(*Ore*) a bird gave voice towards the stream of Levadia
and was looking (my lads) at Dístomo.
(*Ore*) it lamented (my lads) and said, (*óre*) it laments and says,
'At Dístomo (my lads) they are killing people. . .'

These examples, by their relative rarity, make the exception that
proves the rule. Invasions and wholesale killings by an occupying power
are events that recur throughout Greek history. In these cases the tradition may still have the power to transform history into myth and thus
to relegate such terrible and irreversible events to a place in a timeless
pattern. But most of the events and situations with which the Greek
villager has been faced in this century have been the consequences of
new economic and social conditions: neither drastic enough, usually,
to call forth this kind of response, nor, without irrelevance or quaint-
ness, assimilable into an existing pattern of song.

(iii) Andártika

The same period of the Second World War and the civil war which followed in the Greek mainland, gave rise to a great many songs among
the various partisan groups in the mountains. Known generally as
andártika (partisan songs) these songs were banned from public performance in Greece after the civil war and did not surface again until
1974, when legal recognition was again granted to the Communist
Party. The same censorship which can be used to block any mention of
narcotics on gramophone records also continues to impede the issue of
andártika on record, presumably because of the political content of
very many of them, and at least until 1977 the only record of these
songs to have appeared was in a French translation. The songs that have
recently reemerged have mostly been those of the E.A.M.–E.L.A.S.
groups which from the beginning had been dominated by the Greek
Communist Party,[5] and the purpose of the revival has been overtly
political. The content of these songs is all too often militaristic, jingling
propaganda, and their tunes tend to be military or popular tunes borrowed from elsewhere. The majority of these must be counted as 'popular song' rather than folk song (cf. I.F.M.C., 1955, p. 23), but it is
interesting to discover that *some* songs of E.A.M.–E.L.A.S., as well as

of the more right-wing E.D.E.S group, appear to have been composed by guerrilla fighters in the field, in circumstances probably very similar to those of the klefts more than a hundred years before. The forms, attitudes and themes of kleftic songs are sometimes revived among the *andártika*, and it is probable that this was not an artificial revival but a natural expression of partisans who had grown up hearing and singing traditional kleftic songs, subsequently finding themselves in closely parallel circumstances.

The song of Nikos Pakos is composed entirely of traditional formulas. The interjections addressed to the hero of the song, breaking the continuity of the lines, are also traditional in kleftic songs as they are sung.

Τ' ἔχουν τς' Ἠπείρου τὰ βουνά,

         καημένε Νίκο Πάκο μ'

καὶ στέκουν βουρκωμένα,

         Νίκο Πάκο μ' ἀντρειωμένε.

Μήνα χαλάζι τὰ βαρεῖ,

         καημένε Νίκο Πάκο μ'

μήνα βροχὴ τὰ δέρνει

         Νίκο Πάκο μ' ἀντρειωμένε.

Οὔτε χαλάζι τὰ βαρεῖ

         καημένε Νίκο Πάκο μ'

οὔτε βροχὴ τὰ δέρνει

         Νίκο Πάκο μ' ἀντρειωμένε.

Κλαῖνε τὸν καπετάνιο τους

         καημένε Νίκο Πάκο μ'

ὅπου εἶναι σκοτωμένος

         Νίκο Πάκο μ' ἀντρειωμένε.

(Anon., 1975, p. 59)

What is the matter with the mountains of Epiros,
         my poor Nikos Pakos
that they are shrouded so,
         Nikos Pakos my brave man.
Perhaps they're lashed with hail, perhaps they're whipped with rain.
It's not that they're lashed with hail, nor that they're whipped with rain.
They're weeping for their *kapetánios* who has been killed.

200

Other songs of the partisans show varying degrees of a hybrid style, evidently based on traditional forms but often with a refrain which seems to belong to popular song (cf. Anon, 1975, pp. 12, 56, 69).

(iv) Distichs

The most lasting type of folk song has proved to be the rhyming distich. The many lyrical songs which are still composed using traditional material (love songs, wedding songs and funeral laments) are very often now cast in this form, and the use of the rhyming couplet, which in Fauriel's day was confined to the islands and towns, has now spread throughout the mainland of Greece as well. The art is still most developed, however, in Crete, the islands of the Dodecanese and Cyprus. In the villages in all three places a substantial part of a wedding feast or *paniyíri* consists of impromptu *mantinádes* or *tshiattísmata* sung usually by the men, either in dialogue form or in rotation. In Karpathos it is the custom on the second day of a wedding feast for each of the male guests (often the whole male population of the village) to toast the bride and sing a *mantináda* in her honour. Most of the men are able to provide a suitable *mantináda* of their own, either put together on the spot or perhaps, if they are less inspired on the occasion, or less inventive, one that they have used before; while a man who is unable to express himself with the required tact and humour in couplet form will use a traditional, well-known couplet of praise to accompany his toast. (He may not, however, use a couplet which is *known* to have been composed by someone else in the village.)

One of the reasons for the survival of the distich as a medium for traditional composition is its extreme versatility. To make a song of any length, using largely given formulas and themes, is difficult if not impossible outside a relatively restricted range of subject matter. But to compose a two-line epigram using the same structural techniques is hardly more difficult whatever the theme chosen. Most of the distichs published in folk song collections are innocent enough compliments addressed by young men to young girls. But there is a possibility of humour and amusing word-play in these couplets which a skilled singer will use to the full, as in this *mantináda* told me by a singer and *lýra*-player from Crete, which makes tongue-twisting use of the very similar words in the Cretan dialect for a boy and a girl:

Θέλει καρύδι καρυδιὰ καὶ μέλισσα τὸ μέλι,
θέλει κοπέλι κοπελιὰ καὶ κοπελιὰ κοπέλι.

A walnut needs a walnut tree and the honey-bee the honey,
a boy needs a girl and a girl a boy.

Or a *mantináda* may sum up, slightly ruefully, an infinite wisdom which is refreshingly untraditional in its lack of reverence for a traditional past:

Τοῦτον τὸν κόσμο, νούρι μου, ἄλλοι τὸν εἶχαν πρῶτα,
ἐδὰ τὸν ἔχομε κι ἐμεῖς, μὰ δὲ μᾶς τὸν ἐδῶκα.

(Lioudaki, 1936, p. 251, No. 32)

This world, young man, belonged to others before us,
now it's ours, but they didn't give it to us.

An equal diversity is found in the Dodecanese and in Cyprus, where the competition between opposing *tshiattistés* is still held as part of the *Kataklysmós* (Ascension) celebrations in Larnaca on 1 July. The subjects most favoured in Cypriot *tshiattísmata* today are as various as in the *mantinádes* of Crete and the Dodecanese. Organised competitions have encouraged a fluency of direct personal insult, and alongside the ubiquitous theme of love there flourish many fine *tshiattísmata* dedicated to the elaboration of sexual fantasy. There is nothing that cannot be expressed in this form, no matter how serious or banal. In 1975 I was present at a festival in the Cypriot village of Ormidia, where there was a large encampment of refugees from the Turkish invasion of the year before. The occasion was no means a melancholy one, for all that, and the *tshiattísmata* were declaimed vigorously, with characteristically loud amplification. In this 'couplet' (in fact it spills over into three rhyming lines) the word *foussáto* (army) is a Byzantine military term going back to the ninth century, and now obsolete except in popular tradition, while 'NATO' with which it rhymes requires no explanation.

Γιὰ νά 'ρθει ἡ ζωὴ παλιὰ ἐν ἔν' τωρὰ δυνάτον,
μ' ἔξι χιλιάες πού 'φαεν τὸ τούρκικο φουσσᾶτο,
μῆτε ἀθ θέλετε κι ἐσεῖς, ἡ χοῦντα καὶ τὸ ΝΑΤΟ.

To bring back the old life is now not possible,
with six thousand victims of the Turkish army –
not even should *you* wish it, [Greek] junta and NATO.

Notes

CHAPTER 1

1 It cannot be established exactly when Fauriel began seriously to plan his collection. Ibrovac believes that the project was 'very probably' not conceived before the 1821 uprising. But Fauriel's acquaintance with the prominent expatriates Korais and Basilis goes back to 1793 (Ibrovac, 1966, p. 114).

2 Traditionally regarded as above reproach, Passow seems to have been guilty in a small way of the practice of conflating two or more variants to arrive at an 'established text' of a song, for which N. G. Politis has been justly criticised (Politis, A., 1973, p. vii). But it is worth remembering that very few texts published in the nineteenth century are likely to be *exact* reproductions of oral performances.

CHAPTER 2

1 The attempt is frequently made, all the same. Professor Linos Politis, otherwise eminently sane in his judgements, has even written of their 'guileless demotic charm' (1973, p. 39).

2 The grounds for these accusations are slight. The question of idolatry is presumably open to theological debate, although the profound Christian faith of the Anastenarides is not in doubt. The charge of orgiastic behaviour is quite unfounded and seems to be based on the (non-proven) theory of the ritual's Dionysian origin.

3 It is interesting to note that, although names of characters in Greek songs are by no means stable and substitution of one name for another is commonly found, the name Kostantinos rarely varies in versions of this song. In the brief Sarakatsan version (Tziatzios, 1928, p. 31) the hero is called Yannis, and in the Pontic version (Lampsidis, 1960, pp. 40-3) Marandon (probably meaning the 'unwithered one'), but St Constantine is still his patron saint.

4 While in most of the versions so far discussed the sheep, dogs, etc. come by their fine accoutrements, if they have any, miraculously, in examples 1 and 5 they are given them by the shepherd–wife as here; and in example 3 there is an interesting verbal parallel with this song, in the word *asimogioúrtanou* (silver ribbon). The word *giortánia*, or *gioúrtanou*, interestingly enough echoes the *Yordáni potamó* (River Jordan) which is only found in the Anastenaria version.

5 The relation between song texts and ritual in a Greek example and its implications for the existing scholarly taxonomy of folk songs has been discussed from the anthropologist's point of view by Michael Herzfeld (1974; 1977). See also Chapter 8, on ritual songs, whose content and structure are specifically determined by their ritual function, and whose performance is wholly restricted to the ritual context.

CHAPTER 3

1 Sources for the numbered examples in this chapter are as follows. (1) Petropoulos, 1959, p. 227, No. 27A, l. 7; (2) *Laografía* 3, 1911, p. 266, No. 8, l. 2; (3) Ioannou, 1966, p. 424, l. 4; (4) Passow, 1860, p. 257, No. 353, l. 3; (5) *Laografía* 5, 1915, p. 107, No. 96B, l. 3; (6) *Laografía* 5, 1915, p. 71, No. 37B, l. 4; (7) von Haxthausen, 1935, p. 48, l. 3; (8) Jeannaraki, 1876, p. 94, No. 72, l. 12; (9) *Laografía* 19, 1961, p. 373, No. 24, l. 8; (10) Passow, 1860, p. 388, ll. 1–11; (11) Petropoulos, 1959, p. 65, No. 47, l. 1; (12) Spandonidi, 1939, p. 3, No. 1, l. 4; (13) Tziatzios, 1928, p. 52, No. 126, l. 5; (14) Petropoulos, 1959, p. 45, No. 16A, l. 6; (15) Tziatzios, 1928, p. 65, No. 159, l. 1; (16) *Laografía* 1, 1909, pp. 224–5, l. 12; (17) = ex. 13, l. 8; (18) Hasiotis, 1866, p. 155, l. 1; (19) Jeannaraki, 1876, p. 149, No. 155, l. 1; (20) *Laografía* 8, 1921, pp. 533–4, l. 2; (21) = ex. 16, l. 8; (22) Passow, 1860, p. 379, No. 497, l. 1 (cf. l. 10); (23) *Laografía* 5, 1915, pp. 180–2, l. 47; (24) Passow, 1860, p. 338, No. 458, l. 32; (25) Petropoulos, 1958, pp. 19–20, l. 24; (26) Petropoulos, 1959, p. 67, No. 55, l. 1; (27) = ex. 24, l. 34; (28) Fauriel, 1825, p. 4; (29) Petropoulos, 1958, p. 169, No. 29; (30) Pasayanis, 1928, p. 13; (31) Manousos, 1850, I, p. 79; (32) Passow, 1860, p. 5, No. 1; (33) Fauriel, 1824, p. 98; (34) Passow, 1860, p. 97, No. 122; (35) *Laografía* 6, 1917, p. 363, No. 3; (36) Passow, 1860, p. 66, No. 80; (37) Manousos, 1850, I, p. 110; (38) Passow, 1860, p. 30, No. 35, l. 2; (39) Passow, 1860, p. 41, No. 46, l. 1; (40) Hasiotis, 1866, p. 105, l. 6; (41) Petropoulos, 1959, pp. 80–1, No. 88, l. 2; (42) Fauriel, 1824, p. 288, l. 5; (43) Fauriel, 1824, p. 296, l. 8; (44) Passow, 1860, p. 158, No. 216; (45) Fauriel, 1824, p. 194, l. 4; (46) Academy of Athens, 1963, p. 237, No. 5, l. 6; (47) Academy of Athens, 1963, p. 202, No. IVa, l. 1; (48) Academy of Athens, 1963, pp. 200–1, l. 11; (49) *Laografía* 5, 1915, p. 71, No. 37, l. 2; (50) Petropoulos, 1958, pp. 107–8, l. 16; (51) Kyriakidis, 1926, pp. 140–9, l. 17; (52) Passow, 1860, p. 83, No. 102, l. 2; (53) *Laografía* 1, 1909, pp. 600–2, l. 7; (54) Jeannaraki, 1876, pp. 203–4, l. 3; (55) *Zográfios Agón* 1, 1891, p. 73, l. 3; (56) Destouny, 1877, l. 103; (57) Petropoulos, 1958, pp. 124–5, ll. 11–12; (58) Jeannaraki, 1876, p. 154, No. 170, ll. 2–3; (59) = ex. 31, ll. 2–3; (60) Petropoulos, 1958, pp. 134–5, l. 24; (61) Passow, 1860, pp. 394–6, l. 39; (62) Dawkins, 1934, pp. 113–14, l. 11; (63) Lampsidis, 1960, pp. 60–1, No. 17, l. 1; (64) Passow, 1860, p. 28, No. 32, l. 5.

2 The early history of this metre and some of the controversial problems of its development will be mentioned in Chapter 5. A useful critical guide to the literature on the subject is to be found in Alexiou and Holton, 1976.

CHAPTER 4

1 Legrand, 1880, p. 17; Passow, 1860, p. 262, No. 367 (translations by Alexiou). The first passage, said by Alexiou to be of the twelfth or thirteenth centuries, is by the Cypriot monk Neophytos Enkleistos who flourished at the end of the twelfth century (Tsiknopoulos, 1952, pp. 45-6). Interestingly enough it was the same Cypriot monk who recorded, and then re-worked in a poem of his own, the earliest known fragment of a modern folk song (see p. 78).

2 Sources for numbered examples in this chapter are as follows. (1) Petropoulos, 1959, p. 105; (2) Petropoulos, 1958, p. 35, No. 18, l. 6; (3) Petropoulos, 1959, p. 250, No. 82B, l. 6; (4) Politis, N. G., 1885, pp. 229-31, ll. 44-9; (5) *ibid.* pp. 235-6, ll. 29-30; (6) *ibid.* pp. 239-41, ll. 29-30; (7) *ibid.* pp. 241-2; ll. 28-33; (8) *ibid.* pp. 243-5, ll. 50-2, 58-60; (9) *ibid.* pp. 255-6, ll. 29-34; (10) *ibid.* pp. 256-7, ll. 24-6; (11)-(13) see note 3; (14) Petropoulos, 1958, pp. 3-4, ll. 20-3; (15) Petropoulos, 1958, p. 4, ll. 9-14; (16)-(22) see note 3; (23) and (24) Jeannaraki, 1876, pp. 122-4; ll. 2, 46; (25) Jeannaraki, 1876, pp. 237-8, l. 49.

3 Unpublished material from the University of Ioannina Archive is included here by kind permission of the Director, Folk Museum and Archive, University of Ioannina.

4 For a detailed analysis of such thematic patterns in the ballads of north-east Scotland see Buchan, 1972, pp. 87-144.

5 cf. the interesting comments on what he calls *ars combinatoria* in this song by Dronke (1976, pp. 29-32).

CHAPTER 5

1 Professor Linos Politis, whose views on the Escorial manuscript are generally in agreement with my own, suggests that the folk songs of the death of Diyenis, in which Diyenis is *actually named*, may derive from the epic, since the name must have been invented by the author of the epic (1970, p. 578). I agree with him on the literary origin of the name, but apart from this the songs in question have very little to do with the epic. There is no reason why the name alone should not have gone into the folk tradition, and become central to a song otherwise composed of entirely traditional elements.

2 The only manuscript of 'Armouris' to be published in full is that of St Petersburg (Destouny, 1877; reprinted in *Athínaion* 8, 1879, pp. 385-94). This has been republished subsequently in considerably amended versions by Kyriakidis (1926, pp. 119 ff.), Kalonaros (1941, II, pp. 213-17), and Grégoire (1942, pp. 204-12), all apparently without recourse to the original manuscript. Of the dated manuscript, Codex 35 (Topkapı Palace, Istanbul) only a critical apparatus, listing divergences from the St Petersburg manuscript, has been published (Bouboulidis, 1964, pp. 138-44). Some doubt has been cast on the accuracy of Bouboulidis' readings (Papathomopoulos, 1974, pp. 466-7), and a brief reply to this challenge (Bouboulidis, 1975) is no substitute for a full publication of the text.

The second text is interesting because it mentions the date of copying, 1461, implying that the song was then current in this form. The divergences between the texts and the significance of their having been written down at all are questions for further study. All references to 'Armouris' here are to the original reading of the St Petersburg manuscript by Destouny.

CHAPTER 6

1 The version published by N. G. Politis (1914, p. 11 = Petropoulos, 1958, p. 151, No. 2) is a conflation of this song with the opening lines of Manousos, 1850, II, p. 119, on which see p. 98.

2 This last song (Petropoulos, 1958, pp. 155–6 = Ioannidis, 1870, p. 287, No. 20) was thought by its first editor to refer to the sack of Trebizond in 1461. It is clear from the text, however, which refers to *i Póli* and *Romanía*, unambiguously Constantinople and the Byzantine Empire respectively, that its subject is the sack of the latter city.

3 See, respectively, Kriaris, 1920, p. 44 and Herzfeld, 1973, *passim*; Passow, 1860, p. 365; Spandonidi, 1939, p. 3; Petropoulos, 1958, pp. 161–2; Fauriel, 1825, p. 4; Passow, 1860, p. 364, No. 485a.

4 See, respectively, Kyriakidis, 1965, p. 92; Petropoulos, 1958, p. 169; Petropoulos, 1958, pp. 169–70.

CHAPTER 7

1 On the 'Dead Brother' see, for example, Wollner, 1882; Psichari, 1884; Politis, N. G., 1885; Impellizzeri, 1944; Lavagnini, 1953; Dronke, 1976, pp. 23–9; and the critical bibliography by Katerina Krikos (1975). See also Brewster and Tarsouli (1961) which typifies the dangers and limitations of applying the 'historical-geographical' approach to comparative material. The authors discuss *similarities* between the Greek 'Handjeris' (Harzanis) ballad and two Child ballads 'without', in their own words, 'however, attempting to establish any influence or relationship' (p. 3). The result, perhaps inevitably, is desultory and inconsequential.

2 The instinct to claim national ownership of ballads is not confined to scholars whose work is otherwise of a high standard, such as Vargyas and Megas. An apparently 'official' claim to Albanian ownership of the 'Bridge of Arta' ballads attacks simultaneously on two fronts – first showing the alleged primacy of the Shkodër (Skutari) versions and then, to reinforce the point, claiming that even if this were not so and Arta were the 'original' location of the ballad, the region round Arta has belonged culturally to the Albanians (or Illyrians) since prehistoric times (Sako, 1966).

3 In Cypriot versions which begin thus or with a vaguer indication ('Down at the five rivers, down at the five roads') the bridge is often called the Bridge of Hair at the *end* of the song (Papadopoullos, 1975, pp. 28, 176; Megas, 1971, p. 81, summary of a text from Athens Academy Archive). These instances have not been included in Megas' statistical summary.

4 I have been unable to find any reliable information about the building of the present bridge outside the town of Arta. According to the *Megáli Ellinikí*

Enkyklopaídia it was built either in 1602 or 1606, but the source of the author's information (Karamanos, 1928) seems to be a folk tradition (Politis, 1904, II, pp. 774–5; Megas, 1971, p. 91).

5 Baud-Bovy thought that the 'Bridge of Hair' was the most frequent but disregarded its importance on the grounds that 'ce nom, lui non plus, ne doit pas être primitif' (1936, p. 169). The suggestion was taken up again by K. Romaios, who correctly saw the song as essentially mythical in nature but made the mistake of assigning its *origin* to a specific local ritual, the Rousalia (Romaios, 1952). In fact, as Megas has shown, 'Arta' occurs considerably more frequently in the recorded variants of the song, although this need not diminish the importance of the 'Bridge of Hair'.

As to the distribution of the 'Bridge of Hair', this is found in Epiros, the Peloponnese, the Cyclades, Thrace, Asia Minor and offshore islands, the Dodecanese, Pontos, Cappadocia (Megas, 1971, p. 93) and Cyprus (see note 3). It is not found in Crete, although the opening of this Cretan version conveys a similar sense:

Κάτω 's τὸ μαῦρον ποταμὸ καμάρα θεμελιόνουν,
Καμάρα θενὰ χτίσουνε μὴν πνίγουντ' οἱ διαβάταις.

(Jeannaraki, 1876, p. 209)

Down at the black (unhappy) river they are digging the foundations for an arch,
they're going to build an arch so that travellers won't drown.

To save travellers from drowning is an improbable reason for building a bridge, unless it is in fact the 'Bridge of Hair', which serves precisely that purpose.

6 The hybrid form τριχογιόφυρο (hairbridge) is also found in one version of the song from the Peloponnese (Megas, 1971, p. 92).

7 That the popular belief about the hair bridge had a Turkish origin was first suggested by B. Schmidt (1871, p. 240) and rejected out of hand by N. G. Politis as 'most improbable' (1901, p. 623).

8 Even the most objectively constructed models, where the constituent elements of a myth are represented by + and − signs, involve the choice of a criterion for awarding these values, and this may often be more arbitrary, or external to the myth, than we would like to think. See, for example, Maranda and Maranda, 1971, and the comments by Herzfeld on a specific case (1974a). It would be as well, perhaps, to think of such complex mathematical models for mythical structures more as a modern extension of the mythical process than as an ultimate solution to the problems of myths.

9 Fauriel, 1824, 1825; Passow, 1860; Kind, 1861; Jeannaraki, 1876; Kanellakis, 1890; Anagnostou, 1903; Louloudopoulos, 1903; Pahtikos, 1905; Mihailidis-Nouaros, 1928; Pasayanis, 1928; Tziatzios, 1928; Odeon, 1930; Baud-Bovy, 1935, 1938; Perdika, 1940; Tarsouli, 1944; Argenti and Rose, 1949; Petropoulos, 1958, 1959; Yangas, 1959; Ioannou, 1966; *Laografía*, 1909–74; *Arheíon Póntou*, 1938–46.

CHAPTER 8

1 Athenaeus, VIII 360b–d. This whole passage in Athenaeus is, or purports to be, a quotation from Theognis' *Rhodian festivals*. Almost nothing is known of this writer or when he wrote. Athenaeus himself wrote in the second or third centuries AD, and his source may well be a few hundred years older.

2 The word *helidónisma*, now the accepted term for these songs, is not found in ancient sources or in modern songs, but is a scholarly invention (Herzfeld, 1977, p. 29). The *helidónisma* was first discussed by Fauriel (1824, p. cix), and recently a detailed study of these songs was made by Herzfeld in an unpublished thesis (1972). Some of his conclusions have now been published (1974; 1977).

3 On the relation between the literary and oral laments in Byzantine and modern tradition, see Alexiou, 1975, *passim*.

4 The pattern of question and answer, and even part of the wording in the reply are also echoed in the apocryphal prose *Acta Pilati* which as Alexiou has shown 'constitutes a remarkable link between some of the earlier Byzantine material and modern folk tradition' (1974, p. 68; cf. Bouvier, 1976, pp. 229–30).

5 The Cretan poet Sahlikis was the first to use the couplet form consistently, and Morgan dates his career to roughly 1470–95 (1960, p. 86). But it has recently been argued that Sahlikis lived a full century earlier, in the *fourteenth* century (Manoussakas and van Gemert, forthcoming).

CHAPTER 9

1 I use the word 'professional' in this sense throughout the chapter. The status of many of these poets is usually only vaguely defined – most are unlikely to be full-time professionals, or necessarily to subsist on their professional earnings. Such poets are often described elsewhere as 'professional or semi-professional'.

2 Not all of these devices will be used by every professional singer. The importance of topical, historical narrative, however, is constant in British minstrel and broadside ballads (Wells, 1950, p. 210; Shepard, 1962, *passim*; 1973, p. 39) and in Greek professional songs or *rímes* from several areas (Politis, N. G., 1915, p. 505), so that it is not surprising to find certain of the accompanying devices recurring throughout these distinct traditions.

3 cf. W. B. Yeats: 'In primitive times the blind man became a poet, as he became a fiddler in our villages, because he had to be driven out of activities all his nature cried for, before he could be contented with the praise of life' (1924, p. 344).

4 For a cross-section of this material, mostly composed and recorded in the nineteenth century, see Jeannaraki, 1876, pp. 1–89, and Kriaris, 1920, pp. 7–184. These sections include briefer songs which belong to the demotic tradition and a small number of songs which appear to be hybrid, but all the longer songs appear to be the work of *rimadóri*.

5 Petropoulos, 1954; Notopoulos, 1954. With the collaboration of Professor D. Petropoulos, Notopoulos collected a large amount of 'epic' material from Crete and Cyprus during 1953. The recordings, of which almost all remain unpublished, were deposited in the Folklore Archive of the Academy of Athens and in the J. A. Notopoulos collection in the Milman Parry Archive, Widener Library, Harvard.

6 For texts of these long Cypriot narrative songs both professional and traditional, see Sakellarios, 1891; Farmakidis, 1926; and Papadopoullos, 1975. Songs of *pyitárides* with their music have been transcribed by Kallinikos, 1951, pp. 130-5; 154-97.

7 This situation has begun to be remedied with the publication of Yangoullis, 1976.

8 Marshall, following Fauriel (1824, pp. 169-71), gives the date of Andonis' death as 1807, but A. Politis, basing his account on a variety of sources, puts it later, in 1808 or 1809 (Politis, A., 1973, p. 61).

9 The text, which was transcribed with chaotic orthography, was reprinted twice by Legrand (1870; 1874, pp. 108-14). The portions here reproduced follow the Stephanopolis' line divisions, according to which each political line of fifteen syllables is printed as two lines.

10 Of the sixty-two formulas noted by Jeffreys (1973) with more than eight occurrences in the poem, all but a few are of the type,

ὁ πρίγκιπα Γυλιάμος	Prince William
ἐκείνην τὴν ἡμέραν	that day,

that is, inexpert 'padding' of a proper name or commonly recurring noun to fill one half of the political line. Formulas of this type are also found in abundance in the historical tradition although they tend to be scrupulously avoided in the 'traditional' demotic songs. The following examples from Jeffreys' list can also be paralleled in the historical tradition:

μικροί τε καὶ μεγάλοι	great and small,
πεζοὶ καὶ καβαλλάροι	footmen and horsemen (also in the
demotic tradition),	
καθὼς/ὡσὰν σὲ τὸ ἀφηγοῦμαι	just as I'm telling you,
κι ὁ ρήγας ὡς τὸ ἤκουσε	and when the king heard (also in the
demotic tradition),	
τῆς γῆς καὶ τῆς θαλάσσης	by land and sea,
Φράγκοι τε καὶ Ρωμαῖοι	Franks and Greeks.

CHAPTER 10

1 I am grateful to Dr C. J. Wickham for bringing this passage to my attention.

2 I am grateful to Dr M. Alexiou, who made the recording on a field trip, for this information.

3 Greece had been a signatory to a series of international agreements restricting the use of narcotics, in particular of opium, since 1912. Of these by far the most radical was that of the 'Convention pour la Répression du trafic illicite

des droghes luisibles', drawn up in Geneva on 26 June 1936, less than two months before the Metaxas regime came to power. Although the agreement was not ratified by Greece for another two years, there is no doubt of Metaxas' zeal in implementing its terms, which included the imposition of severe penalties for the use of hashish.

4 The most useful and the only really scholarly work on the *rebétika* is a doctoral thesis by E. Gauntlett (1978), as yet unpublished. I am grateful to Dr Gauntlett and to Mr R. Conway Morris for a great deal of information, and many useful discussions, on this subject.

5 For an account of the different partisan groups and the events in which they were involved, see Woodhouse, 1976.

Glossary of Greek words Transliterated in the Text

akritiká – term used by scholars to describe narrative ballads, said to be connected with the hero of the medieval epic, *Diyenis Akritis.*

amanés (pl. *amanédes*) – rhyming couplet, often resigned or lugubrious in character (Asia Minor).

andártika – songs of the partisans of the Second World War and Greek civil war of 1944–9.

armatolíki (pl. *armatolíkia*) – locally recruited armed bands, used by the Ottoman authorities to contain brigandage in parts of Greece in the seventeenth and eighteenth centuries.

armatolós (pl. *armatolí*) – one who serves in an *armatolíki.* By the end of the eighteenth century often indistinguishable from a kleft.

bouzoúki – plucked instrument of the pandore family, popular with singers of *rebétika* from about 1930 onwards.

derbendérissa – a woman of irrepressible individuality, selfishness, energy and perhaps glamour (*rebétika*).

devletli (Turkish) – an honorary title.

helidónisma (pl. *helidonísmata*) – term used by scholars to describe the 'swallow song' traditionally sung on 1 March.

kálanda – carols; folk songs for various religious festivals.

kapetános (pl. *kapetánii*) – leader of a band of klefts or insurgents.

katharévousa – the 'purifying' form of the Greek language, in contrast to *dimotikí*, the vernacular.

kléftika – songs of the klefts.

kléftis – kleft; a 'social bandit' of the Greek highlands.

kondýli – a slate-pencil used by children in primary school.

kontákion – a type of hymn of the early Byzantine church.

leventiá – manliness, including youth, courage and vigour.

lýra – a three-stringed bowed instrument of the rebec family, especially popular in Crete.

lyráris – a player of the *lýra.* Sometimes, but not necessarily, equivalent to a *rimadóros* (Crete).

mánges – characters of the urban underworld in the early twentieth century: proud, flamboyant, frequently antisocial in behaviour (*rebétika*).

mantináda (pl. *mantinádes*) – rhyming couplet (Crete, Dodecanese).

pallikári (pl. *pallikária*) – a brave, handsome young man.

211

paniyíri – (village) festival.

paraloyés – term used by scholars to describe narrative ballads on a range of subjects.

poústika – appropriate to perverts.

pyitáris (pl. *pyitárides*) – a professional singer–composer (Cyprus).

rebétika – songs of the urban lower classes, mostly known from the period between 1920 and the mid-fifties.

rimadóros (pl. *rimadóri*) – a professional singer–composer (Crete).

rímes – long narrative songs on topical or historical subjects.

rizítiko (pl. *rizítika*) – traditional song of west Crete.

tambourás – a plucked instrument of the pandore family, common in the nineteenth century, similar to the modern *bouzoúki* and Turkish *tanbur saz*.

tshiáttisma (pl. *tshiattísmata*) – rhyming couplet (Cyprus).

tshiattistés – contestants improvising rhyming couplets (Cyprus).

Bibliography

Abbott, G. F., 1903. *Macedonian folklore*. Cambridge.

Academy of Athens, 1963. Ἀκαδημία Ἀθηνῶν. Ἑλληνικὰ δημοτικὰ τραγούδια (ἐκλογή). Τόμ. Α΄. Athens.

Alexiou, L., 1956. Ἀλεξίου, Λ. "Ριμάδα γιὰ τὴ θρόνιαση τῆς μητρόπολης τοῦ Ἁγίου Μηνᾶ." *Kritiká Hroniká* 10, 101-33.

Alexiou, M., 1974. *The ritual lament in Greek tradition*. Cambridge.

1975. 'The lament of the Virgin in Byzantine literature and modern Greek folk-song.' *Byzantine and Modern Greek Studies* 1, 111-40.

1978. 'Modern Greek folklore and its relation to the past: the evolution of Charos in Greek tradition.' In *Proceedings of the 1975 Symposium of Modern Greek Studies,* University of California Press, 211-26.

Alexiou, M. and Holton, D., 1976, 'The origins and development of *politikos stichos*: a select critical bibliography.' *Mandatofóros* (Birmingham) 9, 22-34.

Anagnostou, 1903. Ἀναγνώστου, Σ. *Λεσβιακά, ἤτοι συλλογὴ λαογραφικῶν περὶ Λέσβου πραγματείων*. Athens.

Anon., 1975. *Τραγούδια τῆς ἀντίστασης καὶ τοῦ ἐμφύλιου*. Ἑλληνικὰ θέματα 15, Athens.

Apostolakis, 1929. Ἀποστολάκης, Γ. *Τὰ δημοτικὰ τραγούδια. Οἱ συλλογές*. Athens.

1950. *Τὸ κλέφτικο τραγούδι· τὸ πνεῦμα καὶ ἡ τέχνη του*. Athens.

Aravantinos, 1880. Ἀραβαντινός, Π. *Συλλογὴ δημώδων ἀσμάτων τῆς Ἠπείρου*. Athens.

Argenti, P. P. and Rose, H. J., 1949. *The folk-lore of Chios*. Vol. 2. Cambridge.

Baud-Bovy, S., 1935, 1938. *Chansons du Dodécanèse*. 2 vols. Athens.

1936. *La chanson populaire grecque du Dodécanèse, I. Les textes*. Paris.

1946. 'Sur le Χελιδόνισμα.' *Byzantina–Metabyzantina* 1/1, 23-32.

1956. 'La strophe de distiques rimés dans la chanson grecque.' In *Studia Memoriae Belae Bartok Sacra,* pp. 365-83. Budapest.

1973. "Ἡ ἐπικράτηση τοῦ δεκαπεντασύλλαβου στὸ ἑλληνικὸ δημοτικὸ τραγούδι." *Ellinika* 26, 301-13.

Bellaire, J. P., 1805. *Précis des opérations générales de la division française du Levant*. Paris.

Bouboulidis, 1964. Μπουμπουλίδης, Φ. Κ. "Ἀνέκδοτοι παραλλαγαὶ δημώδων μεσαιωνικῶν κειμένων." *Athiná* 67, 107-44.

1975. "Παρατηρήσεις εἰς Διορθώσεις σὲ κείμενα τῆς δημώδους λογοτεχνίας." *Athiná* 75, 49-53.

Bibliography

Bouvier, B., 1960. Δημοτικὰ τραγούδια ἀπὸ χειρόγραφο τῆς Μονῆς τῶν Ἰβήρων. Athens.

1976. *Le mirologue de la Vierge. Chansons et poèmes grecs sur la Passion du Christ.* Bibliotheca Helvetica Romana XVI, Rome.

Brewster, P. G. and Tarsouli, G., 1961. '"Handjeris and Liogenniti" and Child 76 and 110. A study in similarities.' *FF Communications* (Helsinki) 74/ 183.

Bronson, B. H., 1954. 'The morphology of ballad tunes.' *Journal of American Folklore* 67, 5-6.

Buchan, D., 1972. *The ballad and the folk.* London.

Büdinger, M., 1866. *Mittelgriechisches Volksepos. Ein Versuch.* Leipzig.

Butterworth, K. and Schneider, S., 1975. *Rebetika: songs from the old Greek underworld.* Athens.

Cameron, A., 1973. *Porfyrius the charioteer.* Oxford.

1976. *Circus factions. Blues and greens at Rome and Byzantium.* Oxford.

Campbell, J. K., 1964. *Honour, family and patronage: a study of institutions and moral values in a Greek mountain community.* Oxford.

Child, F. J., 1957. *The English and Scottish popular ballads.* 5 vols. New York. Reprint of first edition, Boston, 1882-97.

Chomsky, N., 1964. *Current issue in linguistic theory.* The Hague.

Clogg, R., 1976. *The movement for Greek independence, 1770-1821. A collection of documents.* London.

Dakin, D., 1972. *The unification of Greece, 1770-1923.* London.

Dawkins, R. M., 1934. 'Modern Greek folk songs from Cappadocia.' *American Journal of Archaeology* 38, 112-22.

De Lusignan, F. E., 1580. *Description de toute l'isle de Cypre.* Paris. Photographic reprint, Les Editions l'Oiseau, Famagusta, 1968.

Destouny, G., 1877. Τοῦ 'Αρμούρη. Ἆσμα δημοτικὸν τῆς βυξαντινῆς ἐποχῆς. St Petersburg. Reprinted in *Athínaion* 8, 1879, 385-94.

Dimaras, C. T., 1974. *A history of modern Greek literature.* English edition, London.

Dodwell, E., 1819. *A classical and topographical tour through Greece, during the years 1801, 1805, and 1806.* 2 vols. London.

Dorson, R. M., 1964. 'Current folklore theories.' *Current Anthropology* 4, 93-112.

Doulyerakis, 1956. Δουλγεράκης, Ε. Ι. '"Ανέκδοτοι δημοτικαὶ ιπαραλλαγαὶ τῆς ''Ερωφίλης' καὶ τῆς 'Βοσκοπούλας'.'' *Kritiká Hroniká* 10, 241-72.

Dronke, P., 1976. 'Learned lyric and popular ballad in the early middle ages.' *Studi Medievali, 3rd Series* (Spoleto) 17/1, 1-40.

Eliot, T. S., 1928. Introduction. In Ezra Pound, *Selected poems,* pp. 7-21. London.

1932. *Selected essays, 1917-1932.* London.

Emeneau, M. B., 1966. 'Style and meaning in an oral literature.' *Language* 42, 323-45.

Entwistle, W. J., 1939. *European balladry.* Oxford.

Evlampios, 1843. Εὐλάμπιος, Γ. 'Ο ἀμάραντος ἤτοι τὰ ῥόδα τῆς ἀναγεννηθείσης 'Ελλάδος. St Petersburg.

214

Bibliography

Fardys, 1888. Φαρδύς, N. B. "Ύλη καὶ σκαρίφημα ἱστορίας τῆς ἐν Κορσικῇ ἑλληνικῆς ἀποικίας. Athens.

Farmakidis, 1926. Φαρμακίδης, Ξ. Κύπρια ἔπη μετὰ σημειώσεων καὶ σχολίων. Nicosia.

Fauriel, C., 1824, 1825. Chants populaires de la Grèce moderne. 2 vols. Paris.

Finnegan, R., 1977. Oral poetry, its nature, significance and social context. Cambridge.

Frangakis, 1950. Φραγκάκης, Ε. Κ. "Τὸ δημοτικὸ τραγούδι τῆς Κρήτης." Elliniki Dimiouryía 5, 768-72.

Gauntlett, E., 1978. 'To rebetiko tragoudi.' Unpublished thesis, University of Oxford.

Gill, H. A. R. and Kramers, J. H., 1953. Shorter encyclopaedia of Islam. Leiden and London.

Goody, J., 1968. Introduction. In Literacy in Traditional Societies, ed. J. Goody, 1-26. Cambridge.

Goody, J. and Watt, I., 1968. 'The consequences of literacy.' In Literacy in Traditional Societies, ed. J. Goody, 27-68. Cambridge.

Grégoire, H., 1942. Ὁ Διγενὴς Ἀκρίτας. New York.

Griffiths, J., 1805. Travels in Europe, Asia Minor and Arabia. London.

Hasiotis, 1866. Χασιώτης, Γ. Συλλογὴ τῶν κατὰ τὴν Ἤπειρον δημοτικῶν ἀσμάτων. Athens.

Haviaras, 1910. Χαβιαρᾶς, M. Δ. "Περὶ τοῦ κάστρου τῆς Σουριᾶς μετὰ παραλλαγῶν τοῦ εἰς αὐτὸ ἀναφερομένου ἄσματος." Laografía 2, 557-74.

Haymes, E. R., 1973. A bibliography of studies relating to Parry's and Lord's oral theory. Cambridge, Mass.

Herzfeld, M., 1972. 'The khelidonisma - a study in textual and ritual variation.' Unpublished thesis, University of Birmingham.

—— 1973. 'The "Siege of Rhodes" and the ethnography of Greek oral tradition.' Kritiká Hroniká 25, 413-40.

—— 1974. "Προφορικὴ παράδοση καὶ κοινωνικὴ συνέχεια στὶς ἀνοιξιάτικες τελετὲς τῶν νοτιοροδιτικῶν χωριῶν." Dodekanisiaká Hroniká (Athens) 2, 1-19.

—— 1974a. 'Cretan distichs: "The Quartered Shield" in cross-cultural perspective.' Semiotica 12/3, 203-18.

—— 1977. 'Ritual and textual structures: the advent of spring in rural Greece.' In Text and Context: the Social Anthropology of Tradition, ed. R. K. Jain, 29-50. Institute for the Study of Human Issues, Philadelphia.

Hesseling, D. C. and Pernot, H., 1913. Ἐρωτοπαίγνια (Chansons d'amour). Paris and Athens.

Hobsbawm, E. J., 1972. Bandits. 2nd edition, Harmondsworth.

Holland, H., 1815. Travels in the Ionian Isles, Albania, Thessaly, Macedonia, etc. during the years 1812 and 1813. London.

Hughes, T. P., 1885. A dictionary of Islam. London.

Hustvedt, S. B., 1930. Ballad books and ballad men. Raids and rescues in Britain, America and the Scandinavian North since 1800. Cambridge, Mass.

I.F.M.C., 1955. 'Proceedings of the seventh conference.' Journal of the International Folk Music Council 7, 6-47.

Bibliography

Ibrovac, M., 1966. *Claude Fauriel et la fortune européenne des poésies populaires grecques et serbes.* Paris.

Impellizzeri, S., 1944. 'Il motivo del revenant nella superstizione e nei canti popolari greci.' *Atti dell'Accademia di Palermo, Serie IV*, 4/2, 1–43.

Ioannidis, 1870. 'Ιωαννίδης, Σ. 'Ιστορία καὶ στατιστικὴ Τραπεζοῦντος καὶ τῆς περὶ ταύτην χώρας, ὡς καὶ τὰ περὶ τῆς ἑλληνικῆς γλώσσης. Constantinople.

Ioannou, 1965. 'Ιωάννου, Γ. "Δημοτικὰ τραγούδια τῆς Κυνουρίας." *Diagónios* (Salonica) 1, 1–10.

1966. Τὰ δημοτικά μας τραγούδια. Athens.

Jeannaraki, A., 1876. Ἄσματα κρητικὰ μετὰ διστίχων καὶ παροιμίων. Leipzig.

Jeffreys, M., 1973. 'Formulas in the Chronicle of the Morea.' *Dumbarton Oaks Papers* 27, 165–95.

1974. 'The nature and origins of the political verse.' *Dumbarton Oaks Papers* 28, 141–95.

Jones, G. and Jones, T., 1974. *The Mabinogion.* Revised edition, Everyman's Library. London and New York.

Joss, P. M. L., 1826. Παραδείγματα ῥωμαϊκῆς ποιήσεως. *Specimens of Romaic lyric poetry with a translation into English.* London.

Kairofylas, 1952. Καιροφύλας, Κ. "'Ο Σολωμὸς καὶ τὸ δημοτικὸ τραγούδι." *Ellinikí Dimiouryía* 9, 209–12.

Kallinikos, 1951. Καλλίνικος, Θ. Κυπριακὴ λαϊκὴ μοῦσα. Nicosia.

Kalonaros, 1941. Καλονάρος, Π. Π. Βασίλειος Διγενὴς 'Ακρίτας: τὰ ἔμμετρα κείμενα. 2 vols. Athens.

Kanellakis, 1890. Κανελλάκης, Κ. Ν. Χιακὰ ἀνάλεκτα. Athens.

Karamanos, 1928. Καραμάνος, Κ. Μ. "'Άρτα - λαογραφία." In Μεγάλη 'Ελληνικὴ 'Εγκυκλοπαίδεια, Vol. 5, 680–1. 2nd edition, Athens.

Kind, T., 1861. *Anthologie Neugriechischer Volkslieder.* Leipzig.

Koromilas, 1835. Κορομηλᾶς, Α. 'Ανθολογία ἢ συλλογὴ ἀσμάτων ἡρωϊκῶν καὶ ἐρωτικῶν. Μέρος Α'. Athens.

Kouyeas, 1913. Κουγέας, Σ. Β. "'Έρευναι περὶ τῆς ἑλληνικῆς λαογραφίας κατὰ τοὺς μέσους χρόνους, Α'. Αἱ ἐν τοῖς σχολίοις τοῦ 'Αρέθα λαογραφικαὶ εἰδήσεις." *Laografía* 4, 236–70.

1932. "'Ο Γκαῖτε καὶ ἡ νεωτέρα 'Ελλάς." *Nea Estía* 11, 621–31.

Kraeling, C. H. and Mowry, L., 1957. 'Music in the Bible.' In Wellesz, 1957, 283–312.

Kriaras, 1965. Κριαρᾶς, Ε. 'Ανακάλημα τῆς Κωνσταντινόπολης. 2nd edition, Salonica.

Kriaris, 1920. Κριάρης, Α. Πλήρης συλλογὴ κρητικῶν δημωδῶν ἀσμάτων. 2nd edition, Athens.

Krikos, K., 1975. 'The "Song of the Dead Brother": a bibliography.' *Mandatofóros* (Birmingham) 6, 23–30.

Kyriakidis, 1915. Κυριακίδης, Σ. Π. "Οἱ ποιητάρηδες τῆς Κύπρου." *Laografía* 5, 650–1.

1926. 'Ο Διγενὴς 'Ακρίτας. 'Ακριτικὰ ἔπη - ἀκριτικὰ τραγούδια - ἀκριτικὴ ζωή. Athens.

Bibliography

1934. Αἱ ἱστορικαὶ ἀρχαὶ τῆς δημώδους νεοελληνικῆς ποιήσεως. Salonica.
1947. Ἡ γένεσις τοῦ δίστιχου καὶ ἡ ἀρχὴ τῆς ἰσομετρίας. Salonica.
1965. Ἑλληνικὴ λαογραφία, Μέρος Α'. Μνημεῖα τοῦ λόγου. Revised edition, Athens.

Lampsidis, 1960. Λαμψίδης, Π. Δημοτικὰ τραγούδια τοῦ Πόντου, Α'. Τὰ κείμενα. Athens.

Laourdas, 1947. Λαούρδας, Β. Μπάρμπα-Παντζελιοῦ, Τὸ τραγούδι τοῦ Δασκαλογιάννη. Iraklion.

Lavagnini, B., 1953. 'Alle fonti di un canto popolare: la ballata neogreca del fratello morto e il miracolo dei Santi Confessori de Edessa.' In Προσφορὰ εἰς Σ. Π. Κυριακίδην, ed. Xyngopoulos et al., 399–404. Salonica.

Legrand, E., 1870. Τῆς Ρούμελης τὸ τραγούδι. Collection de monuments pour servir à l'étude de la langue néo-hellénique, 8. Paris and Athens.

1874. Recueil de chansons populaires grecques. Collection de monuments pour servir à l'étude de la langue néo-hellénique. Nouvelle série, 1. Paris and Athens.

1880. Bibliothèque grecque vulgaire. Vol. 1. Paris. Photographic reprint, Grigoriadis, Athens, 1974.

1881. Bibliothèque grecque vulgaire. Vol. 3. Paris. Photographic reprint, Grigoriadis, Athens, 1974.

Lévi-Strauss, C., 1968. 'The structural study of myth.' In C. Lévi-Strauss, Structural anthropology, 206–31. Penguin University Books, Harmondsworth.

1972. The savage mind. 2nd English edition, London.

Lioudaki, 1936. Λιουδάκι, Μ. Κρητικὲς μαντινάδες. 2nd edition, Athens.

Lloyd, A. L., 1975. Folk song in England. Paperback edition, Paladin, London.

Lord, A. B. 1954. 'Notes on Digenis Akritas and Serbocroatian epic.' Harvard Slavic Studies 2, 375–83.

1960. The singer of tales. Cambridge, Mass.

1968. 'Homer as oral poet.' Harvard Studies in Classical Philology 72, 1–46.

1975. 'Perspectives on recent work on oral literature.' Forum for Modern Language Studies 10/3, 187–210.

1977. 'Parallel culture traits in ancient and modern Greece.' Byzantine and Modern Greek Studies 3, 71–80.

Louloudopoulos, 1903. Λουλουδόπουλος, Μ. Α. Ἀνέκδοτος συλλογὴ ἠθῶν, ἐθίμων, δημώδων ᾀσμάτων, προλήψεων, δεισιδαιμονίων, παροιμίων, αἰνιγμάτων κτλ. τῶν Καρύων, ἐπαρχίας Καβακλῆ. Varna.

Maas, P., 1912. 'Metrische Akklamationen der Byzantiner.' Byzantinische Zeitschrift 21, 28–51.

McNeish, J., 1965. Greece in music and song (gramophone record). Argo DA29.

Mango, C., 1954. 'Quelques remarques sur la chanson de Daskaloyannis.' Kritiká Hroniká 8, 44–54.

Manousos, 1850. Μανοῦσος, Α. Τραγούδια ἐθνικά. 2 vols. Corfu. Photographic reprint, Elias Rizos, Athens, 1969.

Manoussakas, M. and van Gemert, A., forthcoming. '"Ὁ δικηγόρος τοῦ Χάντακα Στέφανος Σαχλίκης, ποιητὴς τοῦ ΙΔ' καὶ ὄχι τοῦ ΙΕ' αἰῶνα."' In Πρακτικὰ τοῦ 4ου Διεθνοῦς Κρητολογικοῦ Συνεδρίου (Proceedings of the 4th International Cretological Congress). Iraklion.

Bibliography

Maranda, E. K. and Maranda, P., 1971. *Structural models in folklore and transformational essays. Approaches to Semiotics*, ed. T. A. Sebeok, 10. The Hague and Paris.

Marshall, F. H., 1935. 'Four klephtic songs.' In Εἰς Μνήμην Σπυρίδωνος Λάμπρου, 42–9. Athens.

Martin-Leake, W., 1814. *Researches in Greece*. London.

Mavrogordato, J., 1956. *Digenes Akrites*. Oxford.

Megas, 1961. Μέγας, Γ. Α. "'Αναστενάρια καὶ ἔθιμα Τυρινῆς Δευτέρας εἰς τὸ Κωστῆ καὶ τὰ πέριξ αὐτοῦ χωριὰ τῆς 'Ανατολικῆς Θράκης." *Laografía* 19, 472–534.

— 1971. "Τὸ τραγούδι τοῦ γεφυρίου τῆς Ἄρτας. Συγκριτικὴ μελέτη." *Laografía* 27, 25–212.

Melahrinos, 1946. Μελαχρινός, Α. Δημοτικὰ τραγούδια. Athens.

Menardos, 1921. Μενάρδος, Σ. "Τὸ τραοῦδιν τῆς Ζωγγραφοῦς." *Laografía* 8, 181–200.

Mihail-Dede, 1973. Μιχαήλ-Δεδέ, Μ. "Τὸ 'Αναστενάρι – ψυχολογικὴ καὶ κοινωνιολογικὴ θεώρηση." *Thrakiká* 46, 23–177.

Mihailidis-Nouaros, 1928. Μιχαηλίδης-Νούαρος, Μ. Δημοτικὰ τραγούδια Καρπάθου. Athens.

Morgan, G., 1960. *Cretan poetry: sources and inspiration*. Offprint from *Kritiká Hroniká* 14, Iraklion.

Nagler, M. N., 1967. 'Towards a generative view of the oral formula.' *Transactions of the American Philological Association* 98, 269–311.

Notopoulos, J. A., 1952. 'Homer and Cretan heroic poetry: a study in comparative oral poetry.' *American Journal of Philology* 73, 225–50.

— 1954. 'Homer as an oral poet in the light of modern Greek heroic oral poetry.' *Yearbook of the American Philosophical Society, 1953,* 249–53.

— 1959. 'Modern Greek heroic oral poetry and its relevance to Homer.' Text accompanying Folkways record FE 4468. New York.

Odeon, 1930. 'Ωδεῖον 'Αθηνῶν. 50 δημώδη ἄσματα Πελοποννήσου καὶ Κρήτης. Athens.

Oriental Herald, 1825. Sheridan's *'Songs of Greece'* (review). 5, 604–9.

Pahtikos, 1905. Παχτίκος, Γ. Δ. 260 δημώδη ἑλληνικὰ ἄσματα, Τόμ. Α'. Athens.

Pantelidis, 1910. Παντελίδης, Χ. Γ. "'Ακριτικὰ ἄσματα τῆς Κύπρου." *Laografía* 2, 60–81.

— 1923. "Οἱ ποιητάριδες τῆς Κύπρου." *Laografía* 7, 115–20.

Papadopoullos, 1967. Παπαδόπουλλος, Θ. *Un monument de littérature populaire chypriote*. Publications of the Cyprus Research Centre, 1. Nicosia.

— 1975. Δημώδη κυπριακὰ ἄσματα, ἐξ ἀνεκδότων συλλογῶν τοῦ ΙΘ' αἰῶνος. Publications of the Cyprus Research Centre, 5. Nicosia.

Papathomopoulos, 1974. Παπαθωμόπουλος, Μ. "Διορθώσεις σὲ κείμενα τῆς δημώδους λογοτεχνίας." *Parnassós* 16, 464–8.

Parry, M., 1930. 'Studies in the epic technique of oral verse-making, I: Homer and the Homeric style.' *Harvard Studies in Classical philology* 41, 73–147.

— 1932. 'Studies in the epic technique of oral verse-making, II: The Homeric language as the language of oral poetry.' *Harvard Studies in Classical Philology* 43, 1–50.

Bibliography

Pasayanis, 1928. Πασαγιάνης, Κ. Μανιάτικα μοιρολόγια καὶ τραγούδια. Athens. 1958.

Passow, A., 1860. *Popularia carmina Graeciae recentioris*. Leipzig. Photographic reprint Nikas and Spanos, Athens, 1958.

Paz, O., 1971. *Claude Lévi-Strauss: an introduction*. English edition, London.

Percy, T., 1765. *Reliques of ancient English poetry*. London.

Perdika, 1940. Πέρδικα, Ν. Λ. Σκῦρος, Τόμ. Α'. Athens.

Pernot, H., 1918. *Nos anciens à Corfou. Souvenirs de l'aide-major Lamare-Picquot (1807-1814)*. Paris.

1931. *Chansons populaires grecques des XVe et XVIe siècles*. Paris.

Petropoulos, 1954. Πετρόπουλος, Δ. "Οἱ ποιητάρηδες στὴν Κρήτη καὶ στὴν Κύπρο." *Laografía* 15, 374-400.

1954a. "Τοῦ Δασκαλογιάννη τὰ τραγούδια." *Kritiká Hroniká* 8, 227-37.

1958, 1959. Ἑλληνικὰ δημοτικὰ τραγούδια. 2 vols. Athens.

Petropoulos, I., 1968. Πετρόπουλος, Η. Ρεμπέτικα τραγούδια. Athens.

Politis, A., 1973. Πολίτης, Α. Τὸ δημοτικὸ τραγούδι: κλέφτικα. Athens.

Politis, L., 1956. Πολίτης, Λ. Ὁ Σολωμὸς στὰ γράμματά του. Athens.

1970. 'L'épopée byzantine de Digénis Akritas; problèmes de la tradition du texte et des rapports avec les chansons akritiques.' In *Atti del Convegno Internazionale sul tema: La poesia epica e la sua formazione*, pp. 551-81. Accademia Nazionale dei Lincei, Rome.

1973. *A history of modern Greek literature*. Oxford.

Politis, N. G., 1885. Πολίτης, Ν. Γ. "Τὸ δημοτικὸν ἀσμα περὶ τοῦ νεκροῦ αδελφοῦ." *Deltíon tis Istorikís ke Ethnoloyikís Eterías tis Elládos* 6, 193-261.

1901. Μελέται περὶ τοῦ βίου καὶ τῆς γλώσσης τοῦ ἑλληνικοῦ λαοῦ – Παροιμίαι, Τόμ. Γ'. Athens. Photographic reprint, Erganis, Athens, 1965.

1904. Μελέται περὶ τοῦ βίου καὶ τῆς γλώσσης τοῦ ἑλληνικοῦ λαοῦ – Παραδόσεις. 2 vols. Athens. Photographic reprint, Erganis, Athens, 1965.

1909. "Ἀκριτικὰ ἄσματα· ὁ θάνατος τοῦ Διγενῆ." *Laografía* 1, 169-275.

1911. "Δημώδη βυζαντινὰ ἄσματα." *Laografía* 3, 622-52.

1914. Ἐκλογαὶ ἀπὸ τὰ τραγούδια τοῦ ἑλληνικοῦ λαοῦ. Athens.

1915. "Γνωστοὶ ποιηταὶ δημοτικῶν ἀσμάτων." *Laografía* 5, 489-521.

Pouqueville, F. C., 1813. *Travels in the Morea, Albania and other parts of the Ottoman Empire*. English edition, London.

Prousis, 1945. Προύσης, Κ. "Τὰ ἱστορικὰ κυπριακὰ τραγούδια." *Kypriaké Spoudé* 7, 21-46.

1972. "Ὁ Διγενὴς Ἀκρίτας στὴν Κύπρο." *Parnassós* 14, 192-214.

Psichari, J., 1884. 'La ballade de Lénore en Grèce.' *Revue de l'Histoire des Religions* 9, 27-64.

Romaios, 1952. Ρωμαῖος, Κ. "Δημοτικὰ τραγούδια Σέρβων καὶ Βουλγάρων δανεισμένα ἀπὸ ἑλληνικὰ πρότυπα." *Arheíon tou Thrakikoú Laografikoú ke Glossikoú Thisavrou* 17, 307-65.

1958. "Ἡ πάλη τοῦ Διγενῆ καὶ τοῦ Χάρου." *Arheíon Póntou* 22, 167-78.

1963. Ὁ 'νόμος τῶν τριῶν' στὸ δημοτικὸ τραγούδι. Athens.

1964. "Διγενής – τὸ μεγάλο πρόβλημα τῆς καταγωγῆς τῶν ἀκριτικῶν τραγουδιῶν." *Arheíon Póntou* 26, 197-230.

1968. Ἡ ποίηση ἑνὸς λαοῦ. Athens.

219

Bibliography

Russo, J. A., 1966. 'The structural formula in Homeric verse.' In *Homeric Studies*, ed. G. S. Kirk and A. Parry. Yale Classical Studies 20, 217–40.

St Clair, W., 1972. *That Greece might still be free. The philhellenes in the War of Independence*. Oxford.

Sakellarios, 1868. Σακελλάριος, Α. Α. Τὰ κυπριακά, Τόμ. Γ΄. Ἡ ἐν Κύπρῳ γλῶσσα. Athens.

1891. Τὰ κυπριακά, Τόμ. Β΄. Ἡ ἐν Κύπρῳ γλῶσσα. Revised and expanded, Athens.

Sako, Z., 1966. 'Eléments balkaniques communs dans le rite de la ballade de l'emmurement.' *Studia albanica*, 3e année, 2, 207–13.

Saunier, G., 1972. 'Le combat avec Charos dans les chansons populaires grecques.' *Ellinikà* 25, 119–52; 335–70.

Schmidt, B., 1871. *Das Volksleben der Neugriechen*. Leipzig.

Schmitt, J., 1904. *The Chronicle of Morea*. London. Unchanged reprint, Bouma's Boekhuis, Groningen, 1967.

Schneider, M., 1957. 'Primitive music.' In Wellesz, 1957, pp. 1–82.

Schorelis, 1977, Σχορέλης, Τ. Ρεμπέτικη ἀνθολογία, Α΄. Athens.

Shepard, L., 1962. *The broadside ballad*. London.

1973. *The history of street literature*. Newton Abbot.

Sheridan, C. B., 1825. *The songs of Greece, translated from the Romaic text, edited by M. C. Fauriel, with additions*. London.

Simopoulos, 1975. Σιμόπουλος, Κ. Ξένοι ταξιδιῶτες στὴν Ἑλλάδα. Τόμος Γ1, *1800–1810*. Athens.

1975a. Ξένοι ταξιδιῶτες στὴν Ἑλλάδα. Τόμος Γ2, *1810–1821*. Προμηνύματα τοῦ ξεσηκωμοῦ. Athens.

Smith, J. D., 1977. 'The singer or the song? A reassessment of Lord's "oral theory".' *Man* 12/1, 141–53.

Soyter, G., 1921. 'Das volkstümliche Distichon bei den Neugriechen.' *Laografía* 8, 379–426.

Spandonidi, 1939. Σπανδωνίδη, Ε. Τραγούδια τῆς Ἀγόριανης (Παρνασσοῦ). Athens.

Sperber, D., 1975. *Rethinking symbolism*. English edition, Cambridge.

Stephanopoli, D. and N., 1800. *Voyage de Dimo et Nicolò Stephanopoli en Grèce pendant les années V et VI*. 2 vols. Paris.

Swales, M., 1975. *Goethe: selected poems*. Oxford.

Tarsouli, 1944. Ταρσούλη, Γ. Μωραΐτικα τραγούδια - Κορώνης καὶ Μεθώνης. Athens.

Thompson, S., 1946. *The folktale*. New York.

1955–8. *Motif-index of folk-literature*. 6 vols. Revised and enlarged edition, Copenhagen and Indiana.

Tillyard, H. J. W., 1912. 'The acclamations of Emperors in Byzantine ritual.' *Annual of the British School at Athens* 18, 239–60.

Tommaseo, N., 1842. *Canti popolari, toscani, corsi, illyrici, greci. Vol. III. Canti del popolo greco*. Venice.

Tournefort, M., 1713. *A voyage into the Levant*. English edition, London.

Tsiknopoulos, 1952. Τσικνόπουλος, Ι. Π. "Ἡ ποιητικὴ παραγωγὴ τοῦ Ἐγκλείστου Ἁγίου Νεοφύτου." *Kypriaké Spoudé* 16, 39–49.

Tziatzios, 1928. Τζιάτζιος, Ε. Τραγούδια τῶν Σαρακατσαναίων. Athens.

Bibliography

Vakalopoulos, 1964. Βακαλόπουλος, A. Ἱστορία τοῦ νέου ἑλληνισμοῦ. Τόμ. A'. Salonica.

Vamvakaris, 1973. Βαμβακάρης, M. Αὐτοβιογραφία, ed. A. Καΐλ. Athens.

Vansina, J., 1973. Oral tradition: a study in historical methodology. English edition, Penguin University Books, Harmondsworth.

Vargyas, L., 1967. Researches into the medieval history of folk ballad. Budapest.

Vasdravellis, 1952. Βασδραβέλλης, I. Ἱστορικὰ ἀρχεῖα Θεσσαλονίκης. Salonica.

Vayakakos, 1970. Βαγιακάκος, Δ. Οἱ Μανιᾶται τῆς Διασπορᾶς. A'. Οἱ Μανιᾶται τῆς Κορσικῆς. Athens.

Vlahoyannis, 1938. Βλαχογιάννης, Γ. "Κλέφτικα καὶ ναυτικὰ τραγούδια, B'." Néa Estía 23, 165-9.

Von Haxthausen, W., 1935. Neugriechische Volkslieder. Münster.

Vyzantios, 1972. Βυζάντιος, Δ. K. Ἡ Βαβυλωνία, α' καὶ β' ἔκδοση, ed. S. Evangelatos. Athens.

Wagner, G., 1874. Carmina graeca medii aevi. Leipzig. Photographic reprint, Spanos, Athens, n.d.

Wellesz, E., 1949. A history of Byzantine music and hymnography. Oxford.

1957. New Oxford history of music, Vol. 1. Ancient and oriental music. Oxford.

Wells, E. K., 1950. The ballad tree. New York.

Wilgus, D. K., 1959. Anglo-American folksong scholarship since 1898. New Brunswick, N.J.

Wollner, W., 1882. 'Der Lenorenstoff in der slavischen Volkspoesie.' Archiv für Slavische Philologie (Berlin) 6, 239-69.

Woodfill, W. L., 1953. Musicians in English society from Elizabeth to Charles I. Princeton.

Woodhouse, C. M., 1976. The struggle for Greece, 1941-1949. London.

Wordsworth, W., 1815. Essay, supplementary to the preface. In The prose works of William Wordsworth, ed. J. B. Owen and J. Worthington Smyser, 62-107. Oxford, 1974.

Yangas, 1959. Γιάγκας, A. Ἠπειρώτικα δημοτικὰ τραγούδια, 1000-1958. Athens.

Yangoullis, 1965. Γιαγκουλλῆς, K. Γ. "Κυπριῶτες ποιητάρηδες." Kypriaká Hroniká 4/45, 75-85.

1970. "Τὸ ἔργο τοῦ ποιητάρη Ἀριστοτέλη Νικολάου." Kypriaké Spoudé 34, 35-46.

1976. Οἱ ποιητάρηδες τῆς Κύπρου. Προλεγόμενα-βιο-βιβλιογραφία (1936-76). Salonica.

Yeats, W. B., 1924. Essays. Collected works, Vol. 4. London.

Zakythinos, D. A., 1976. The making of modern Greece: from Byzantium to Independence. English edition, Oxford.

Zambelios, 1852. Ζαμπέλιος, Σ. Ἄσματα δημοτικὰ τῆς Ἑλλάδος. Corfu.

Index

songs (2) – *cont.*
  'Swallow Song' (*helidónisma*) **137–40,** 144, 145, 208
  'The Virgin's Lament', **141–4,** 145
  'The Wife who Came to Grief', 134
songs (3), *by place of origin*
  Aegina, 23–4, 145–6
  Anoyia, 162
  Mt Athos, 78, 86–7, 98
  Balkans, 116, 117, 118, 120–1, 122, 128
  Bulgaria, 32, 120, 121
  Corfu, 22–3, 97–8
  Corsica, 138–9
  Crete, 24, 29–30, 97–8, 207
  Cyprus, 20–1, 24–6, 29
  Dodecanese, 114
  Epiros, 26–7, 192
  Hios, 28
  Karpathos, 31, 83, 184
  Kavakli, 32
  Kythira, 174
  Larnaca, 202
  Lefkás, 67
  Macedonia, 23, 33
  Pontos, 26, 31–2, 78, 99, 203
  Thrace, 24, 29, 34
  Zagori, 145–6
Sperber, D., 125–7, 135
Stefanopoulos family, 88
Stephanopoli, D. and N., 5–6, 172
Stournaris (*armatolós*), *see* songs (1)
structuralism, 39, 113–14, 125–6, 129, 207
structure
  of the demotic tradition, 3, **35–73,** and *passim*
  of distichs, 148–9
  of the historical tradition, 157–62
  of myth, 129–30
  of ritual songs, 136, 139–40, 145
  of urban songs, 194
'Swallow Song' (*helidónisma*), *see* songs (2)
symbolism, 126–8, 131–5
syntactical patterns, 44, 51–3, 54, 55, 56

table songs, 34; *see also rizítika*
taxonomy, *see* classification of folk songs
Tenedos, 99
themes, 3, **65–9,** 70
  in Scottish ballads, 181
  in urban songs, 193–8
Thrace, 19; *see also* songs (3)
Tommaseo, N., 9
Tournefort, M., 88
transmission
  of broadside ballads, 180
  of the demotic tradition, 35–6, 69–71, 74
  of folk tales, 125
  of the historical tradition, 159–61, 174–5, 185–8
  of ritual songs, 145
  see also memorisation, oral tradition
Trebizond
  Diyenis Akritis discovered at, 78, 79
  sack of (1461), 206
Tripolitsá (Tripolis), 100
tshiattísmata, 148, 177, **201–2;** *see also* Cyprus, distichs
Tsitsanis, V., 197
Tsopanakos (Panayiotis Kalas), 168–9
Turkey, 1, 194–5
Turks
  influence of, 102, 207
  and Islamic legend, 123
  and klefts, 2, 102–11 *passim*
  lament for, 100
  rule of, in Greece, 5–6, 86–9, 95, 140–1, 184
  and St George, 65–8

urban folk songs, *see rebétika*

Vamvakaris, M., 196–7
variants of folk songs, 2, 11, **21–34,** 69–71, 112–15, 118, 120
'verbal tradition', 181–2, 184
'Virgin's Lament, The', *see* laments, songs (2)
Vyzantios, D., 94

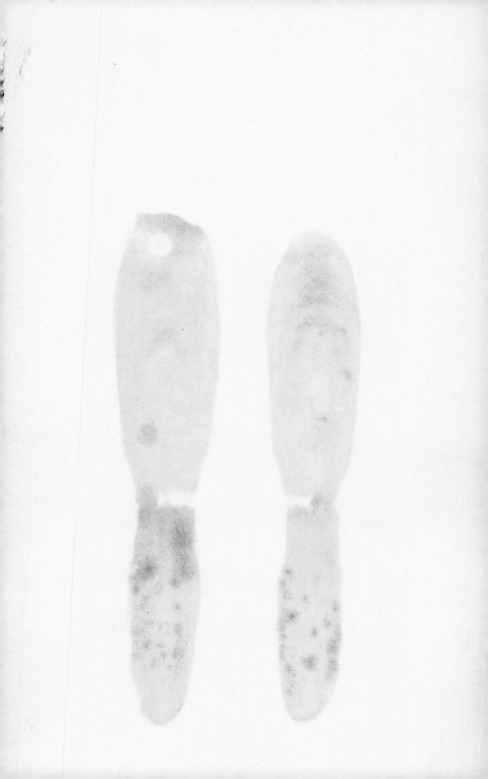